Royal
Weddings

Royal
Weddings

Dulcie M. Ashdown

ROBERT HALE · LONDON

ISBN 0 7091 9383 1

Robert Hale Limited
Clerkenwell House
Clerkenwell Green
London EC1R 0HT

Photoset by
Kelly Typesetting Limited
Bradford-on-Avon, Wiltshire
Printed in Great Britain by
St Edmundbury Press, Bury St Edmonds, Suffolk
Bound by Weatherby Woolnough, Northants

Contents

Illustrations

PICTURE CREDITS

Acknowledgements

Material from the Royal Archives is here quoted by the gracious permission of Her Majesty the Queen, republishing from *The Letters of Queen Victoria*, first series, ed. A. C. Benson and Viscount Esher (John Murray, 1907), second series, ed. G. E. Buckle (John Murray, 1926); J. Pope-Hennessy, *Queen Mary* (George Allen & Unwin Ltd, 1959); the broadcast speech of HRH the Duke of Windsor, 1936; Sir John Wheeler-Bennett *King George V* (Macmillan, 1958).

Permission to quote from copyright material has been granted by:

George Allen & Unwin Ltd: P. M. Kendall, *The Yorkist Age* (1962)

Her Majesty's Stationery Office: *The Hastings Papers*, ed. F. Bickley (The Historical Manuscripts Commission, 1947)

Hodder & Stoughton Ltd: *The Diaries of a Duchess*, ed. J. Greig (1926)

John Murray: *The Letters of Queen Victoria*, third series, ed. G. E. Buckle (1930); *My Dear Duchess*, ed. A. L. Kennedy (1956); *Life with Queen Victoria*, ed. V. Mallet (1968)

Michael Joseph Ltd: The Duchess of Windsor, *The Heart has its Reasons* (1956)

Oliver & Boyd: *Early Sources of Scottish History*, collected and translated by A. O. Anderson (1922)

Oxford University Press: *The Complete Works of George Savile, Marquess of Halifax*, ed. W. Raleigh (Clarendon Press, 1912); R. L. Arkell, *Caroline of Anspach* (1939)

Routledge & Kegan Paul Ltd: M. Young and P. Willmott, *Family and Kinship in East London* (1957)

Introduction

There are certain headlines that could be 'guaranteed to sell millions of extra newspapers: 'WAR DECLARED', 'MARTIAN INVASION IMMINENT' and 'INCOME TAX ABOLISHED'. Just slightly less inviting is 'ROYAL WEDDING SPECIAL EDITION'.

In late-twentieth-century Britain, the royal family is so popular that the wedding of one of its members causes many people as much excitement as a wedding in their own family. But it was not always so. Until this century, royal weddings were celebrated much more privately, with only family, courtiers and certain dignitaries present—where now millions of people are admitted through the eye of the television camera; until the advent of the newspaper, news of any royal event would permeate the country only very slowly and, even so, be of little interest to the millions who regarded the king only as the ultimate landlord.

This book sets out to trace the history of royal weddings for more than a thousand years, crossing the gulf between private royal weddings and those of today in their blaze of publicity, between royal matches made for political or international considerations and today's, which are made for love. The child's plea at the end of the fairy-tale: 'And did they live happily ever after?' is so natural a query after the story of any wedding that we here pursue the married lives of many of England and Scotland's monarchs, and those of their brothers and sisters—some of them through happy years to the tranquillity of 'Darby and Joan', others through stories of marital strife and even murder that rival anything in fiction.

Here royal weddings are set against the background of the 'ordinary' weddings and marriages of the same periods, comparing and contrasting customs and ceremonies but also, hopefully, keeping a check on that ever-present temptation to treat a royal family, in marriage as in so much else, as 'apart from', 'above', the foibles and trials of Everyman and his wife. And because history—even 'history in stories'—is so often a picture of life that today we cannot quite believe in, of people whom we cannot regard as common humanity with ourselves, here many of them come forward to tell their own stories, in the journals and letters which have survived them, along with their own recorded views of the royal weddings of their times. 'Voices from the past' bring home to us the humanity that we share far more then any mere statement of fact could.

So here is *Royal Weddings*, the author's labour of the year 1980, in which a royal wedding—that of the Prince of Wales—became a subject of speculation in the news media which seemed at times to eclipse all the problems of the nation's ills and the world's wars. Now that the news has broken, with the nation's enthusiasm for the coming wedding, people are recalling their memories of royal weddings of times past, perhaps seen on television, perhaps witnessed from a roadside cheering crowd, and as they tell their stories, so here are a few more, from years far beyond living memory.

The Middle Ages

"The Great Bond of Matrimony"

When Julius Caesar visited Britain, some forty years before the birth of Jesus Christ, he noticed communities in which ten or twelve people of the same family lived together in one hut, the men sharing the women between them. A century or so later, the Roman historian Tacitus noted that polygamy was practised in certain German tribes—tribes which invaded Britain in the fifth century and made the practice common there. In fact, anthropologists, studying primitive societies, have found this mating-pattern common throughout the world: first incest, then polygamy within the tribe; the next step is the search for brides in other tribes, which involves first warfare for possession of nubile women ('marriage by capture') and then a system of inter-tribal purchase of them. Alternatively, after a war between tribes, a woman might be handed over to seal the peace. In the Early English poem *Beowulf* there is a description of such a match: "Young and decked with gold, she is promised to the gracious son of Frodan. This has been brought about by the Scyldings' friend, the protector of the realm, who counts it gain that, by means of this woman, he should settle their share of bloody feuds and strife." But, the poet admits, "It seldom happens that, after the fall of a prince, the deadly spear draws back for even a little while from battle, no matter how worthy the bride be."[1]

When St Augustine brought his mission to England in 597, 'marriage by purchase' was superceding 'marriage by capture', and his first convert, King Ethelbert of Kent, made a law that bridged the two systems: if a man carried off a girl by force, he had to pay her father a 50-shilling fine and then buy her from him to marry at an agreed price; if the girl was already betrothed, a fine of 20 shillings was due to her fiancé; if she was married, the abductor could keep her if he paid her husband enough money to buy a replacement.

Under normal circumstances, marriages were arranged by the elders of a community or negotiated between a man and the father of the girl he wanted. The prospective bridegroom would offer the girl's father a 'foster lean' as surety that he would marry her; if he did not, within two years, he forfeited the money to her father, but if the fault was on the bride's part, or her family's, the foster lean had to be repaid to him two- or three-fold. Originally, whatever a bride brought with her from her own family, the 'fader-fiod', was hers to keep, and so was the 'morning-gift' made to her by her husband after their wedding-night, but she lost it if she married within a year of his death.

The ceremony of uniting man and woman was called by the Anglo-Saxons 'hand-fasting', for, after the handing-over of the groom's payment to the bride's father, and the bride's father handing her over to the groom, the couple joined hands to repeat their promises. The vows used in the later Middle Ages contain so many Old English words that they are generally accepted as coming from the centuries before the Norman Conquest:

> The man: "I take thee to my wedded wife, to have and to hold, for fairer, for fouler, for better, for worse, for richer, for poorer, in sickness and in health, from this time forward, till death us do part, and thereto I plight thee my troth.
> "With this ring I thee wed, and this gold and silver I give thee, and with my body I thee worship, and with all my worldly chattels I thee honour."
> The woman: "I take thee to my wedded husband, to have and to hold, for fairer, for fouler, for better, for worse, for richer, for poorer, in sickness and in health, to be blithe and obedient in bed and at board, till death us do part, and thereto I plight thee my troth."

After the wedding, both families would feast in the bride's home for several days, and on the first night the bride and groom would be given some privacy (unusual in those days under normal circumstances) to consumate the marriage. On the second day, the bride would go off to her new home, teased along the road by youths pitching dirty water at her, to rouse her husband to fight them (a mimicry of the 'marriage by capture' of earlier years).

While the transaction of bride for money remained the central factor in the wedding, the Church had little part to play in the proceedings, and it was difficult for the clergy to establish the right even to perform a blessing after the vows had been exchanged, let alone to make a church wedding obligatory. But as the years passed, it became customary to read the contract and exchange the vows at the church door (or at its lych-gate) and then to proceed into the church for a Nuptial Mass.

By threatening to withhold the blessing and then, if the couple still married, to excommunicate them, the Church attempted to enforce certain rules. Chief among them was its insistence that no one should marry a close relation. Christendom had always had an 'incest taboo', and the Germanic practice of a man marrying his widowed stepmother was always condemned; although in the early Saxon period marriages with all but the closest relations were allowed, more and more 'prohibited degrees' of consanguinity were laid down over the centuries that followed—so that by 1215 a couple could not marry if they had a common great-great-grandfather.

Worse, there were 'degrees of affinity' too: a widower could not marry anyone in his late wife's family who stood within the prohibited degrees to her, since he and she had been 'of one flesh'; nor could a man marry anyone related to his mistress, for the same reason, or anyone related to a woman to whom he had once been betrothed. At the utmost absurdity, a man who was godfather to a child could not marry its godmother, because they had a 'spiritual affinity'.

It was all very confusing, but where anyone could pay the necessary fee to the Church courts for a 'dispensation', permission to marry even a first cousin was rarely refused. Kings could pay, of course, and they and other members of the ruling caste of Christendom were the most frequent applicants to the Papacy, the supreme court of appeal, for dispensations to marry within the prohibited degrees. The ancestry of royal and noble families was carefully documented and recorded, and whenever a marriage between two such families was proposed, genealogies could be consulted to see if a dispensation would be required. For the illiterate peasantry there were, obviously, no such records, and folk memory would be the only witness to past marriages and ancestry. This gave rise to the (still used) request for anyone knowing any impediment to the marriage to come forward before it was performed; when that request was made, outside the church, in full view of the public, anyone with a knowledge of family history could state an objection. For the peasantry, the way to evade an ecclesiastical ban on a marriage of close relations was simply not to marry by Church law at all but to take the vows that had been used before the Church began to enforce its control over weddings. Since serfs were generally required by their lord to marry someone on the same manor (lest the lord should lose the profit of their or their children's labour to another landowner), more often than not the peasant did marry someone who was related to him in some way.

Just as lords of the manor had the power to supervise their serfs' marriages, so the great landowners had a measure of control over those of their tenants who held land from them on certain terms (by 'feudal dues' rather than cash rents), and the king had the right to control the marriages of the orphan children (and the widows) of his tenants-in-chief. The lords always grudged the kings this power, mainly because kings were in the habit of selling off heirs and heiresses for their own profit, but there was a way of circumventing the system of 'wardship and marriage': a vassal of the king could contract his children very young, to his own profit, so that if he died before they came of age, they were already safely bound to a future partner and could not be 'bestowed' at the king's will—and to *his* profit. Thus there were numerous infant marriages among the nobility in the Middle Ages. Kings married off their children 'in the cradle' too, but for a different reason—to gain immediate foreign allies or support from their own nobles, to seal a treaty of peace after war or to win additional estates, without having to wait for the children to grow up to fulfil these functions.

These 'espousals' of infants were made *per verba de futuro*, a promise for the future, that the children would marry when they reached the age of consent (twelve for girls, fourteen for boys). Theoretically, the child could repudiate an espousal when it reached the age of consent; in practice, the child, being still in the power of its family, had no independent voice, and the vast majority of repudiated espousals were effected by the child's family—if, for example, a better match had been found elsewhere. However, if the young couple went to bed together, the *de futuro* promise automatically became a full marriage.

If a couple, both over the age of consent, made their vows *per verba de praesenti* (that is, coming into effect immediately), they were bound to each other, whether they made the vows in a church service or privately, with or without parental consent.

When, in the fifteenth century, Margery Paston fell in love with her father's bailiff, Richard Calle, they married *per verba de praesenti*, without the knowledge of the girl's family. When the Pastons found out, they tried to bully her into saying that she had not done so (there had been no witnesses present), but she would not. Though they shut her up, to force her to repudiate Calle, she was faithful—and so was he. He wrote to her:

> Mine own lady and mistress, and before God very true wife,
> I, with heart full sorrowful, recommend me unto you, as he that cannot be merry nor nought till it be otherwise with us than it is yet, for this life that we lead now is neither pleasure to God nor to the world, considering the great bond of matrimony that is made betwixt us and also the great love that hath been, and as I trust yet is, betwixt us, and as on my part never greater. . . .
> I suppose they deem we be not ensured together [properly espoused], and if they do, I marvel, for then they are not well advised, remembering the plainness that I broke to my mistress [Margery's mother] at the beginning, and I suppose [by you too if] ye did as ye ought to do of very right. . . . Though I tell them the truth, they will not believe me as well as they will do you; and therefore, good lady, at the reverence of God, be plain to them and tell the truth, and if they will in no wise agree thereto, betwixt God, the Devil and them be it. . . .[2]

When the Pastons invited the Bishop of Lincoln to examine the couple (and to put pressure on them to deny the espousal), he found the marriage true, but Margery was disowned by her family, and there is no evidence that she and her husband were ever forgiven—though her mother did leave some money to their eldest son in her Will.

Margery Paston and Richard Calle were exceptions to the rule. Most people in the Middle Ages did not expect to marry for love. A peasant might—if his lord allowed it; a citizen might, though he would be ridiculed if he turned down a well-dowered woman for one who brought him no financial advantages; few nobles did, for there were estates to be preserved or augmented, political alliances to be forged by judicious marriages; and kings?—when King Edward IV was so eccentric as to marry for love, he was roundly condemned for having thrown away a foreign match advantageous to the kingdom.

However, even among the apparently heartless arranged marriages of the period, we may come upon those in which there was a real wooing of affection—even if it did come after the match had already been made by the families and the couple bound to each other whether they could find love or not. In the fifteenth century, when Thomas Betson was contracted to his little cousin Kathryn Stonor, several years his junior, he used the years before their marriage to court her, and surely any child would be won over by such a letter as this, which he wrote her when he was away from home on business:

> Mine own heartily beloved cousin Kathryn,
> . . . I understand right well that ye go in good health of body and merry at heart, and I pray God heartily of His pleasure to continue the same. . . . And if ye would be a good eater of your meat always, that ye might wax and grow fast to be a woman, ye should make me the gladdest man of the world, by my troth. . . .
> I pray you, greet well my horse and pray him to give you four of his years to help you withal, and I will at my coming home give him four of my years and four horseloaves [as] amends. . . .
> [Written] at great Calais on this side of the sea, the first day of June, when every man has gone to his dinner and the clock smote nine and all our household cried after me and bade me come down, come down to dinner at once! And what answer I gave them, ye know it of old.[3]

(They were married in 1478, when Kathryn was twelve, but sadly Thomas died ten years later, leaving her with five children.)

Not every girl was as fortunate as Kathryn, of course: many were contracted by their parents to men to whom they had taken a dislike for some reason. Few were as obstinate as Elizabeth Paston in refusing to marry such a man. Her suitor, Stephen Scrope, was a widower in his fifties (she was in her teens), and he was somewhat disfigured. When she refused to marry him, her parents tried coercion. "She was never in so great sorrow as she is nowadays," wrote a cousin to Elizabeth's brother, "for she may not speak with no man, whosoever come, nor with servants . . . and she hath since Easter been beaten once in the week or twice, and sometimes twice on one day, and her head broken in two or three places. . . . Think on this matter, for sorrow oftentime causeth women to beset themselves otherwise than they should do, and if she were in that case, I wot well ye would be sorry."[4] Fortunately it did not come to such a crisis, for Elizabeth was allowed to marry another, one whom she found "full kind" to her.

It was not only child marriages that were made for money; a young man independent of his family and able to seek his own bride would also have an eye to a girl's prospects. Richard Cely, a London wool-merchant, was typical . . .

In April 1482 Cely was touring the Cotswolds buying fleeces when a dealer friend, William Midwinter, told him that he had heard of a girl of the Lemeryke family who had been left £40 a year by her late mother and whose father was the richest man in those parts. Midwinter suggested that Cely might go to Northleach, where the girl was accustomed to go to church and where he, Midwinter, could arrange a meeting. Accordingly Cely and his friend William Breton, a wool-packer, turned up for Matins on the appointed day and took a good look at the girl. After the service they had a drink with her and her stepmother, and later he wrote home that "The person pleaseth me well, as by the first communication. She is young, little and very well favoured and witty; and the country speaks much good of her. All this abideth the coming of her father to London, that we may understand what sum he will depart and how he likes me."[5] Maybe Master Lemeryke did not like Master Cely; maybe they could not agree on the financial settlement; perhaps Lemeryke preferred another of his daughter's suitors—there could be any number of reasons, but certainly the match did not transpire.

By the time of the Celys, Pastons and Stonors, the late-fifteenth century, the wedding ceremony had become more or less standardized. The couple met at the church door, listened to the reading of the contract (which stipulated the bride's dowry and, usually, the 'jointure' allotted to her in case of widowhood), paused a moment to allow any objections to their marriage to be voiced, then made their vows *per verba de praesenti*. Proceeding into the church, the priest would go before them, reciting the 128th Psalm: "Your wife shall be like a fruitful vine in the heart of your house; your sons shall be like olive-shoots round about your table. This is the blessing in store for the man who fears the Lord." After the Nuptial Mass, bread, wine and sweets were served to the couple, and then came the final blessing: "Look with favour, O Lord, on this Thy man-servant and this Thy handmaiden, that in Thy name they may receive the heavenly benediction and in safety see the sons of their sons and their daughters, even to the third and fourth generation."[6]

One curious custom in medieval weddings was the use of the 'care-cloth', a sort of canopy held over the couple while Mass was celebrated: children born to them before the wedding would be 'legitimated' by standing under it with their parents.

For most couples, however, the consummation had still to come, and for any timid virgin the ritual bedding by parents and friends, amid broad and lewd joking, must have been an ordeal—but one to be endured for generations, even into the eighteenth century.

Though only a small minority of medieval couples may have 'fallen in love' before their marriage, many arranged marriages proved remarkably happy and resulted in real marital love. There occurred, says one modern historian, "the birth of love from the womb of worldly goods. The delicate balance of the two forces was adjusted by an inner logic, known to everyone then but since well nigh lost."[7]

In the upper classes, however, where the material advantages of matches most obviously outweighed all else, men and women came to seek an alternative to married love in the convention of 'courtly love'. It offered the delightful picture of a knight passionately in love with his lady—not with his wife, for she had been married for gain and for sons; not with a maiden, for her 'maidenhead' was strictly guarded; but with someone else's wife, a mature woman who could cope discreetly with a lover's attentions. In its highest concept, courtly love was a spiritual thing and stopped short at the knight's sentimental sighings and his fervent protestations of adoration, the lady merely accepting his love with only token acknowledgement. Who is to say, however, how many ladies consented to secret embraces, or more, from their knights?

The fourteenth-century poet Geoffrey Chaucer was well versed in courtly love conventions (being the translator into English of the *Roman de la Rose*, which epitomized courtly love poetry), but his own work, the *Canterbury Tales*, offers a wide variety of views on love and marriage, from the bawdiness of the Wife of Bath through the Merchant's cautionary tale of a dotard and his young wife, and the Clerk's praise of women's constancy in the story of 'Patient Griselda', to the Franklin's tale, in which Chaucer turned courtly love topsy-turvy to prove that true love could exist between husband and wife.

For most couples, affection, at least, might grow from shared interests, shared work and a family, but then, as now, there were marriages in which one partner, or both, found the other intolerable. A peasant or a citizen could just abscond, disappear into a distant place and, conscience permitting, marry again with no one any the wiser—of course, land-owners, or nobles in the public eye, could not. Their first hope might be a partner's death: so many people died young in those centuries (men in battle, women in childbirth, even more in epidemics) that many a husband or wife was freed from an unhappy marriage by Providence. Some few might take matters into their own hands, and back in 1072 a Church council meeting at Rouen declared that, "It is forbidden anyone who, in the lifetime of his wife, has been charged with adultery, after her death to marry the woman with respect to whom he was accused, for great mischief has ensued from this practice, and men have even murdered their wives."[8]

But such cases were few, for it was possible for couples to obtain an annulment of their marriage on several grounds (though not a divorce as we know it, for incompatibility or adultery). First, there was the compara-tively easy repudiation of a fiancé, after a *de futuro* espousal—usually, as we have seen, by a boy or girl betrothed as a child who revoked vows at the age of consent. A marriage (i.e. vows *de praesenti*) could be annulled by the Church if it had not been consummated or if one or both partners petitioned on grounds of consanguinity or affinity previously unknown (or conveniently ignored)—that was more difficult, but it could be done, even if there were children of the marriage, and in fact, if both parties swore that they had married in good faith, their children would still be regarded as legitimate.

More unusual were cases were one partner declared that he, or she, had been married forcibly. At the beginning of the thirteenth century, one Margaret fitzGerold claimed that King John had married her to his military commander Fawkes de Bréauté against her will and to her disparagement; she won her divorce.

The case of another Lady Margaret (surname unknown), in 1270, was more complex and far more distressing than most appeals. She informed Pope Alexander III that, as a child, she had been espoused to a knight, but three or four years later their families had agreed that the espousal should be annulled, as the couple were related within the prohibited degrees. Her husband had then taken her away by force, imprisoned her for three years and turned the betrothal into a marriage by raping her. Pregnant, she had escaped from him, but while her family were trying to obtain her divorce in the Bishop of Lincoln's court, the knight was appealing to the Archbishop of Canterbury to validate the marriage. When the Archbishop ordered him to pay for Margaret's board in a convent until her child was born, he refused and, with drawn sword, chased her through Lincoln into St Margaret's Church, where she claimed sanctuary. Terrified, she had promised to abide by the decision of lay arbitrators to be chosen by both parties, but now the Pope decreed that, if the arbitrators pronounced against her plea, she should be absolved from that promise, and then the original case for annulment should be considered. The Bishop of St Asaph's, whom the Pope put in charge of the case, was to see that the knight did not harass Margaret any more.

And that is all that we know of that divorce. Its outcome was never recorded.

That is how it is with the Middle Ages: what evidence we have on weddings and marriages is fascinating—but incomplete. How many couples were there like Lady Margaret and her violent knight? How many like Thomas Betson and his Kathryn? How many girls dared defy their parents, as Elizabeth Paston did, when faced with a repellent suitor? And what of the great mass of the peasantry, illiterate and therefore unheard today, who loved or hated a partner, mourned or rejoiced at a partner's death? The medieval voices that still echo today are so few compared with those that will be forever silent.

Anglo-Saxons and Danes

When the missionary St Augustine arrived in England in 597, he found his task of converting the English made considerably easier by the fact that his first host, King Ethelbert of Kent, had a Christian wife, Bertha of France; a few years later, the faith spread northwards with another royal marriage, that of Ethelbert and Bertha's daughter Ethelburga and Edwin of Northumbria. However, even in Kent some continued in the old pagan ways, and the second-generation Christian King Eadbald horrified his clergy by reverting to the pagan practice of marrying his stepmother. As we have seen, it was some time before the Church was able to assert its authority over marriage customs, but in the ninth century King Ethelbald of Wessex was forced by St Swithin to give up *his* stepmother-wife.

Until the ninth century, England was divided into seven small kingdoms, but now and then one of the kings managed to impose authority over all the others. One such was Offa of Mercia, whose power was recognized by the great Emperor Charlemagne in 789, when he proposed a marriage between one of Offa's daughters and his son Charles. Offa may have been gratified, but he was also wary, suspecting that Charlemagne mistrusted a united England and had plans to subjugate it—using the Mercian princess as a hostage to prevent English resistance. To test the Emperor's good faith, the King declined the proposal but countered it with one for his own heir, Egfrith, to marry a daughter of Charlemagne. When the Emperor refused, relations between England and the Empire deteriorated to such a point that a trade-embargo was imposed.

A century later, when England had been finally united by the House of Wessex, there were Continental marriages in plenty. King Alfred married a daughter to a count of Flanders; Edward 'the Elder' gave his daughter Edgiva to Charles 'the Simple', King of France, and King Athelstan sent four of his sisters abroad to marry. The first to go was Edhilda, whose hand was solicited in 926 by Hugh, Duke of the Franks. Hugh certainly knew how to persuade Athelstan to give him his bride: the English King was an avid collector of holy relics, so when Hugh sent his proposal, appropriate gifts went with it—not only jewels and horses and "perfumes such as never had been seen in England before" but also an iron nail from the Crucifixion, set in the pommel of a sword, "the banner of the most blessed martyr St Maurice", "part of the holy and adorable Cross enclosed in crystal" and "a small portion of the crown of thorns".[1] Two years later, Edhilda's sisters Edith and Elgiva were shipped off to the Emperor Henry I, for him to select one as his son Otto's bride—the reject to marry a Burgundian prince; the fourth princess, Edgiva, married the King of Provence.

But international marriages brought problems as well as gifts and prestige. These were years of war in Europe, war between the kings of France and dukes of the Franks, between the French and subjects of the emperors, and more than once King Athelstan was called upon to take sides among his sisters' husbands. Such divided loyalties, the direct result of royal marriages, were to bedevil the lives of generations of the royal family, even into the twentieth century.

For the most part, however, English kings were content to marry into the native nobility, the class of 'ealdormen' (later called 'earls') who ruled in the shires. These matches attracted little attention from the chroniclers—except when something went wrong.

There was King Edwy (955-9), for example, and his 'irregular' marriage to one Elgiva—irregular in that the couple were related within the 'prohibited degrees'. Since the Church would not sanction their marriage, Elgiva could not be crowned with her husband, but she had, it seems, no intention of missing the festivities altogether. When the King suddenly disappeared from his coronation banquet, and the Archbishop sent a bishop and his kinsman St Dunstan to seek him, the two prelates came upon a shocking scene: 'God's anointed' was found reclining between his wife and her mother, "embracing them wantonly and shamelessly by turns"; he had already discarded his crown, which had rolled away across the floor. Horrified, Dunstan "dragged the lascivious boy from the chamber",[2] clapped the crown back on his head and bore him off to report to the Archbishop. But nothing the churchmen could say or do could persuade Edwy to renounce his wife; indeed, they only lost influence to her, and she had Edwy banish Dunstan.

That stern saint reappeared, however, in the reign of Edwy's brother Edgar—and again challenged a royal marriage . . .

When Edgar was left a widower, in about the year 960, he sought to marry a daughter of the ealdorman of Devon, a girl of reputedly wonderful beauty, named Elfrida. To propose for him, he sent a close friend, Ordgar, Ealdorman of East Anglia, but so beautiful was Elfrida that Ordgar betrayed the King's trust and made love to her on his own account. Reporting back to Edgar, Ordgar said that Elfrida was so ugly that the King would be dishonoured if he were to marry her, but that he, Ordgar, would be willing to do so, to save offending the girl's father. In the months that followed their wedding, Edgar was perplexed to hear further reports of Elfrida's beauty, and at last, unable to contain his curiosity, he set off for Ordgar's manor. When the Ealdorman heard that the King was coming, he was terrified; he tried to persuade his wife to disguise herself, even to mar her own beauty. Now one source says that Elfrida was more afraid of being found out in subterfuge than of facing up at once to Edgar's anger; another claims that she did not care for Ordgar and was eager to attract the King—but all agree that she defied her husband, put on her best clothes to meet Edgar and "omitted nothing which could stimulate the desire of a young and powerful man".[3] The inevitable happened: when Edgar saw Elfrida, he wanted her. For a while, he pretended to have forgiven the Ealdorman and accepted his hospitality, but while the two men were out hunting, Edgar ran Ordgar through with his spear—as if by accident, killing him.

The wedding of the King and Elfrida took place almost immediately after the murder, but it did not long go unchallenged. St Dunstan appeared at the foot of the couple's bed and recited to them their sins. They ignored him; they were not ashamed; the marriage stood.

Elfrida proved as bad a character as Edgar. When he died and was succeeded by his son Edward, by his first marriage, she contrived the boy's murder, to put her own son, Ethelred, on the throne. He was the king called 'the Unready'—that is, 'redeless', meaning 'lacking counsel' or 'unadvised', and certainly the King seemed powerless to prevent the conquest of England by the Norsemen (Danes and Norwegians) that troubled his reign. The Norse King Swein deposed Ethelred for a time in 1013, and his son Canute overthrew Ethelred's son Edmund and ruled England himself (as well as Norway and Denmark) between 1016 and 1035.

In an attempt to gain a maritime ally against the Norsemen's powerful fleets, Ethelred had married Emma, daughter of Richard, Duke of Normandy, but after Ethelred's death, Emma married Canute. To complicate matters, the new King had a wife already, Elgiva of Northampton, but in view of Emma's higher rank, Elgiva was sent off to Denmark, where she reigned as queen consort, visited from time to time by Canute, who was apparently not the least ashamed of his bigamy.

Like their predecessors on the English throne, the Norse kings always had an eye to a foreign alliance, and in 1036 Canute's daughter Gunhilda became the wife of the Emperor Henry III. Almost immediately, the young Empress was charged with 'spouse-breaking' (adultery) and under the crude law of the time had to prove her innocence not by reason and explanation but by force. Indeed, she was fortunate not to have to undergo the test of the hot irons, which were said not to burn the hand of a faithful wife; instead, she was allowed to choose a champion to do battle to the death with her accuser. So confident was Gunhilda of virtue prevailing that she chose not a seasoned warrior but a puny boy, one of her own pages. She was vindicated when the boy killed the false witness—of course described by the chroniclers as a Goliath to his David. Thus exonerated, Gunhilda might have been reinstated, but she refused to return to the husband who had so mistrusted her and took herself off to a convent, where she died two years after her wedding.

With the death of Gunhilda's brother Hardicanute, the crown of England was restored to the Anglo-Saxon line, to Ethelred's son Edward, later called 'the Confessor'. As a monarch, he was little stronger than his father, dependent for years on Earl Godwin of Wessex to keep the peace in the shires. To strengthen his hold on the King, Godwin married him to his daughter Edith—not with any great success, for Edward refused to consummate the marriage. Why, is not clear. Even the historian William of Malmesbury, writing just two centuries later, could not find out the truth of it:

> When she became his wife, the King so artfully managed that he neither removed her from his bed nor knew her after the manner of men. I have not been able to discover whether he acted thus from dislike of her family, which he prudently dissembled from the exigency of the time, or out of pure regard to chastity; yet it is most notoriously affirmed that the track of my history is here but dubious because the truth of the facts hangs in suspense. [1]

When, in 1051, Edward quarrelled with Godwin, Queen Edith shared in her family's disgrace, and for a time, before peace was restored between King and Earl, she was left in a convent. The price of the reconciliation was Godwin's delivery to Edward's cousin William of Normandy of one of his sons and a grandson, as surety for the Earl's good behaviour.

The sympathy between the cousins Edward and William led—at least so William said—to the childless King's offering him the crown of England, as his heir. The Norman was also to declare, years later, that Godwin's son Harold had promised to support his claim to the throne, in return for the freeing of the hostages and a marriage with William's daughter Agatha. Be that as it may, when Edward died, in 1066, Harold Godwinsson had himself proclaimed King of England, dealt with a threat from a Norse claimant and led out an English army to meet the invading Normans.

The two armies clashed at Hastings in October 1066, and Harold was killed in the battle. Thus, by conquest, if not (as he always protested), by right, William the Norman became King of England.

There is a postscript to the story, however. When William's son Henry came to the throne, in 1100, one of the first things he did was to marry one of the last surviving members of the Anglo-Saxon royal dynasty. His wife Matilda was the daughter of the Scots King Malcolm III and of St Margaret, great-grand-daughter of Ethelred 'the Unready'. Through that marriage, today's royal family can claim descent from a line of English kings that stretches back to the dawn of the nation's history.

Normans and Plantagenets

Marriage was one of the first duties of kings in the Middle Ages—to beget sons to succeed to their throne. In a world that regarded women as unfit to rule, it was essential for the stability of a kingdom for its king to have a *male* heir. Henry I's lack of a son, and the attempt by his daughter to rule, brought England to virtual anarchy in the twelfth century.

A second consideration prompting kings to marry was their desire to win foreign allies and for "the extinction of wars and the strengthening of friendship among loving princes, for by such means tranquillity is often produced among discordant minds,"[1] as Henry VI once put it. A match with the daughter of a Continental neighbour could seal a pact of friendship or a peace-treaty, ensure an ally against a common enemy or gain trade advantages for merchants in foreign markets. Of course, there was no guarantee that the alliance would be honoured: England and Scotland were frequently at war throughout the Middle Ages, despite the regular intermarriage of their royal families.

In Scotland it was common for the sons and daughters of kings to be matched with the native peerage, as often as not to bind a disloyal clan to the Crown or to win support for a king against another clan. It was not so in England. There such marriages were looked upon with suspicion: Henry III was severely censured for marrying his sister Eleanor to the controversial statesman Simon de Montfort; Edward III alienated his lords by marrying his sons to heiresses whose lands those lords coveted for themselves.

Most of England's kings had never set eyes on their brides before the marriage contract was completed, because it was the terms of the marriage, the political advantages of it, that mattered, not the looks and personality of the bride and how the couple liked each other. Nor did the majority of English princesses have a chance to assess their bridegrooms before marriage but were despatched 'sight unseen' to their weddings.

Cruel as it may seem now to use young people as bargaining-counters in diplomacy, or as mere breeding-stock, those matches must be seen in the context of their time. Arranged marriages were the norm in royal circles: children were brought up in full knowledge of their eventual fate, with duty to 'king and country' their priority. Nor was the wrench from home as great as it would be today, for there was no real family life in the ruling classes at any level, to be missed and pined for by an 'exported' bride. Indeed, some infant princesses were sent abroad to their future husbands' countries, to learn the manners, language and customs, before they could form any close ties with their homeland. Henry I's daughter Matilda was sent to her German bridegroom when she was only eight, and when she returned to England, a widow, at twenty-two, her father's courtiers found her thoroughly German.

The youngest princess to come into England as queen consort was Richard II's second wife, Isabelle of France, only seven years old when she was married but already appreciative of her prestige and responsibilities. When told of her destiny, the little girl is reported to have said: "An it please God and my lord my father that I shall be Queen of England, I shall be glad thereof, for it is showed me that I shall then be a great lady."[2]

Even when kings and princes were free to choose their own wives, they would rarely take advantage of the opportunity to marry for love: the results of a diplomatic marriage were far too valuable to be given up for mere personal considerations. King John was one of the exceptions: he fell in love with the twelve-year-old Isabelle of Angoulême, so the story goes, and married her despite the fact that she was engaged to another man—a man so furious at the King's 'theft' of his bride that he rebelled against him. When, in the fifteenth century, Edward IV fell in love with Elizabeth Woodville, he married her secretly, even while negotiations were in train in France for him to marry the French King's sister-in-law. France did not retaliate—though it had good excuse, but Edward's ambassador arranging the match, the Earl of Warwick, added his humiliation to a list of grudges he bore the King that one day prompted him to treason: he temporarily dethroned Edward before he was killed in battle.

Negotiations between royal families for a marriage often began when the couple were still in their cradles: one of Edward I's daughters was only four days old when her father discussed with the Count of Burgundy's envoys her future marriage with the Count's son. (It never transpired: she died before her fifth birthday.) But while it is true that many royal children were betrothed very young, in England at least child-marriages were in a small minority. An analysis of the ages at which kings of England married in the Middle Ages shows that the average was twenty-four; their younger sons' average age at marriage was twenty, their daughters' sixteen.[3]

Except when royal match-making was prompted by a specific event— such as the end of a war, it was usually begun with a hint from resident ambassadors, sounding out the feasibility of an alliance, or the arrival of special envoys with a formal proposal. When Emperor Henry V sent to ask for the hand of Henry I's daughter Matilda in 1110, his representatives were "persons of tall stature, remarkable for their polished manners, of noble rank and surpassing wealth".[4] Nevertheless, no one saw anything incongruous in the Duke of Burgundy's sending his own illegitimate son to ask Edward IV for his sister Margaret, to be the Duke's wife. Margaret presented herself for inspection "richly apparelled, accompanied with a great multitude of ladies and gentlewomen . . . with so sober demeanour, so fair a visage, so loving a countenance and so princely a port that she was worthy to match in matrimony with the greatest prince of the world",[5] so an observer wrote, but even had she been plain and gauche, the match would probably have transpired.

Sometimes negotiations between the two parties would drag on for months, even years, while commissioners haggled over the dowry or when a new turn in international relations changed circumstances. When the Count of Armagnac was urging Henry VI to accept one of his daughters in 1442, offering him "silver hills and gold mountains" as her dowry, Henry was told that the Armagnac girls were "pre-eminent in splendid virtues, in comeliness of manners, as well as in the perfect gifts of nature and nobility of birth", but though he was generally indifferent to women, he would not accept until his Court painter had been to Armagnac to take their portraits, which the King stipulated should be drawn "in their kirtles simple, and their visages like as ye see, and their stature and their beauty, the colour of their skin and their countenances".[6] In the event, the affair never came to a wedding for his Council decided in favour of a French match that would bring peace to the two nations after long war.

Sometimes a princess had already been sent to her future bridegroom, already betrothed, when a match was called off. In 1338 Edward III handed his four-year-old daughter Joan over to the Emperor, to live in Germany until she was old enough to marry the Duke of Austria, but the following year she was sent home, when the boy's guardian repudiated the match. King Louis of France sent his daughter Alice to Henry II, when she was only an infant, to be betrothed to his son Richard, but years later, long after they were old enough to marry, she was still in Henry's custody: he had fallen in love with her himself; some said she even had children by him—in any event, when Henry II died and Richard succeeded him, he made no move to marry Alice and in the end sent her home.

When a king of England sent his eldest daughter to her wedding, he called in a customary 'feudal due' from his barons, a tax to provide her with a dowry, but his younger daughters were dowered at his own expense. Sometimes a bride brought a dowry of land, as well as cash, plate and jewels. In 1173 Henry II contracted his youngest son, the future King John, to the heiress of the Count of Maurienne, with the contract stipulating that she would bring the Prince 4,000 marks in silver and the county of Maurienne if her father did not produce a son before he died; if he did, then she was to have certain lands stipulated very carefully in the dowry. However, she died a couple of years later, so all the haggling, and the clerks' careful phrasing of the documents, was wasted.

Very occasionally, a bride would be accepted without a dowry, as when Henry VI turned down the Armagnac treasure in favour of peace with France. Anne of Bohemia, who married Richard II in 1382, was another bride who brought nothing but her kinfolks' good will, but then she was the daughter and sister of emperors; in fact, England offered the Emperor a £15,000 loan for the privilege of calling Anne its queen.

The financial settlement was not the only documentation of a royal marriage: almost invariably a papal dispensation had to be invoked, to permit cousins to wed. Since royal families regularly intermarried, and since the 'prohibited degrees' stretched so far, few royal matches were made without recourse to the Papal Curia. This is the letter which Pope Alexander VI sent to Henry VII's daughter Margaret in 1500 to allow her to marry James IV of Scotland:

> We, anxiously watching over the state of all the faithful in Christ, and more especially of those possessing generous royal blood, are careful to accede willingly to those prayers by which the people, and especially the Catholic kings and princes, may be able to obtain fortunate success. Since, therefore, as the petition lately shewn to us from you averred, you, the firstborn daughter of our dearest son in Christ, Henry, the illustrious King of England, being now about 10½ years of age, cannot contract marriage with our dearest son in Christ, James, illustrious King of Scotland, according to the desire of the said King James, to whom you are related in the third and fourth degree of consanguinity and affinity, unless the authority of the apostolic see be granted for this: we, wishing fitly to provide thereupon, inclining to your applications on this behalf by our apostolic authority and of certain knowledge, by the tenor of these present letters, as a gift of especial favour, grant a dispensation to you and the said King James, freely and lawfully to contract matrimony together from this time forth and to remain therein when it shall have been contracted.[7]

When Henry I wanted to marry Matilda of Scotland, in 1100, it was not consanguinity that put doubts about the match into churchmen's minds but the fact that Matilda was thought to be a nun. Archbishop St Anselm hastily convened a Church council to examine the girl, and to receive depositions from her guardians, and a strange story came to light. The Princess *had* worn the veil of a nun, said the prioress of the convent where she had been educated, but only to protect her from the dubious attentions of Henry's elder brother William II when he came to visit her. (Obviously the prioress had heard of William's evil reputation—but not that he was homosexual.) Matilda had kept the veil on after William had left, but only until her father, King Malcolm of Scotland, arrived: when Malcolm saw Matilda dressed as a nun, he was furious and tore the veil from her head and trampled on it. The Princess corroborated the story, so she and King Henry were allowed to marry. (Even so, years later, people brought up the business of the veiling, when they wanted to cast doubts on the legitimacy of the couple's daughter.)

Another requirement of the Church was, of course, the consent of the bridal pair themselves—not at the betrothal, when they were under age, but when they were old enough to marry. Only rarely was that consent refused, and when it was, it was usua'ly for political reasons on the parents' part rather than personal reservations by the young couple. In 1346, however, one brave soul, Louis of Flanders, did not wait to have his consent demanded . . .

Louis had no cause to love his prospective father-in-law, Edward III, who had caused the death of his, Louis's, father; besides, the young man had had an offer from France of help in gaining the restoration of his county if he would accept a marriage with a daughter of Brabant. When Edward III and the Flemish guardians of Louis's inheritance got wind of his plans to change brides, he was put in prison, but he soon convinced them of his change of heart and actually went through the betrothal ceremony with Edward's daughter Isabel. But all the time Louis was still plotting with the French, and in the very week of the wedding he managed to escape, riding hell for leather into France, where he married the Brabant girl. The English Princess Isabel's reaction to this jilting is not recorded.

It may only be legend—it probably is—but there is a good story about Matilda of Flanders, the prospective bride of Duke William of Normandy ('William the Conqueror'), refusing to marry him because he was illegitimate. When William heard that she had withheld her consent to their marriage, he had his own way of dealing with her: he presented himself at her home in Bruges, stormed into her chamber and beat and kicked her until she was almost unconscious—not hard work, since, it is said, William was nearly 6 feet tall, Matilda only some 50 inches. Perversely, this treatment impressed her: even while she was recovering, she was heard to declare that she would marry the Norman and no other. And marry they did.

So—the bride has been chosen; negotiations have been concluded; a contract has been signed, stipulating the dowry; maybe a dispensation has been obtained from Rome. Sometimes the next step is a proxy betrothal or even a proxy wedding, often a requirement when a bride's parents refused to send her from home while still a child. Margaret Tudor, eldest daughter of Henry VII, was promised to James IV of Scotland when she was only ten, but since her parents wanted to keep her in England until she reached puberty, her own promise to the marriage had to be solicited when she reached the legal age of consent. It took the form of a proxy wedding with the Earl of Bothwell, representing James, and the Princess's curious vow ran:

> I, Margaret, . . . wittingly and of deliberate mind, having twelve years complete in age in the month of November last, contract matrimony with the right excellent, right high and mighty prince James, King of Scotland, for the person of whom, Patrick, Earl of Bothwell, is procurator; and take the said James, King of Scotland, unto and for my husband and spouse, and all

other for him forsake, during his and mine lives natural; and thereto I plight
and give to him, in your person as procurator aforesaid, my faith and troth.[8]

Even stranger is the tale of Philippa of Lancaster's proxy wedding to the
King of Portugal: the Archbishop of Braganza, representing the King, not
only recited his master's vows but had to undergo the ordeal of being
'bedded' with Philippa, though only to the extent of being laid beside her
on a bed in full gaze of the Court, to signify the consummation of the
marriage which made it even more binding on the King and new Queen
of Portugal. In 1282 there had been a similar proxy wedding and bedding
in Spain, when Sir John de Vescy acted the part of the bride, Edward I's
daughter Eleanor, lying down beside the bridegroom, Alfonso of Aragon.
But there that marriage ended, for before Eleanor could go out to join
Alfonso, he was laid under papal ban and deprived of his kingdom by the
Pope. When Aragon's problems were at last solved, at the end of the
decade, Alfonso sent for his 'wife'—but too late: before she could embark,
he died.

Spain seems to have been unlucky for English brides. William I's
daughter Agatha died on her way to be married there, and in 1348
Edward III's daughter Joan (who had had such bad luck in Germany, as
we have seen), having stopped to rest at Bordeaux on her way to marry
Pedro, heir of Castile, contracted that terrible plague known as 'the Black
Death' and died there.

When a princess did arrive at a foreign Court for her wedding, her
worth was reckoned only minimally from her looks and character, far
more by her dowry and the furniture, plate, gowns and jewels she
brought with her. The records of the trousseaux of English princesses
show them to have been well provided for. Henry II's daughter Matilda
took fifty-six silver coffers of various goods with her to Germany as a
bride; her niece Isabel, sent to wed Emperor Frederick, had fourteen
robes, all fur-trimmed, and two beds, one with arras (tapestry) hangings
and one draped with cloth-of-gold. Edward II's daughter Eleanor carried
with her to Guelders a trousseau that included a mantle and hood of blue
cloth, ermine-trimmed; two pelisses in green, with gold beading; a
surtunic of cloth-of-gold, embroidered with a hunting-scene; a coronal of
260 large pearls and another of 420 pieces of silver; among her household
effects was a bed hung with green velvet embroidered with the arms of
England and Guelders in gold, its curtains of Tripoli silk also embroidered
with gold, and a crimson cover with another embroidered hunting-scene.
Of the five 'chariots' she took with her, the finest was painted all over
with coats-of-arms, and it was lined with purple velvet 'powdered' with
gold stars, each of which had a gem at its centre.

The famous London mercer and Lord Mayor Richard Whittington was
responsible for gathering the trousseau of Henry IV's daughter Blanche,
aged ten, when she went to marry Emperor Rupert's son Louis in 1402.
Dozens of gowns and mantles are listed in her account-book, including a

gown of cloth-of-gold from Cyprus, worked with white flowers and edged with miniver, another of red velvet embroidered with pearls, a red cloth-of-gold of Cyprus embroidered with roses, and one of green cloth-of-gold with a blue train, worked with golden eagles.

Unfortunately no medieval chroniclers (all men, most of them monks) deign to describe a royal wedding-dress; were it not for the brides' account-books, this most fascinating of items would elude us. As it is, we know what only a few royal brides wore. Edward I's daughter Elizabeth's gown was of embroidered silk with silver-gilt buttons—thirty-five tailors, working four days and four nights, had made it; her coronal was of gold set with rubies, emeralds and pearls. Her niece Eleanor was married in a robe of Spanish cloth-of-gold embroidered with vari-coloured silks, under a tunic and mantle of crimson velvet embroidered with gold. When Edward IV's sister Margaret married the Duke of Burgundy, in 1468, she was wearing a surcoat and mantle of white cloth-of-gold, furred with ermine. But apparently more resplendent than any of the royal brides was King Richard I at his wedding to Berengaria of Navarre, in 1191: he appeared in a tunic of rose samite, a cape embroidered with golden crescents and silver sunbursts, a scarlet cap embroidered with gold animals and birds, and cloth-of-gold boots with silver spurs. (So dazzled was the chronicler then that he completely forgot to mention the bride's dress.)

The arrival of a royal bride-to-be was usually the occasion of tremendous festivities, not only at her bridegroom's Court but along her road from coast to capital. Henry VI's bride, Margaret of Anjou, was greeted by a peasantry sporting daisies in honour of her name, and when she came to London, on 28th May 1445, she was met by a 'pageant-car' at the end of London Bridge, on which was staged an allegory of Peace and Plenty. On the bridge itself was a representation of Noah's Ark, at Cornhill a tableau of St Margaret with angels, and at Chepe conduit one of the Wise and Foolish Virgins. The men of Chepe had also built a 'Heavenly Jerusalem', and at St Michael's in Querne citizens staged their impression of the Resurrection and Last Judgement. (These pageants were a fashion from the Continent and became extremely popular in London. In fact, their descendants can still be seen in London once a year, during the Lord Mayor's procession, the tableaux now mounted on lorries touring the streets.)

When Henry II's daughter Joan reached Palermo, for her wedding to the King of Sicily in 1177, the whole city welcomed her by illuminating the night: ". . . lamps, so many and so large, were lighted up that the city seemed almost to be on fire".[9] When her niece Isabel arrived at Cologne to meet her bridegroom, the Emperor Frederick, "there went out to meet her, with flowers, palm branches and in festive dresses, about ten thousand of the citizens, mounted on Spanish horses, who put them to full speed and engaged in jousting with one another."[10] Isabel responded with a courtesy that guaranteed her popularity: ". . . learning that everyone, and especially the noble ladies of the city, who sat in balconies, were desirous of seeing her face, she took her cap and hood from her head, for all to get a sight of her, for doing which everyone praised her and, after they had gazed at her, gave her great commendation for her beauty as well as her humility."[11]

Some of England's medieval kings married at home—Henry I at Westminster and at Windsor, Henry III in Canterbury Cathedral, Edward III at York Minster, Henry VI at the little Benedictine abbey of Titchfield, in Hampshire; others married abroad, in France or in Spain, and Richard I leads the field with his wedding on the island of Cyprus, when he was on his way to the Crusade in the Holy Land. But wherever the kings married, their chroniclers give no account of the ceremony itself, and we must presume that it was basically that used by all, perhaps with the addition of music and choirs. Only one royal wedding service really caught the chroniclers' attention, and that was at Henry I's marriage (his second), in 1121, to Adelicia of Louvain. Since the King was then staying at Windsor Castle, and Windsor was in the diocese of Salisbury, the Bishop of Salisbury reasonably thought it his right to officiate at the royal nuptials, and he was actually donning his robes when he was informed by the Archbishop of Canterbury that *he* would be conducting the service. To settle what threatened to become an acrimonious dispute, a Church council was convened, and it did not take long to decide that Canterbury had precedence. Though the Archbishop had his way with the wedding, the King, who had some fondness for the Bishop, invited Salisbury to crown him and his bride a week later. Then Canterbury struck again—this was, after all, the most important of royal ceremonies, one traditionally the right of the primate; but he arrived too late: there were the royal couple already crowned and enthroned by Salisbury. Tactfully, King Henry suggested that, if the Archbishop thought the crowning had not been done properly, he could do it again himself. He did.

In the centuries after the Norman Conquest the bride of an English king was usually crowned after her wedding—but it had not always been so. In the years after the unification of England (in the ninth century), there was a marked antipathy to the practice of allowing royal state to a woman, and more than one chronicler puts this down to the infamy of a certain crowned Queen Consort of Wessex, Eadburga of Mercia, who had given queens a bad name. For some years afterwards, the king's wife went uncrowned and was called merely 'the lady'. Some Anglo-Saxon consorts were subsequently crowned, but it was only after the Norman Conquest that it became customary. Often kings were re-crowned at their brides' coronations.

A thirteenth-century monk, Matthew Paris, was an eye-witness at the coronation that followed Henry III's wedding to Eleanor of Provence in 1236:

There was assembled at the King's nuptial festivities such a host of nobles of both sexes, such numbers of religious men, such crowds of the populace and such a variety of actors, that London, with its capacious bosom, could scarcely contain them. The whole city was ornamented with flags and banners, chaplets and hangings, candles and lamps, and with wonderful devices and extraordinary representations, and all the roads were cleansed from mud and dirt, sticks and everything offensive. . . .

The Archbishop of Canterbury, by the right especially belonging to him, performed the duty of crowning, with the usual solemnities.[12]

The banquets that followed royal weddings were gargantuan feasts. When Margaret of England married Alexander of Scotland at York in 1251, the citizens and neighbouring landowners contributed all the bread, two hundred deer, three hundred does, two hundred young bucks and a hundred boars; the King of England's fishermen brought in 230 fish, and the Archbishop of York donated more than sixty fat oxen. After the coronation of Henry V's bride, Catherine of France, in 1420, the feast was of 'Lenten fare', almost totally of fish, but so richly sauced and seasoned as to tempt any faster's appetite to gluttony. Just one of the three courses included carp, turbot, tench, perch, fresh sturgeon with whelks, eels roasted with lamprey, roast porpoise and prawns, flanked by dates 'in compost', a cream mould and that famous medieval confection named 'the subtelty', here in a form of a man on horseback, a tiger whelp in his arms. The English chronicler of Margaret of York's wedding to the Duke of Burgundy, in 1468, was in raptures at the feast: "a swan roasted and silvered . . . a peacock of like form, . . . a unicorn bearing trussing-coffers full of comfits; an hart charged with a basket filled with oranges, and many dishes of delicates, marvellous to me . . .".[13]

For days on end a royal Court would feast the bridal couple, and there would be dancing and singing and, for the knights, jousting for prizes. When Edward IV's five-year-old son Richard 'espoused' the six-year-old Anne Mowbray, in January 1478, the little girl reigned as 'Princess of the Feast' and handed out the jousters' prizes of jewelled trinkets, the chief of which was a gold brooch in the form of an 'A' (for 'Anne'), set with a diamond.

Despite all the careful planning, the weighing of this or that alliance, the provision of dowry and trousseau, the church ceremonial and Court festivities, the climax of the wedding came not between a king and queen, or prince and princess, but between a man and woman; not in fine clothes and crowns but in nakedness; not with a crowd of prelates and courtiers in attendance but with two people alone in the dark.

A royal wedding is a matter of a few months' planning, a few days' festivities; a marriage demands years of careful nurture.

Some royal couples, meeting as strangers on their wedding-day, built up marriages of affection, companionship and trust—as did Edward I and Eleanor of Castile, his faithful companion on military expeditions in Europe and the Near East, the mother of a fine brood of children; when she died, Edward erected monuments to her that were expressions of his real grief; there can still be seen, along the route of her funeral cortège from Lincolnshire to London, some survivors of the numerous 'Eleanor crosses' he raised in her memory. Richard II's grief for a beloved wife took a different form: he razed to the ground the Palace of Sheen, her favourite home, unable to bear looking on the place where they had been so happy together. Some couples, however, blighted their marriages with fierce mutual antipathy and even violence: Eleanor of Aquitaine supported her sons in a civil war against her husband, Henry II; Isabelle of France was so humiliated by her husband's treatment of her (he was homosexual and allowed his 'minions' to rule through him and to insult his wife) that she took a lover, raised an army against the King, dethroned him and instigated his murder.

It was taken for granted that kings should have mistresses—though their wives were not allowed similar latitude. Henry I is reputed to have had twenty-odd children by various women, and Edward IV, even though he had married for love rather than policy, kept his mistresses openly at Court. But let a prince marry his mistress, and it was a scandal. When Edward III's son John of Gaunt took as his third wife his mistress of many years, Catherine Swynford (by whom he already had four children), the ladies of the Court "were greatly shocked and thought the Duke much to blame. They said he had disgraced himself by thus marrying his concubine. . . . They themselves would be disgraced if they suffered such a baseborn duchess . . . to take precedence, and their hearts would burst with grief were it to happen. . . . They considered the Duke of Lancaster a doting fool. . . ."[14]

When Lancaster's grandson Humphrey, Duke of Gloucester, abandoned his wife Jacqueline, Countess of Hainault and Holland, simply because he was finding it too difficult to keep control of her lands, and married her lady-in-waiting Eleanor Cobham, the scandal spread even beyond the Court:

> . . . one Mistress Stokes, with diverse other stout women of London, of good reckoning and well apparelled, came openly to the upper Parliament and delivered letters to the Duke of Gloucester and to the Archbishops and to the other lords there present, containing matter of rebuke and sharp reprehension to the Duke of Gloucester, because he would not deliver his wife Jacqueline out of her grievous imprisonment [over on the Continent] . . . and for his public keeping by him of an adultress, contrary to the law of God and the honourable estate of matrimony.[15]

Parliament would not see another such female demonstration until the Suffragette riots at the beginning of this century—and, needless to say, this was equally ineffective. But perhaps Mistress Stokes and her friends had their triumph when, some years later, Duchess Eleanor was found guilty of witchcraft and sentenced to do public penance through the streets of London.

Marriage, birth, inheritance—these were vital factors in the political life of the Middle Ages, but they would be even more vital to England's peace and stability in the sixteenth century . . .

Medieval Scotland

The marriages of the Anglo-Saxon kings of England were, as we have seen, often of interest to the chroniclers. It was not so in Scotland in that period, when historical records on any subject are sparse. In fact, until the eleventh century it is hard to find even the name of a Scottish king's consort. Among the first is that of Gruoch, herself a member of the House of MacAlpin which had ruled the kingdom from the mid-ninth century; she married her cousin Macbeth, king between 1040 and 1057—the evil character given to her by Shakespeare is not historical.

Let us begin then with King Malcolm III, who reigned from 1058 to 1093 and who married first a noblewoman from the Orkneys, Ingeborg, and then St Margaret, one of the last members of the Anglo-Saxon dynasty.

Margaret had come to Scotland soon after the Norman Conquest, with her brother Edgar, who had been elected king by the English in 1066 but could not maintain his claim against the Norman armies. She married Malcolm in about 1069.

Since Margaret was later (in 1249) declared a saint, her life-story was well recorded, and one of the most interesting passages in a contemporary biography is that which tells of the depth of the Scottish King's love for her. By all accounts Malcolm was a rough man, and illiterate, but he was proud of his cultured and cosmopolitan consort (born in Hungary, educated at the frenchified Court of Edward 'the Confessor'), and he respected her love of books:

> . . . although ignorant of letters, he used to handle and gaze on the books in which she had been accustomed either to pray or to read; and when he heard from her which of them was dearest to her, to hold it dearest too, to kiss it and fondle it often. Sometimes also he called in a goldsmith and gave orders that the book should be adorned with gold and jewels; and the King himself used to bring it back, decorated, to the Queen, as a mark of his devotion.[1]

Malcolm raided England in 1070, during the general unrest there after the Norman Conquest, but thereafter relations improved between the neighbouring kingdoms, and his daughter Matilda's marriage to Henry I in 1100 opened the way for others—and for an influx of Norman guests into Scotland, many of whom stayed to take posts in government, to become Scottish barons and to add their quota of 'refinement' to the northern Court. It was a two-way traffic: Matilda went to the English King, and her sister Mary to a count of Boulogne, but in about the year 1107 their brother Alexander I married one of Henry I's illegitimate daughters, Sybilla, and a few years later the future King David married a great-niece of the Conqueror, Matilda, Countess of Huntingdon. (Obviously the English alliances were highly valued for a king to marry a royal bastard instead of a 'real' princess, especially as Sybilla herself was apparently not what a queen should be: "When she died, he [Alexander] did not much lament her loss," wrote a near-contemporary, "for there was, as they affirm, some defect about the lady, either in correctness of manners or elegance of person".[2])

In 1186 William 'the Lion' sealed a new peace with England by marrying a protégée of King Henry II, Ermengarde de Beaumont, whose father was a Norman lord, her mother one of Henry I's illegitimate daughters. They were married in Henry II's presence, at his manor of Woodstock in Oxfordshire, with four days of festivities at the expense of the English. Part of Ermengarde's dowry was Edinburgh Castle, which the English had taken from the Scots when they defeated them in war in 1173.

Later it became the custom for the English and Scots to meet at York for royal weddings. Alexander II and Henry III's sister Joan were married in the Minster in 1221, and thirty years later Henry took his daughter Margaret there, to marry Alexander III. This was a case where the *de futuro* vows were used, for Alexander was only ten, Margaret eleven, and for some years afterwards the Scottish regents housed them separately. By 1255, however, Margaret was becoming bored with her quiet life and angry that she was not allowed to be with her husband, and she complained to her father's envoys that she was "improperly kept in custody, or rather imprisoned, in . . . a sad and solitary place, devoid of wholesome air and out of sight of the green fields . . . neither was her husband permitted access to her or to enjoy the privileges of a husband".[3] Firm pressure from England brought the young couple together soon after.

When Margaret died, in 1275, she left Alexander a son to succeed him on the Scottish throne, but the young man died in 1284, and in an attempt to save his dynasty from extinction, Alexander married again. Perhaps he did so too hastily, for Yolande of Dreux, a connection of the dukes of Brittany, arrived in Scotland in 1285 under suspicion that she had broken strict vows to become the King's wife. As one chronicler put it, "Many people declare that, before her engagement beyond the sea, she had changed her dress in a convent of nuns, but that she altered her mind with the levity of a woman's heart and through ambition for a kingdom."[4] The urgent wedding went ahead, but then, when it had already been celebrated, when the festivities were underway, a warning omen occurred: a skeleton appeared from nowhere and began to dance among the courtiers. It was, of course, taken to portend a royal death—and so it did. In March 1286 Alexander was in the midst of a convivial evening in Edinburgh when he suddenly took it into his head to join his wife out at Kinghorn; it was a dark night, blowing a gale, and in the gloom he became separated from his companions; his horse stumbled and threw him over a cliff—his dead body was found later, the neck broken.

Queen Yolande swore that she was pregnant, that she was carrying the next king of Scotland, and for a while Court and Council believed her—until she was caught in an attempt to smuggle in a 'common' baby to pass off as her own. Her departure for France was not long delayed.

The one surviving descendant of Alexander III, his daughter Margaret's child, Margaret of Norway, was despatched from her home in Scandinavia to take the throne and, by treaty with England, to marry Edward I's heir. Had she arrived and married the future Edward II, the two kingdoms would have been joined some three centuries before the actual union of the crowns, under James VI and I; as it was, the three-year-old Margaret died on the voyage. And so there came the moment dreaded in every nation—that of a kingdom without a king. In fact, there were a dozen 'competitors' for the Scottish crown, through female lines descended from earlier kings, and their rivalry brought civil war, with England mixing in in an ostensible attempt to arbitrate. It was only some thirty years later that one of the claimants, Robert Bruce, defeated Edward II's army at Bannockburn and gave Scotland independence again. As undisputed king, he made peace with England and accepted the English princess Joan as his son David's bride.

Joan 'Makepeace', they called her, this seven-year-old girl matched with the four-year-old Scots boy, but the peace did not last long. When David and his brother-in-law Edward III went to war in 1333, David was defeated, forced to seek refuge in France for seven years and then, after an unsuccessful invasion of England, to spend eleven years in captivity there. Nor was the marriage itself successful: Joan was childless, and after her death in 1362 the King married his longtime mistress, Margaret Drummond, but she too gave him no children, and so, in 1371, the House of Bruce gave way to the House of Stewart, in the person of David's nephew, Robert II.

All through this period, members of the Scottish royal family had been marrying into the native nobility, 'condescending' to mate with mere knights and ladies—matches that would have been scorned by the Plantagenets but which in Scotland served to make allies for the kings in the factional warfare to which the realm was always prone. But where some matches bound clans to the Crown, they inevitably alienated others. For example, when George, Earl of Dunbar, offered Robert III a huge dowry with his daughter, to have her marry the King's heir, David, the head of the clan Douglas was heard "disdaining the Earl [of Dunbar's] blood to be advanced before his stock",[5] and Douglas outbid Dunbar to make his own daughter the bride—though not a queen, for David died before his father.

Dunbar demanded his down-payment back, of course, and when King Robert gave him only "frivolous and trifling answers",[6] the Earl turned to England for help. Robert thereupon deprived him of his earldom and demanded that Henry IV of England return the miscreant forthwith; when he did not, one of those futile little wars between the neighbours broke out yet again.

Henry IV had the good fortune to capture Robert III's son, and eventual heir, Prince James, when the boy was on the way to France to be brought up away from the factional dangers in Scotland. James stayed in England, comfortably housed, honourably treated, carefully educated, through the last years of his father's life and the first of his own reign, and when at last, in 1424, he was allowed to return to Scotland, he took an English bride with him—a young woman whom, it was said, he dearly loved.

In later years James wrote a fine poem entitled 'The Kingis Quhair' ('The King's Book') in which he recounted how, during his captivity, he had been sitting alone in his tower room meditating his sad exile when he caught sight of a beautiful girl walking in the garden below: he fell in love with her on sight. Then comes the dream-sequence conventional in love-poetry of the time, in which James describes a visit to the Court of Venus, the goddess of love, who promises help to win the lady. When he awakes, he is given his freedom and the lady and lives happily ever after, in "bliss with her that is my sovereign".

James may well have based his poem on an actual event in his life; he may well have fallen in love with Joan Beaufort, but romance apart, it would be typical of the ambitious Beaufort family, so powerful in the early years of Henry VI's reign, to marry one of their girls to the Scots King.

In December 1423 James was a signatory to the Treaty of London, by which he gained his freedom for the price of 60,000 marks—under the 'polite fiction' that this was the cost of his 'visit' to England (twenty-one hostages were sent from Scotland to stand surety for the payment), and he had to promise that Scotland would send no more military aid to France. Then, on 2nd February 1424, he married Joan Beaufort, whose 10,000-mark dowry went towards paying off his debt, and that spring the newly married couple went north.

James may have lived "in bliss" with Joan for the thirteen years that remained to him, but his promise to be faithful to England, against France, was not kept. France was at war with England again, and as in times past, a French king found it useful to have an ally in the north, so when negotiations were in train for James to send Scottish troops against England, the alliance between the two kingdoms included the marriage of his eldest daughter, Margaret, to the Dauphin Louis. The Princess was only an infant at the time, and it was not until she was eleven that she sailed to her wedding, but for years English naval patrols kept an eye open for the Scottish wedding-fleet, to capture Margaret and prevent the marriage; when they did spot her ships, however, a Flemish merchant vessel was also in view, and the thought of its rich booty induced the English commander to chase the easier, unarmed prey.

Thus, in mid-April 1436, the bride landed safely at La Rochelle, greeted by the town's dignitaries, who presented her with a set of silver plate; in early May she made a state entry into Poitiers, met by the mayor and corporation, university professors, judges and clergy—more appropriately, as she rode through the gate, a little girl came forward to crown her with flowers. At last, on 24th June, Margaret came to Tours, where members of the royal family were waiting, her twelve-year-old bridegroom, Louis, among them. He was an uncouth-looking boy, his legs different lengths, which upset his balance and gait; his narrow eyes peered out shiftily on either side of a long, hooked nose.

The next day, when the King, Charles VII, had joined the party, the children were married in the castle's chapel. Margaret wore velvet and cloth-of-gold, a mantle of state and a golden crown, while Louis was in blue-grey velvet embroidered with gold leaves, wearing the sword of the great Robert Bruce which King James had sent him. After the wedding, the children were housed separately, and the marriage was not consummated until July 1437.

The French King and Queen made the little Dauphine something of a pet, but apparently Louis never took to her, and one chronicler says it was because she was "of such nasty complexion and evil-savoured breath that he abhorred her company as a clean creature doth a carrion".[7] Margaret was intelligent, however, full of taste in fashion, a patroness of poets and musicians—and reputedly something of a poet herself, and if accusations against her may be believed, some men found her attractive, for while she was still in her teens there were rumours that she was taking lovers; it was even said that she made attempts at contraception by drinking vinegar and eating sour apples and induced miscarriages by lacing her clothes too tightly. When she died, in August 1445, it was given out that she had taken a chill, but one story had it that she was poisoned by one of the women who accused her of adultery—though on her deathbed the Dauphine swore that she had never been unfaithful to Louis. Whatever the truth was, it seems to have been a sad episode.

Margaret's sister Isobel had joined her in France in 1442, to marry François, Duke of Brittany. Compared with Margaret, Isobel had "pleasant breath", the chronicler said, but "as for wit, womanhood and civil behaviour, she never had nor exercised [them]. Wherefore, when the Duke before his marriage was by his Council admonished to refuse and forsake so innocent a creature, he, more moved with her fair face than her womanly wisdom, answered that it was enough for a woman to judge the difference between the shirt and doublet of her husband and to know him in the dark from another man".[8] And so they were married.

The girls' brother, King James II, sought a French match for himself, but Charles VII persuaded him that an alliance with Duke Philip of Burgundy was desirable, to strengthen the anti-English pact, so the Duke's niece,

Marie of Guelders, was despatched in 1449, and very satisfactory she proved. But none of the Scots kings of this period lived to old age, and eleven years after his wedding James II was killed when one of his own cannons exploded while he was besieging the English at Roxburgh: he, who had come to the throne at the age of six, was succeeded by his eight-year-old son, James III.

Nine years later, the new King married outside the usual 'system' of French and English matches. His bride was the twelve-year-old Margaret of Denmark, valuable for the Orkney and Shetland islands which her father, King Christian I, was forced to hand over to Scotland when he could not pay her dowry. The wedding was remarkable mainly for the political upheaval which coincided with it, whose roots lay back in the King's minority when the Boyd family had seized power as his guardians, marrying Lord Boyd's son Thomas to James's sister Mary. It was Lord Boyd who arranged the Danish marriage, sending Sir Thomas to collect the bride, while he himself went off on an embassy to England. Such an opportunity was not to be missed by their enemies, who overthrew the Boyd party and prepared to imprison their leader and his son on their return. When the Danish fleet landed at Leith, however, Princess Mary was there to meet her husband, and they used one of the bridal ships to make their escape to the Continent.

Margaret of Denmark proved an excellent wife, and she provided an heir to the kingdom in 1473, when she was only sixteen, but, like his immediate forefathers, James III reigned only briefly: in 1488 he was killed in flight from the battle of Sauchieburn, defeated by his own rebellious subjects.

His fifteen-year-old successor, James IV, would one day marry Margaret Tudor, daughter of Henry VII of England—a match in which lay the beginning of the end of Scotland as a separate kingdom.

The Sixteenth Century

"His Pretty Pussy to Huggle"

It was King Henry VIII's desire to be rid of his first wife, Catherine of Aragon, which sparked off the Reformation of the English Church in the 1530s—a reformation which, over the years that followed, went far, far beyond anything the King had envisaged initially. For centuries Rome had wielded the ultimate power over matrimonial disputes, and when Rome refused to annul the royal marriage, Henry determined to have Church courts in England freed from Rome's authority, to allow his 'divorce' to proceed. At the same time, he took the opportunity of having his clergy loosed from all the ancient ties that bound them to Rome, but it was only years later, in the reigns of his younger children, Edward and Elizabeth, that changes in doctrine and forms of worship were really effected. In that period, from the 1530s to the 1560s, Church law in England was in the melting-pot—including the law on marriage.

Ironically, some of Henry's own reforms reduced the number of 'divorce' (i.e. annulment) cases brought to Church courts: first, by extending the range of relations who could marry (later, the Elizabethan Church Settlement reduced the 'prohibited degrees' to those listed in the Bible—"A man may not marry his grandmother" etc), so that the convenient loop-holes of consanguinity and affinity could not be used; secondly, de futuro espousals were no longer to be legally binding, so they would not need a court case to break them. However, the law on espousals was so frequently and confusingly changed after Henry's reign that it was difficult to know when they were binding and when they were not. By the end of the century though, the suggested form of betrothal vow was "I, [name], do willingly promise to marry thee, [name], if God will and I live, whensoever our parents shall think good and meet; till which time I take thee for my betrothed wife and thereto plight thee my troth"[1]—which gave everyone some leeway.

The cornerstone of the Elizabethan Church Settlement as regards marriage was the rule that wedding ceremonies should be performed only by Anglican clergy. The Puritans (extremist Protestants) objected to

45

this, just as they objected to the oppression of their break-away congrega-
tions, unauthorized ministers and new forms of worship. The Catholics,
equally oppressed, but for their fidelity to the old ways, did their best to
circumvent the law, often going through the Anglican ceremony but
supplementing it with (what was to them the real wedding) a rite performed by one of the few remaining Catholic priests.

The Puritans were the first to condemn arranged, loveless marriages—
at least, the first to do so formally, in their numerous books and
pamphlets on moral issues. But the Puritans were still in the minority. In
fact, the twentieth-century idea that a couple's happiness comes before
any other consideration would be regarded by almost everyone in the
sixteenth century as the height of selfishness. Loyalty to the family and its
interests came above all else, so that Shakespeare's story of Romeo and
Juliet—who put their love above loyalty to their families' feud—though it
might appeal to the rebellious young, would not find much sympathy
among 'rational' people. Indeed, when Henry VIII sought to divorce
Catherine of Aragon because she could not give him a male heir to his
kingdom (urgently needed), her refusal to co-operate was regarded by
many as unreasonable, selfish, disloyal and unpatriotic. With such a
climate of opinion, an arranged marriage, by which a family gained a
fortune or an estate, was seen as a duty to be accepted cheerfully by a
young man or woman, and most sons and daughters made no complaint
against their parents' choice for them.

If the peasantry (now free of the serfdom of the Middle Ages) did not
marry for money, they were frowned upon for marrying without it. One
Elizabethan Puritan complained that:

> . . . you shall have every saucy boy of ten, fourteen, sixteen or twenty years
> of age to catch up a woman and marry her . . . without any respect how they
> may live together with sufficient maintenance for their callings and estate.
> No, no, it maketh no matter for these things, so he have his pretty pussy to
> huggle withal . . . for that is the only thing he desireth. Then build they up a
> cottage, though but of elder poles, in every lane end almost, where they live
> as beggars all their life.[2]

In the landed classes, where child marriages had always been the most
numerous, they were still acceptable, though less so as the century
passed. The nobility were especially concerned to contract their children
young, for the Tudor monarchs strengthened the Court of Wards, which
controlled the children (and widows) of dead tenants-in-chief of the
Crown. To keep a child out of the Court's power, and so to retain the full
profit of its marriage, the head of the family would certainly take care to
contract his children himself.

Some child marriages were successful. In 1613 Lord Huntingdon told
his son that "I myself was married when a child and could not have
chosen so well myself nor been so happy in any woman I knew"—but, he
added, "because one proves well, it must not beget a conclusion."[3] By

then, there were many to agree with him. Everyone knew of child marriages that were failures, those in which

> when they come once unto the perfection of age and see others whom they could find it in their heart to fancy and love better, then many of them begin to hate [one] another . . . and curse their parents even unto the pit of Hell for the coupling of them together. Then seek they all means possible to be divorced one from another. But if it be so that they remain still together, what frowning, overthwarting, scolding and chiding is there between them, so that the whole house is filled full of these tragedies even unto the top.[4]

Of course, parents had the power to match not only very young children but sons and daughters of any age where they were financially dependent. A young man earning his own money from his own work could marry where he pleased; but the 'gentleman' did not work—he received rents and dues from land, and the gentleman's son would be supported in idleness by his father, so if he wanted to marry, he would have to gain his father's permission or lose his allowance (and maybe the prospect of his inheritance), while if his father demanded that he marry someone, he must obey or suffer the consequences. Daughters had no choice: they were invariably dependent on their families; only as widows, with incomes of their own, could they choose to remain unmarried or select their own husbands—though even then, few would marry without an assurance of advantage as well as affection.

While fathers held the purse-strings, they could make life difficult for disobedient children even from beyond the grave. When Sir Ralph Verney died in 1525, he left 500 marks to each of his daughters, but if any of them would not "be advised nor ruled in the preferment of her marriage by my executors and supervisors, it shall be at their [the executors'] liberty to [di]minish part of the sum bequeathed until she will be reformed".[5] Many Wills contained such provisos.

There were some parents, perhaps the majority, who would not marry their children only for money or status but thought health and character equally important factors. The great Elizabethan statesman William Cecil, Lord Burghley, could have matched his son Robert with any peer's daughter in the kingdom, but he allowed the young man to make his own choice, only offering advice:

> Enquire diligently of her stock and race, from whence she sprang, and how her parents have been affected in their youth. Let her not be poor, how generous soever, for generosity without her support is but a fair shell without the kernel, because a man can buy nothing in the market without money.
>
> As it is safest walking ever between two extremes, so choose not a wife of such absolute perfection and beauty that every carnal eye shall bespeak you injury; neither so base and deformed that she breed contempt in others and bring you to a loathed bed. Make not a choice of a dwarf or a fool, for from the one you may beget a race of pygmies as the other will be to you a daily grief and vexation; for it will irk you so often as you shall hear her talk, and you shall continually find to your sorrow . . . that there is nothing so fulsome as a she-fool.[6]

Other parents still believed that the best they could do for their children was to marry them to money—but how can one blame them for giving their children away without regard to their affections, giving them to strangers, risking incompatibility (or worse), when those very parents, as widows and widowers, themselves married merely for money, security or to have children?

The Tudor century was a time of new ideas, with the old ideas of arranged marriages being gradually superceded by the new, where a couple's attraction to each other was, if not the primary factor, at least one needing consideration. Who can doubt, with the evidence of Shakespeare's plays before us, that many Elizabethans sought love in marriage, that chance meetings, a 'fancy' and a little flirtation were frequently the beginnings of a match, just as they are today? Shakespeare wrote of every kind of marriage, from the conventional arrangement to the most passionate love, and he leaves his audience in no doubt but that affection, esteem, respect and trust are the true ingredients of a marriage.

The couple matched, the contract drawn up, there comes the wedding. A merchant's bride, in the late-sixteenth century, appeared dressed in "a gown of sheep's russet and a kirtle of fine worsted, her head attired with a billiment [circlet] of gold, and her hair as yellow as gold, hanging down behind her, which was curiously combed and pleated".[7] A bride's flowing hair was a customary sign that she went 'a maiden' to her wedding, and when the three daughters of a London scrivener were married on the same day in 1560, they were "in their hair", covered by "three goodly caps garnished with laces, gilt and fine flowers".[8] Poor girls, with no billiments or caps, wore a wreath of fresh flowers, usually with rosemary and myrtle among them.

The bride would go to church attended by her 'bride-maids', her sisters, cousins and friends, and they and the 'groom's men' would wear coloured ribbons called 'favours', which the bride would distribute; at grand weddings, gloves, sometimes perfumed, were passed round among the guests, as carnations are today. In the account of the Newbury merchant John Winchcombe's wedding, we read that his bride went to church with "a fair bride-cup of silver and gilt carried before her, wherein was a goodly branch of rosemary gilded very fair, hung about with silver ribands of all colours. Next was there a noise of musicians that played all the way before her. After her came all the chiefest maidens of the country, some bearing great bride-cakes and some garlands of wheat finely gilded, and so she passed unto the church."[9]

The Reformation had moved the whole of the wedding ceremony into the body of the church and had added a sermon to the proceedings— usually an admonition to the couple to live a 'godly life', and to the bride, especially, to obey her husband.

But solemnity was left at the altar. Once the couple came outside (or even, in the worst-conducted weddings, before they came out), there would be a scramble to tear ribbons from the bride's dress, for luck, and the most impudent young men would snatch under it for her garters, the greatest prize. Escorted back to the bride's home with more music, the couple would pause on the threshold to have the 'bride-cake' broken over their heads, a custom that seems to have come from Ancient Rome, where grain had been thrown, to propitiatiate Hymen, the goddess of prosperity and fertility who presided at weddings. The cake came to be made of small biscuits held together with sweet icing which would fall apart easily and shower the bride and groom—like modern confetti.

Peasant couples who could not afford to feast their friends would hold a 'bride-ale', to which guests contributed food and paid a few pence to the bride for their drink. The richer the couple—or rather, the richer the bride's family, who were expected then as now to 'give her a send-off', the longer the feasting. Some wedding festivities lasted a week, and what was left from the meals was distributed among the poor.

At the grandest weddings, there would be fancy-dress entertainments—when Henry VIII graced a courtier's wedding in 1536, he and his attendants dressed up as Turks. Later in the century, aristocratic weddings featured a play or a masque—that is, music and dancing, elaborately staged and with colourful costumes and scenery, such as that which Shakespeare devised for the betrothal of his Miranda and Ferdinand in *The Tempest*. There would be dancing for the guests too, and not the slow, stately kind but the romping 'branle' or 'brawl', in which the men grasped the women by the waist and swung them up as high as they could, gyrating faster and faster until everyone collapsed, exhausted. A bride's elder, unmarried sister had to dance barefoot at the wedding, it was said, or she would remain an old maid.

Late in the evening the bride would withdraw with her bridesmaids, to be undressed and put into bed. (Every pin from her clothes had to be thrown away; if a bridesmaid kept one, *she* would be the old maid.) Once the bride was in bed, she was joined by the groom, led in by his friends, and the whole party would crowd into the bedchamber to drink the 'benediction posset' of hot wine laced with milk, eggs, sugar and spice. Then came the game of 'flinging the stocking': bridesmaids and groom's men would sit on the end of the bed, their backs to the couple, and fling the bride and groom's stockings back over their shoulders, trying to hit one of them; success meant an early marriage for the thrower. But that was not the end of it, for even when the bridal chamber had been cleared of rowdy, often drunken guests, the couple would be serenaded from the other side of the door with a repertoire of lewd songs—and, like as not, they would awake to the same the next morning.

"Whosoever hath the desire and purpose to be a good wife or to live comfortably," ran a Tudor homily, "let her set down this conclusion within her soul: 'Mine husband is my superior, my better; he hath authority and rule over me'."[10] The wife's promise to obey her husband was taken very seriously, and the beating of disobedient wives was commonplace in Tudor times, as in previous centuries.

From the plentiful evidence we have of sixteenth-century marriages, there were many wives who could accept the subordination of their wills to their husbands', many husbands whose 'rule' was gentle, not irksome to their wives. The picture that emerges from the surviving letters of Tudor men and women is of marriages which were mainly happy and successful, relationships in which the somewhat formal courtesies of the age were balanced by the informality of affection—one Puritan was shocked to hear so many women calling their husbands not 'Master So-and-So' but 'sweeting', 'ducks' and even 'pigsnie'.

But there is evidence of another kind too—marital complaints and accusations such are to be found in every century . . .

In 1569 one Mistress Stanhope, a widow, appealed to William Cecil, Lord Burghley, for support for her daughter Juliana, whose husband, John Hotham, "is so given over to his own will as he forgetteth God, abuseth his own body with evil company and, which is the fruits thereof, hath, of long time, upon a hatred conceived of my daughter, his wife, evil entreated and in sundry sort slandered her . . . and since sueth to be divorced from her" in order to marry his mistress, formerly Juliana's servant.

> O Lord, sir, I pray you [continued Mistress Stanhope], think what discomfort it was to me to receive her in that sort, but how much more grief it is to my heart to hear the sundry slanders he hath most untruly bruited and blasted of her, and how can I live to see him work his tyrannous will against her by way of divorce, especially in Yorkshire, where he may suborn men and women to say what he listeth to serve his devilish purpose . . . the world is given to condemn the woman where any suit of divorce is made. . . .[11]

Then there is the letter of Sir John Clifton to Sir Edward Stradling, of 1573:

> Sir, the bearer hereof, being one that dwelleth somewhat near me, hath requested me to write these few lines unto you in her behalf. That whereas she hath by space of nine years been married to one Richard Love, by occupation a carpenter, the said Richard Love about Whitsuntide last was twelve months departed from this poor woman, his wife, and took with him a lewd concubine, who hath a husband at this present dwelling in Bath. This poor woman hath been informed by some of her friends that the said Richard Love, her husband, inhabiteth in a parish somewhere near you, called Cowbridge; if, therefore, it may please you, for God's sake, as also according to the laws of the realm, to show your favour to this poor woman in taking some good order with the lewd fellow her husband, no doubt you shall do a most godly deed. . . .[12]

The Hungerford case, of 1566-70, with its many depositions of servants against their mistress, reads like a modern 'scandal-sheet'. One servant claimed he had seen Lady Hungerford with her 'friend' William Darrell pretending to play a board-game together, "but leaning over the table and talking together until some person chance to come into the chamber, and then they shuffle the men and cast the dice as [if] they had been playing". Among several servants who claimed to have seen them in bed together, one Alice Jones was adamant that she was not mistaken, because there had been "a fire in the chamber, the moon shining bright and the windows open" so that she could see them clearly. Somehow, despite all the evidence, Lady Hungerford was proved innocent—though not to her husband's satisfaction, for he separated from her, refused to support her, threatened to charge her with attempting to poison him and removed her daughters. As Lady Hungerford wrote to a friend in 1570, she had good reason to fear for the children: "Susan is, as I hear, clean spoiled; she has forgotten [how] to read, and her complexion is clear gone with an itch, and she hath scant to shift her withal. Jane is with a seamstress in Marlborough, very evil too."[13]

By the end of the century, broken marriages had become almost commonplace at Court, and it is estimated that between 1595 and 1620 a third of the peers were estranged from their wives. Worse, two peers, the Earl of Leicester and Lord Howard of Bindon, were suspected of having murdered their wives, and Lady Douglas Sheffield of contriving the death of her husband, though nothing was ever proved.

The divorce law was changed several times between the Henrician Reformation and the end of Elizabeth I's reign. Henry allowed only annulments—and those on fewer grounds than in the Middle Ages; Edward VI's ministers introduced divorce for adultery and allowed the innocent party to remarry; Mary I repealed their laws, and Elizabeth permitted only annulments and separation (with maintenance for the wife, for a husband's adultery).

Death was still the only real relief from an unhappy marriage, and with childbirth still so hazardous, deadly plague so rife and even common ailments often fatal, the death of a partner was a means of release for which anyone might hope. On the other hand, of course, death being 'no respecter of persons', many happily married couples were separated by it too.

The Early Tudors

One of the first aims of any usurper of a throne is to have foreign powers recognize him as king. When Henry Tudor overthrew the last of the Plantagenets, Richard III, in 1485, and became king, as Henry VII, he was fortunate in this respect: though the King of Scotland championed pretenders to the English throne in the first years of Henry's reign, other European monarchs were more amenable, and just three years after he became king, he could pride himself on the friendship of two of Christendom's most prestigious monarchs, Isabel of Castile and her husband, Ferdinand of Aragon, who accepted his proposal that his heir, Arthur, Prince of Wales, marry their youngest daughter, Catherine.

Negotiations were protracted, however, and it was not until May 1499 that the Prince went through a proxy wedding with the Spanish ambassador representing Catherine—repeated fifteen months later when Arthur reached the age of consent, and October 1501 before the Princess was delivered to England. When she did arrive, the King had even more reason to be pleased with the match: Catherine was a healthy, straight-limbed, auburn-haired, grey-eyed sixteen-year-old, a far better specimen of royalty than his own Arthur, ten months her junior, who was frail and rather blank-faced.

London was *en fête* to greet the bride. When Catherine crossed London Bridge, the first of many citizens' 'pageants' was waiting to welcome her, with a tableau of her patron, St Catherine, and a legendary British saint, Ursula. On the north side of the river, in Gracechurch Street, there was a stone-and-canvas 'Castle of Virtue and Nobility', in which stood Policy, Noblesse and Virtue, their speeches at the ready. Next came 'the Sphere of the Moon' and 'the Sphere of the Sun', at conduits in Cornhill and Chepe, and further up Cheapside were a 'Temple of God' and 'Throne of Honour', magnificently spired and pinnacled structures adorned with heraldic devices and containing an assortment of citizens dressed up as angels, sages, prophets, warriors and kings—one of the pageants even had an image of Prince Arthur on its top, with a mechanical cosmos spinning around him.

Two days later, on 14th November, Catherine and Arthur were brought to St Paul's for their wedding. A sort of bridge, 6 feet high, had been constructed from the door of the cathedral to the royal dais in front of the altar, so that the great congregation could observe every part of the ceremony, from the moment when Arthur's brother Henry led in the bride, through the vows and the Nuptial Mass (celebrated by the Archbishop of Canterbury) to the grand procession out again—and a pause at the door, for Arthur to bestow a third of his property on his wife. The young couple were dressed in white satin, and Catherine's gown was swelled out over hoops—the first farthingale worn in England; over her flowing hair she wore a white silk veil bordered with gold and set with jewels.

For days afterwards, Court and City shared the festivities. There were jousts outside Westminster Hall, where a space had been cleared and sanded "for the ease of the horses",[1] and set about with flowers and artificial trees laden with fruit. So many people crowded into the arena and stood watching from walls and battlements that one observer remarked that "there was nothing to the eye but only visages and faces, without the appearance of bodies".[2] Then there were the banquets in Westminster Hall, "not so sumptuous as populous, nor yet so populous as delicate, nor so delicate as of things abundant".[3] And every night there were more pageants and 'disguisings': a castle trundled in on wheels, containing men dressed as animals; a ship on runners that made it seem to float across the hall; an arbour full of dancing knights and ladies; a mountain on which sat people playing and singing—and many, many others; the *pièce de résistance* was a huge lantern, lit by a hundred candles, from which issued ladies to dance. There was, besides, a good share of dancing for the younger members of the royal family: Catherine demonstrated Spanish dances, and her brother-in-law, Prince Henry, led out his sister and other ladies, leaping around so vigorously that "perceiving himself to be encumbered with his clothes, [he] suddenly cast off his gown and danced in his jacket . . . in so goodly and pleasant a manner that it was to the King and Queen great and singular pleasure".[4]

Catherine and Arthur were ritually 'bedded' on the night of their wedding, and the next morning the Prince of Wales boasted to his attendants that he had done his duty well. "Gentlemen," he declared, as he left the bedchamber, "I come out glad this morning, for I have been during the night 6 miles into Spain."[5] But maybe that was only a boy's bravado, for when the fact of the consummation was called into question a few months later, Catherine was ready to deny that Arthur had ever made her truly his wife.

They had not lacked opportunity, for they were together throughout the next few months, at the castle of Ludlow in the Welsh Marches where Arthur's Court had been settled for some years past. But certainly the

Princess was not pregnant when, in April 1502, her husband took a chill and died.

Catherine's response to her husband's death is unrecorded; nor do we know her reaction when, only a few weeks later, she heard that negotiations were already in train for her to marry her ten-year-old brother-in-law Henry, the new heir to England. There were complications, of course, not the least of them the fact that she was related to Henry in the 'first degree of affinity', but Catherine swore that Arthur had never consummated their marriage—which was exactly what everyone wanted her to say, so that an application could be made to Rome for a dispensation. Thus, on 23rd June 1503, Catherine was betrothed to Henry, to marry him a couple of years later when he reached the age of consent.

Four months earlier, Henry VII's queen had died, and for a moment it had seemed that the King was considering marrying Catherine himself, but there was just no precedent for a man marrying his daughter-in-law, and no one could reasonably expect a pope to grant a dispensation for him to do so. Still, with only one son, the King of England could only see it as his duty to marry again, and over the next years he considered several European princesses.

Henry was a cautious and a shrewd man, as his policies for the strengthening of royal power in the kingdom show, and he approached the idea of a new marriage with typically meticulous precautions. When he sent envoys to Valencia in 1505, to take a look at the widowed Queen Juana of Naples, he supplied them with a list of twenty-four points on which he must be satisfied, including her age, her stature, "her visage, whether she be painted or not, whether it be fat or lean, sharp or round, and whether her countenance be cheerful and amiable, frowning or melancholy, steadfast or light, or blushing in communication," if her skin was clear, what colour her hair and eyes were, the length and breadth of nose and forehead, her complexion, the size of hands, arms and fingers, "her breasts and paps, whether they be big or small', the odour of her breath after fasting, what illnesses she had suffered and "whether she be a great feeder or drinker"—all this to be answered, although the envoys were instructed to obtain a portrait too.

In fact, the Englishmen found the Spanish-born Queen of Naples a very attractive woman. She was twenty-seven years old, fair and clear-skinned, with brown hair and eyes, her lips "somewhat round and thick", her nose "a little rising in the midward and a little coming or bowing towards the end", with rounded arms, and fingers that were "right fair and small", her breasts "somewhat great and full . . . trussed somewhat high, after the manner of the country, the which causeth Her Grace for to seem the much fuller and her neck to be the shorter"; they guessed that she was of middle height, but they only saw her wearing a full mantle that hid her shape.[6]

Unfortunately, Juana was not so well endowed in fortune as she was in personal charms, and that may be the reason why Henry did not pursue the matter further, having wasted so many people's energies in assessing her.

Nor, when it came to the point, did he marry his son to Catherine of Aragon; he even had the boy repudiate his betrothal vows. The King was feeling more secure by then, less in need of Spanish support than he had been early in his reign: his elder daughter Margaret had married the King of Scotland in 1503, and there was the chance of a match for the younger, Mary, with Charles of Habsburg, whose paternal grandfather was the Holy Roman Emperor. Thus for the younger Henry, the best plan would be a French match, and while the King was negotiating to marry a French princess himself, the Prince was included in the package. Even so, Henry VII had no intention of sending Catherine back to Spain, and for years she stayed on at the English Court, almost penniless since her dowry had not been paid in full and she had renounced her jointure when she became betrothed to Prince Henry; her letters to her father in these years, begging support and money, make pitiful reading.

However, perhaps Prince Henry admired Catherine, some eight years his senior, perhaps he pitied the plight of her prolonged widowhood, for when his father died, in May 1509, he wasted no time and married her six weeks later. (Of course, there were also more reasonable explanations: a match with Spain was still desirable, and so was the speedy production of an heir to Henry's kingdom.)

Famed though Henry VIII became for marrying six times, only one of his weddings (the fourth) was remarkable for its splendour. Indeed, the first of them, that to Catherine, was a distinctly quiet affair: the couple merely walked out of Greenwich Palace on the morning of 11th June and were married in the nearby chapel of a Franciscan friary. But their coronation, on the 24th, made up for the lack of wedding festivities, being as magnificent as any ever known.

Nevertheless, if Catherine now tasted her first happiness in years, with an apparently devoted husband, the blight on their marriage quickly revealed itself. She had several miscarriages, and of those few babies who did survive birth, all but one, a daughter, died soon after. While Catherine was still young, still conceiving, there was always hope, but by 1520 she was in her late thirties, and by 1522 there were rumours that Henry VIII was thinking of replacing her with a younger woman . . .

In the meantime, Henry's affairs of state included the business of settling outstanding differences with France, and how better to seal an alliance than by that well tried expedient of a royal marriage? The fact that the twice-widowed King of France, Louis XII, was in his fifties and that the proposed bride, Henry's sister Mary, was a teenager, was irrelevant to the issue.

Not for Mary, apparently. Less complaisant than other princesses, who might find queenship a compensation for taking on an elderly husband, Mary wrung a promise from her brother—as she was to remind him only a few months after the wedding:

Dearest brother,

I doubt not but that you have in good remembrance that, whereas for the good of peace and for the furtherance of your affairs, you moved me to marry with my lord . . . King Louis of France, though I understood that he was very aged and sickly, yet for the advancement of the said peace and for the furtherance of your causes, I was contented to conform myself to your said motion, so that if I should fortune to survive [him], I might with your good will marry myself at my liberty without your displeasure.[7]

With Henry's promise, Mary obediently repudiated her betrothal (made in infancy) to Charles of Habsburg and on 13th August 1514 took the hand of the Duke of Longueville in a proxy wedding. Then, clad in a fine nightdress, she was laid on a bed next to the Duke, and their clothes were turned up so that their bare legs could touch, a travesty of the consummation of the union which would make the vows binding.

The French King, receiving his bride and marrying her in person that October, was delighted with Mary, and he boasted after the wedding night that he had 'crossed the river' three times. As one English lord reported home a few weeks later, "The Queen is continually with him, of whom King Louis maketh as much as it is possible for any man to make of a lady."[8] But in the reckoning of his day, Louis was "very aged", as Mary had said, and his health was poor; his attempts to prove to his wife that he could match her in youthful spirits and exuberance weakened him quickly. When Louis died, on New Year's Day 1515, she had almost literally 'danced him into the grave'.

With the news that Henry VIII was intending to marry her to Louis's successor, François I, Mary lost no time by making formal application to her brother with regard to his promise to allow her to choose her second husband but married at once, after only a few weeks of widowhood.

Charles Brandon, Duke of Suffolk, was the English King's closest friend, his companion since childhood, and Mary herself must have been acquainted with him the whole of her life. Whether she had been in love with him before her marriage to Louis or whether she merely wanted an English husband, any English husband, to prevent Henry's marrying her abroad, is hard to say, but Suffolk was an ambitious man (he had earlier aspired to marry the Emperor's sister), and there is evidence that Henry had once made him promise not to marry Mary without permission. But now, sent to France as Henry's envoy to his widowed sister, Suffolk was induced to brave the King's already famous wrath and to marry her without delay.

Sire [he wrote to Henry after the wedding],

So it is that when I came to Paris, the Queen was in hand with me the first day and said she must be short with me and show to me her pleasure and mind, and so she began unto me and showed how good lady she was to me, and if I would be ordered [by her], she would never have none but me. . . . I never saw woman so weep.[9]

Mary wrote home too, reminding her brother of his promise, which he had even confirmed "at the waterside" when she left for France, and trying to exonerate her husband from all blame:

> Now that God hath called my late husband to His mercy, and that I am at my liberty, dearest brother, remembering the great virtues which I have seen and perceived heretofore in my lord of Suffolk, to whom I have always been of good mind, as you well know, I have affixed and clearly determined myself to marry with him; and the same [I] assure you hath proceeded only of mine own mind, without any request or labour of my said lord of Suffolk. . . . And to be plain with Your Grace, I have so bound myself unto him that for no cause earthly I will or may vary or change from the same.[10]

Henry knew when he was beaten: he exacted a considerable fine from the couple and had them re-married in England, but after a while they were given their places at his Court. If the Duke found that he had gained less than he had expected from the match, if the Duchess found her husband less faithful than she could have wished, they had no one but themselves to blame.

Suffolk had discarded a couple of wives in the years before his marriage to Princess Mary; Henry VIII's sister Margaret managed to gain annulments of her second and third marriages with little difficulty; so why should Henry encounter problems when he tried to 'divorce' Catherine of Aragon, to enable him to marry a woman who could give him the son so urgently needed to inherit the throne and to keep the kingdom from harm? But problems there were, problems which were to bedevil the 1520s and to result, in the 1530s, in the English Church's break with Rome; good men, unable in conscience to forswear allegiance to the Pope, would go to the stake and the scaffold for refusing to acknowledge Henry as head of the English Church—and all because a king wanted to rid himself of his wife.

The stumbling-block was the Pope's refusal to declare invalid the dispensation which one of his predecessors had issued to Henry and Catherine to enable them to marry. While Catherine protested that Arthur had never consummated their marriage, that she *had* been free to marry Henry, her nephew the Emperor Charles V was coincidentally holding the Pope a virtual prisoner in Italy, so that he dared not overrule her and accommodate the English King. The Pope did send a Cardinal to England in the end, to hear the royal couple's conflicting evidence, but that envoy had strict orders to procrastinate in order not to bring the case to any embarrassing conclusion.

In the years while 'the King's Great Matter' was being debated, a new factor entered the case: Henry's infatuation with one of his wife's maids-of-honour, Anne Boleyn. To Tudor tastes Anne was no conventional beauty (she was thin, very dark—most men liked them plump and fair), but she had a charm, a fascination, about her that some men called witchcraft. Certainly she bewitched Henry—one has only to read his love-letters to her to know that, and though he might have had a royal French bride to replace Catherine, it was Anne whom he intended to make his second queen. For years she refused to become his mistress, and it was only in the last months of 1532, when the divorce seemed hopeless, that she yielded to him. But then, almost immediately, she became pregnant, and Henry had to act fast if her child were to be born legitimate: first, in January 1533, he married her secretly; then, in the spring, he had his Archbishop of Canterbury pronounce his divorce from Catherine— that is, to say that the marriage had never been valid, so that the wedding with Anne had been completely legal. In doing so, Henry was demonstrating that the Pope had no right to preside over the case, that it was a matter for the English Church alone, and this opened his way to proclaiming himself Head of the Church in England and to instituting reforms which would take it out of Rome's orbit altogether.

Queen Catherine was now locked away, her one surviving child, Mary, declared illegitimate, and on Whit Sunday 1533 Anne was crowned queen. The ceremonies and festivities which Henry ordered could not be faulted, but it was noticed that there were not ten men in the crowd to throw up their hats and cry "God save the Queen!" In later years, Englishmen would look back and say that Catherine should have sacrificed her honour and her marriage for the sake of the kingdom, to allow Henry to beget his heir, but at the time she was popular and her firm stance respected (especially, perhaps, by wives who feared that their husbands might follow the King's example).

But Anne's first child, born in September 1533, was a girl, and afterwards, like Catherine, she seemed prone to miscarrying. Nor, perhaps, did she satisfy the King in bed, for it was not long before the Court noticed that pretty women were interesting him, whereas before she had become his, he had had eyes only for Anne. While Catherine still lived, Henry would be in difficulties if he tried to divorce his second wife—to say that their marriage had never been legal, but Catherine died in January 1536, and three weeks later Anne gave birth to a stillborn child. That combination was her doom: on May Day 1536 she was arrested on a charge of 'treasonable adultery'—which carried the death-penalty.

For some time past, Henry's right-hand man, Thomas Cromwell, had been collecting 'evidence' against the Queen, and he could name several men, her own brother included, who had had 'treasonable relations' with her. They, and Anne, protested their innocence, but it was in no one else's interest to believe them. All were executed before the month was out. Henry also took the precaution of having the marriage annulled and so declaring Anne's daughter Elizabeth illegitimate, on the ingenious grounds that Anne had been related to him in the first degree of affinity, because her sister had once been his mistress.

On the very evening of Anne's execution, 19th May 1536, Henry betrothed himself to Jane Seymour, a girl who had been at Court since the days of Queen Catherine, and on the 30th they were married. Everyone agreed that Jane was virtuous, and it was her solicitude which brought Catherine's daughter Mary back into Henry's favour, but beyond that she had no time to make her mark on the kingdom. On 12th October 1537 the Queen gave birth to a son; on 25th October she died, of puerperal fever.

To date, three women had died for the sake of England's heir—Catherine, reputedly of a 'broken heart', though some murmured about poison; Anne, because she failed to provide Henry with a son, and now Jane, in the exertion of doing so.

Would Henry now rest content? Why should he? He was a free man, eligible in the eyes of at least some of Europe's rulers—even Catholic kings who could overlook the fact that the Pope had excomunicated him. Even the Emperor, Queen Catherine's nephew, looked more warmly on Henry now, hoping for an ally against France. But to marry Charles's niece, the widowed Duchess Christina of Milan, the King would have to apply for a papal dispensation, which would mean capitulation to Rome and maybe even a restoration of the monasteries which he was in the process of dissolving, making a good deal of money in the process.

Against the Emperor, there stood France, and the French King was only too generous in giving Henry his choice of brides: King François's own sister, or one of several daughters and sisters of the dukes of Lorraine, Guise and Vendôme. Encouraged by such munificence, however, Henry VIII overstepped the mark: he suggested to the French ambassador that all the girls should be brought to Calais (still English territory), to be paraded there for the King himself to assess before he made his choice. The ambassador was shocked, but he put the request to François. Inevitably, the French King returned word that such a parade was just not possible. Henry tried to insist, but Ambassador de Castillon asked tentatively: "Sire, would you like to 'mount' these ladies, one after the other, and then keep for yourself the one that suits you best? Did the Knights of the Round Table in times past so treat the ladies of this country?"—"I think this shamed him," the Ambassador reported, "as suddenly he laughed and blushed."[11]

The King's Council was divided in opinion as to who should be Henry's next bride, but Thomas Cromwell was closest to Henry at the time, and he was in favour of an alliance with the block of Protestant princes in Germany. Cromwell's candidates were the daughters of the Duke of Cleves, Anne and Amelia. But still Henry would not marry without some idea of the girls' appearance, whatever the policy and its importance, and so his Court painter, Hans Holbein, was despatched to Cleves, with orders to depict their true likenesses. We can still see Holbein's portrait of Anne today, and very pleasant she looks, albeit not remarkable; Henry must have thought so, for she was his choice.

Courtiers were sent to Germany to fetch the bride, to bring her overland to Calais to avoid, as it was said, "the danger, and also the fear ladies have of the danger, of sea-voyages".[12] Danger-free, the short Channel crossing was accomplished in the last, stormy week of 1539, and on New Year's Day Anne and Henry met at Rochester. The King was disappointed: he admitted that the Princess was "well and seemly", but in no way did she match up to Holbein's portrait. The next day he left her, travelling up to Greenwich, and before she could follow him, he had made his first attempt to be rid of her, asking the German envoys if there was any truth in the rumour that she had been 'pre-contracted' to a Frenchman—no truth at all, they answered; there had been a betrothal, but that had been properly repudiated. So Henry was doomed, though he did say that if Anne had not already come, if all the preparations had not been made, and if the affair would not "ruffle" the world, he would certainly not marry her.

On 3rd January, Blackheath was ready for Anne's ceremonial reception, with "tents and pavilions in the which were made fires and perfumes for her and such ladies as should receive Her Grace; and from the tents to the park gate of Greenwich were all bushes and firs cut down and a large and ample way made for the show of all persons."[13] All round the central open space were ranged the mayor, aldermen and councillors of London, the City and foreign merchants, and the gentlemen, esquires and servants of the Court. At about midday Anne rode up in her chariot, attended by a huge retinue of English lords and ladies, besides her Germans, and while they were warming themselves over the scented fires, the King arrived on horseback from Greenwich. He was dressed in purple velvet and cloth-of-gold, says the chronicler of the day, and Anne was in a cloth-of-gold gown "made round without any train after the Dutch fashion,"[14] with a matching bonnet sewn with pearls. "With most lovely countenance and princely behaviour," Henry greeted Anne and embraced her, and then they rode off together, towards Greenwich. "Oh what a sight was this, to see so goodly a prince and so noble a king to ride with so fair a lady, of so goodly a stature and so womanly a countenance, and in especial of so good qualities. I think no creature could see them but his heart rejoiced."[15] Anne may have had "good qualities", but Henry could not see them for his disappointment with her plain face, and there were many to agree with him and not with the chronicler: "Accordingly to the judgement of several who saw her close to," it was reported, Anne was "not found so young as was thought, nor of such great beauty as everyone affirmed; in stature she is big, and of bearing and countenance very self-confident,"[16] with high spirits and vivacity, by which she attempted to make up for lack of beauty.

Certainly, the following Tuesday, 6th January, when the King was in procession to his wedding, he was still not enthusiastic about his bride, whispering to Cromwell that "were it not to satisfy the world and his realm, he would not do that he must do that day for none earthly thing".[17]

If fine clothes could enhance them, the big, plain Anne and the heavy-jowled, massive-chested Henry should have appeared as Oberon and Titania, for he was in a doublet of cloth-of-gold woven with silver flowers and a crimson coat with a great diamond collar, and she wore a cloth-of-gold dress with pearl flowers, with a jewelled crown on her loose 'yellow' hair. After the wedding and the feast, Anne changed into a lighter-weight gown, of 'tissue', with sable trimmings and narrow sleeves, a pearled and jewelled 'cornet' of lawn on her head.

But night came, and with it the moment when Henry must see his queen without her fine clothes. He did not like what he saw. The next day he told Cromwell that he had "felt her belly and her breasts, and, as he should judge, she should be no maid"—moreover, the King added, "he left her as good a maid as he found her."[18] Nor was he tempted to further intimacy as time passed.

In July, Henry made the excuse of a plague-scare at Court to send Anne away to Richmond—in fact, to allow him to finalize an annulment, on the grounds of that pre-contract to a Frenchman, a solution which no one sought to dispute now. Anne herself, faced with the news at the end of the month, made no complaint, professed herself the King's servant in all things and merely begged to be well treated (did she fear the axe?). With so complaisant a wife, Henry could afford to be generous—and friendly: in the first week in August he dined with her so cheerfully that some courtiers thought he might be having a change of heart; but no, his thoughts were already elsewhere, and as for Anne, she was happy "each day changing into new clothes of a strange sort", paid for by her liberal pension, though the French ambassador could not decide if her serenity was "a wonderful prudence to dissimulate what she thinks or a too great simplicity and stupidity of forgetting so easily what ought to touch her heart so closely".[19] Whatever it was, Anne was left in peace.

However, Cromwell was not. Having made the match, and the German Protestant alliance, he fell with the Queen, and on the day of Henry's fifth wedding his head fell too, under the executioner's axe. The Protestant party, which Cromwell had headed, had lost ground steadily since the arrival of Anne of Cleves, and in its place was the faction headed by the Duke of Norfolk (uncle of the late Anne Boleyn) which sought to appease the Catholic powers and restrain the introduction of Protestant doctrines and forms into the Church of England. Norfolk had managed to insert a pretty young niece, Catherine Howard, into Anne of Cleves' household and to make sure that the King would compare her fresh English beauty with the German woman's defects. The Duke was successful. Long before the marriage with Anne was annulled, Henry was 'toying' with Catherine, and as soon as Anne was out of the way, he made her his fifth queen, that July, at a very 'private' wedding.

This marriage lasted something less than twenty months. Henry doted on Catherine (the French ambassador reported home that the King was "so in love that he does not know by what good treatment he can enough demonstrate the affection he bears to her, which exceeds . . . all the caresses which he has made to the others"[20]), but 'there is no fool like an old fool': just a few months after their wedding, the Queen (still a teenager) was cuckolding her husband at every opportunity. Worse, when this treason was revealed, in November 1541, many of her old friends came forward to declare that she had already had a couple of lovers before she came to Court. The men were despatched to their deaths by the end of the year; Queen Catherine was beheaded on 13th February 1542.

That experience, as much as recent ill health, turned Henry VIII into an old man, though he was only fifty and had always prided himself on his energy. Now the muscular giant turned into a mass of flabby fat, scarcely able to stand unsupported, with suppurating ulcers all over his legs. It was a nurse he needed now, not a bed-fellow, and his realization that he could no longer expect to father children was proved by the fact that, though the woman he took for his sixth wife, in July 1543, been twice married, she had never had a child.

Catherine Parr, Lady Latimer, was the protégée of the Protestant party which dominated Henry's Council in the last years of his life and was herself an enthusiastic champion of the 'New Faith'. Women of her generation, in the upper classes at least, were highly educated, and Catherine was a notable scholar, well able to hold her own in disputation over Christian doctrine. Had Henry lived longer, his sixth queen might well have gone to the stake as a heretic, for despite his rejection of papal authority, the King had a firm distaste for the Protestant doctrines that were seeping into the Anglican Church. Indeed, at one point, the Queen came near to sharing the fate of her friend Anne Askew, burned at the stake for her 'heresy', and she saved herself only by assuring her husband that she argued theology with him only to take his mind off his pain.

Catherine survived. In the early hours of 28th January 1547, Henry VIII went to account to God for a lifetime of political and social crimes—not the least of them a unique history of abuse of holy matrimony.

The Later Tudors

If Henry VIII had set a record for kings by marrying six wives, his widow, Catherine Parr, did the same for queens consort by taking a fourth husband in the spring after Henry's death.

She married Thomas Seymour for love, it seems, for she wrote to him before their marriage that, "I would not have you to think that this mine honest good-will toward you proceed of any sudden motion of passion, for, as truly as God is God, my mind was fully bent, the other time I was at liberty [that is, before she married Henry VIII], to marry you before any man I know."[1]

Seymour's motive was obviously less pure. He was the brother of the late Queen Jane Seymour, and thus uncle of the new king, the nine-year-old Edward VI, but he was forced to rank after his elder brother in the royal Council—a matter of ill-concealed resentment; by marrying the Queen Dowager, whom the boy King adored, Thomas would thus endear himself to the child, entrench his status and have Catherine's sizable jointure at his disposal. In fact, the marriage was so blatant a threat to his brother's position that Thomas was immediately held suspect of intending to usurp the 'Lord Protector's' power. Nor did he allay fears but intrigued with all and sundry to overthrow his brother. In 1549 (a few months after Catherine's death in childbed), Seymour's machinations were brought to light, and he was executed as a traitor—but not before others were implicated in his schemes . . .

One of his pawns had been Thomas Grey, future Duke of Suffolk, who had married Frances Brandon, elder daughter of Princess Mary Tudor and her second husband. Seymour had promised Grey that, in return for his support, he, Seymour, would marry Grey's daughter Jane to her cousin the King—a promise he had not fulfilled by the time of his death. Worse, Edward VI's half-sister Elizabeth was dragged into the affair, albeit only passively. It seemed that Seymour had been paying court to the teenaged girl for some time past, even while his wife was still living; while Elizabeth was staying with him and Catherine at their Chelsea house, he had been in the habit of entering her bedchamber of a morning, kissing her and tickling her. 'Proof' was brought to light (or manufactured) that Seymour had intended to marry Elizabeth, to make her queen and rule with her if anything should happen to her young brother. There was even a rumour, in the months after Seymour's death, that he had got the girl pregnant, and the sixteen-year-old Elizabeth sent an indignant letter to the Lord Protector, his brother, demanding a public denial.

Edward VI seems to have been fond of his uncle Thomas, so much more sympathetic than his dour uncle Edward, the Protector, and Catherine Parr was the only 'mother' he had ever known, but apart from that he was a somewhat cold-blooded child, and one wonders what sort of husband he would have made, with his father's example before him.

In the reign of Henry VIII plans had been put forward for Edward to marry his cousin Mary, the infant Queen of Scotland, thereby uniting the two kingdoms, and on 1st July 1543, when Mary was only seven months old, the Treaty of Greenwich promised her to him. But before the year was out, there was a change of mood in Scotland, a firmer leaning towards France, and in 1544 the English King sent an army over the border for what came to be known as 'the Rough Wooing'—that is, a campaign of devastation which should terrorize the Scots into handing over their Queen. It failed: Mary was removed from the danger-zone and in August 1548 despatched to France, to be married there.

In the last years of Henry VIII's reign, after the probability of the Scottish match had receded, Edward was sought in marriage for several foreign princesses, but after he became king, a definite proposal was made on his behalf to France. The boy recorded the negotiations of 1551 with avid interest in his journal, noting the horror of the envoys when his own commissioners demanded a 1,500,000-crown dowry with the French Princess Elisabeth; the French subsequently beat them down to 200,000 crowns, plus the girl's travelling-expenses and trousseau—she was to be "sufficiently jewelled and stuffed" (apparelled), wrote the boy King with glee.[2] Elisabeth was only six years old at the time, and she was to be brought to England three months before her twelfth birthday, ready for the wedding when she reached the age of consent. That would be in 1557, when Edward VI would be twenty years old.

But Edward did not live long enough to marry. Measles (often fatal in his day, always serious) weakened his constitution, but it seems that it was tuberculosis which killed him, in 1553, some three months before his sixteenth birthday.

The irregularities of Henry VIII's marriages, and those of his sisters, now played a vital part in the problem of naming Edward VI's successor. Henry had decreed his daughter Mary, to be followed by Elizabeth, as the boy's heirs, despite the fact that in the past both of them had been declared illegitimate. But Mary had retained the Catholic faith with stubborn determination, and Edward VI's Council were fearful not only for the Church of England but for their own (avowedly Protestant) lives, should she succeed to the throne. Lord Protector Dudley, Duke of Northumberland, who had overthrown Lord Protector Seymour, had equally little desire to see the Princess Elizabeth proclaimed queen, for there was no love lost between them, and he knew that Elizabeth would have no use for his services. The next heir, by strict heredity, was the Queen of Scotland, but she could be discounted as an 'alien'; then there was her half-aunt, Margaret Douglas, the daughter of Margaret Tudor's second marriage—but, like her cousin Mary of England, she was a Catholic, and besides, there were strong doubts as to her own legitimacy.

There remained the descendants (all female) of Henry VIII's younger sister, Mary, who had married Charles Brandon: setting aside yet more doubts of *her* daughters' legitimacy, they were at least Protestant. The Lord Protector had taken care, in the last months of Edward VI's life, to woo Frances Brandon and her husband the Duke of Suffolk, and just a few weeks before the King's death, Northumberland's son Guilford married the Suffolks' eldest daughter, Lady Jane Grey. It was Jane, fifteen years old, whom he proposed to raise to the throne.

Jane Grey was a clear-sighted girl, educated far beyond the norm, with

The wedding of King Edward II and Isabelle of France in 1308—a
fifteenth-century manuscript illumination.

If a royal bridegroom was already king when he married, his bride would be crowned after their wedding. This illustration of the coronation of a queen consort is from the fourteenth-century *Liber Regalis* in Westminster Abbey.

A thirteenth-century couple married by a bishop.

John of Gaunt's daughter Philippa (sister of the future King Henry IV) married to King John of Portugal in 1387.

The wedding of King Henry V and Catherine of France in 1420.

A medallion commemorating the wedding of Henry VII and Elizabeth of York in 1486.

The betrothal of Henry VII's son Arthur, Prince of Wales, and Catherine of Aragon—a sixteenth-century Flemish tapestry.

Henry VIII's sister Mary with her second husband, Charles Brandon, Duke of Suffolk.

The Holbein portrait of Anne of Cleves which tempted Henry VIII to marry her.

King James V of Scotland with his second wife, Marie of Guise.

IACOBVS.QVINTVS.SCOTTORVM.REX

ANNO.ÆTATIS.SVE.

Z 8

MARIA.LOTHORINGIA.ILLIVS.IN.SECVNDIS.

TIIS VXOR·ANNO ÆTATIS SVE. Z 4

Sir Henry Unton's wedding-feast—a detail from a remarkable pictorial story of his life painted in the late-sixteenth century. In the foreground musicians and brightly costumed dancers present a masque to celebrate the occasion.

a real Tudor pride which she had displayed from an early age. Faced with marriage to Guilford Dudley, Jane exhibited an extraordinary antipathy to the match: she did not plead to be spared it, however—no, this cool, self-possessed girl just refused it, point-blank. The Suffolks were not so calm: the Duke cursed her, the Duchess beat her, and in the end she was forced to submit. Exactly what Jane's objection to the marriage was, we are not told. Certainly, at the time, she had no idea of her prospective father-in-law's plans for her, with regard to the crown of England. It may be that, as the King's cousin, she had expected to marry him—or at least a grand foreign match, or it could be that she knew, and disliked, Guilford Dudley. Certainly he seems to have been a boy of little character, a 'mother's boy', as future events would show. On Whit Sunday, 25th May 1553, Jane and Guilford were married; on 6th July Edward VI died, and three days later Northumberland told his daughter-in-law that she was Queen.

Jane was stunned, appalled, but then, apparently, docile, ready to follow the Duke's orders and wait quietly in the Tower while he made sure of England's acceptance of her. Not so Guilford: he was noisily jubilant, demanding the title of King. When Jane, glad of this new power over him, refused to consider that possibility, the boy burst into tears, ran for his mother and stood by sullenly while the Duchess of Northumberland ranted at the 'ungrateful' girl. When the lady declared that her son should no longer honour his wife's bed and should go home with her, Jane calmly asserted her authority to stop them leaving.

But that was the only pleasure she ever derived from her brief reign. Even in London, Northumberland's stronghold, there was little enthusiasm for Queen Jane, and in the shires her cousin Mary was rallying an army to overthrow her. A few days later Northumberland was captured by Mary's supporters, and subsequently executed, and Jane made a prisoner in the Tower. Seven months later, she and Guilford died by the axe. She had refused to see him before their death, not from any former resentments but because, she said, they would shortly meet "in a better place". He sobbed on the scaffold; she mounted it firmly and serenely.

Queen Mary I had not intended to take such terrible vengeance on her cousin Jane, but she was very much under the influence of the Holy Roman Emperor Charles V, her cousin, and anxious for marriage with his son Philip, so that when the Emperor told her that he could not send Philip to England while there was a chance of insurrection against her, on behalf of Jane Grey, the Queen was forced to sign the death-warrant.

Mary had, it seems, always wanted to be married. As a small child, she had been betrothed first to the Dauphin of France and then to Charles himself, and even in the years after her mother's repudiation, when Mary was deemed illegitimate, several foreign princes asked for her. But Mary knew that her father would never send her abroad, even to marry a Protestant prince, for there was always the danger that her mother's relations would set her up as a claimant to the English throne. As she had said herself: as long as her father lived, "it was folly to think that they would marry her out of England, or even in England", and she would remain "only the Lady Mary, the unhappiest lady in Christendom".[3] Losing any charm she had ever had as the years passed, she became the archetypal 'old maid', passionately fond of other people's children. Now, free at last, queen at last, it was no wonder that she was so often seen to blush with pleasure at the thought of a bridegroom and that she would sacrifice the life of her cousin Jane to gain one.

Mary was, of course, aware that her cousin Philip (ten years her junior and whom she had never met) was not marrying her for love, just as she was fully aware of the unpopularity of the proposed match within her own kingdom, where the Emperor's potential influence was feared and where the restoration of the English Church to Roman allegiance was not welcomed by the majority. Nevertheless, everyone knew that the Queen must marry, that she must attempt to give the kingdom a male heir—even though, in her mid thirties, she seemed unlikely to do so. England had never had a queen regnant (apart from the unsuccessful Matilda, back in the twelfth century), but other countries had, and their queens had always married, to have a man to rule on their behalf, so the desirability of Mary's marriage was not in dispute, only the fact that she had chosen to marry a foreign prince who would make England a satellite of the Habsburg empire. Englishmen's fears were not much allayed by the insertion in the marriage contract of a clause stipulating that Philip would have no authority in England, that he would merely 'assist' in government and that none of his Spanish friends should have a seat in the royal Council.

On 20th July 1554 Philip landed at Southampton, to be greeted not by Mary (who was waiting to receive him formally in Winchester) but by her first gift, a horse so finely caparisoned in velvet and gold that the Prince joked that it was better dressed than he would be in his wedding-suit. Certainly, drenched in pouring rain, he must have cut a poor figure when he entered Winchester, but he changed his suit before proceeding to a thanksgiving in the Cathedral and to his meeting with Mary. Her greeting made up for the unreasonable weather and for the coldness of the English: she was pacing the hall of the Bishop's palace when he entered, and she ran towards him, clasped his hand and kissed it; he responded by kissing her lips.

Winchester Cathedral had been chosen for the wedding, the first public wedding of an English monarch since that of Henry VII and Elizabeth of York nearly seventy years previously. The Cathedral had been hung with cloth-of-gold and tapestries, a wooden platform erected for the ceremony and canopied chairs brought in for the bridal couple. Philip did not have to wear his own despised wedding-suit, for Mary had given him another, a white doublet and breeches, a French mantle of cloth-of-gold trimmed with crimson velvet, lined with crimson satin, embroidered with gold thistles and sporting twenty-four pearl buttons on the sleeves. Mary wore a black velvet gown (black was often worn at weddings in Tudor times, as was red), but it blazed with jewels of all colours and was covered with a cloth-of-gold mantle to match her bridegroom's.

Philip entered the Cathedral first, by the West Door, then Mary, with a large retinue and followed by her bishops. The ceremony began with the announcement by one of Philip's lords that he had been created King of Naples by his father (in order to match his wife in rank), and then the Lord Chamberlain publicly confirmed the marriage contract, before the couple proceeded to their wedding by the revived Catholic rite—under a special dispensation, since England was still formally under papal ban. The Queen was 'given away' by the Marquess of Winchester and Earls of Pembroke, Derby and Bedford, in the name of the kingdom, and she had chosen as her wedding-ring a plain "round hoop of gold", for, she had said, "her desire was to be married as maidens were married in the old time".[4] When the ring was laid on the Bible for the Bishop of Winchester's blessing, Philip put down three handfuls of gold beside it, in token of his endowment of his bride, and Mary was seen to smile as she handed it to her lady to be put in a purse. After the wedding, there was a High Mass, and the couple took Communion together.

The wedding-feast that followed was so lavish that a good deal of the food was left over. One gentleman in attendance later reminisced that "It was my chance to carry a great pasty of a red deer in a great charger, very delicately baked, which for the weight thereof diverse refused, the which pasty I sent unto London to my wife and her brother, who cheered therewith many of their friends."[5]

It seems that everyone at the wedding felt the importance of the bedding that followed—after all, Mary was no young girl, with years ahead of her for child-bearing. But when, the next morning, the Spaniards tried to follow their own custom of greeting the couple in bed, and the English (for once prudish) stopped them from bursting in on their queen and her husband, they had a surprise: Philip had already risen and begun his paper-work. Not that the Spaniard intended any slight to his middle-aged bride: "He treats the Queen very kindly and well knows how to pass over the fact that she is no good from the point of view of fleshly sensuality," wrote one of his retinue. "He makes her so happy that the other day, when they were alone, she almost talked love-talk to him, and he replied in the same vein."[6]

A few weeks later, there were rumours that the Queen was already pregnant, and though Philip was anxious to get away to the Continent to take part in his father's war against France, he decided to remain with his wife until her confinement—he had, after all, been named Regent of England in case she should die while their child was a minor. Everything seemed to be going well, and at Easter Mary 'took her chamber' according to custom. Then, on Tuesday 30th April, there came the news that she had given birth to a son: London and the Home Counties went wild, with bells and bonfires. But it was all a dreadful mistake. There was no child, nor, though everyone continued to wait in expectation, did one appear.

The 'wise women' at Court said they had been mistaken in the date, that the heir to England would be born in May or June, but as time passed, Mary's abdomen, which had been so distended in the spring, began to deflate to its normal shape. In fact, she had never been pregnant at all.

It was a bad time for the Queen, who had been so happy throughout the winter: no child, and now no Philip, for he had at last taken ship for the Continent.

One person who could only rejoice that Mary had not become a mother was her half-sister Elizabeth. The Princess had been imprisoned for a while at the beginning of the reign, but she had come out of the Tower and was now, apparently, taken into the Queen's favour—most likely because Philip and his father, envisaging a future in which Mary was dead, preferred her to her cousin Mary of Scotland as heir to the English throne. In fact, Elizabeth was offered marriage with Duke Philibert of Savoy, a protégé of the Habsburg empire, to make sure of her loyalty to their interests. When she refused the match, Philip railed at his wife for her inability to force her sister to submit to his plans. That was during his second visit to England, in the spring of 1557, and was only one part of Philip's agenda; another was, of course, to make Mary pregnant, but despite revived hopes, again they came to nothing; a third project was to draw England into war with France, and this at least he accomplished—to Mary's eternal shame, for it was at this time that England lost Calais, her last foothold on the Continent.

The reign of Mary I ended in bitterness and horror, not least for Mary herself. Abandoned, apparently, by her husband, unable to bear a child to maintain the succession, she was also branded as the merciless persecutor of Protestant 'heretics': some three to four hundred men and women were burned to death for their faith, and the Queen was reviled as 'Bloody Mary'.

Ironically, the tumour of stomach or womb which had given her the appearance of being with child was the cause of her death. After long pain, the Queen died on 17th November 1558.

Elizabeth Tudor was twenty-five years old when she came to the throne, glad to be still alive, let alone to reign. For the first two years of her life, she had been petted and praised; then, with her mother's disgrace and death, she had been cast into the oblivion that her half-sister Mary had been suffering for years. Her last stepmother, Catherine Parr, had been kind to her, but Elizabeth's involvement with Catherine's husband, the ill-fated Thomas Seymour, had brought the girl her first real taste of fear when she was only sixteen. During Edward VI's reign, Elizabeth had lived quietly, a studious, tensely self-controlled young woman who had already learned to mask her real feelings and to hold herself aloof from political intrigue. Under Mary, her life was in real danger after Wyatt's rebellion, when she was suspected of having conspired to take her sister's throne, but, as we have seen, she survived imprisonment in the Tower, and though she was held in custody or at least under close surveillance for the rest of the reign, though she went always in terror of her sister's suspicions, though she had to give at least token submission to the Catholic Church, she kept her head—in more senses than one.

But the years had left their mark on this last Tudor, and in nothing so much as in the matter of her marriage. As a child, in her father's reign, Elizabeth had been named time and again in 'package deals' of foreign marriages proposed for her, Edward and Mary, but they had all come to nothing; in Mary's reign, the Emperor's plan to marry her to Philibert of Savoy had been matched by secret French proposals, made to secure her alliance in the event of Mary's death, and English dissidents had attempted to unite her with Edward Courtenay, a scion of the old Plantagenet line. But Elizabeth had always refused to commit herself.

It has been said that Elizabeth I had some physical defect that made the prospect of child-bearing a hazard to her life; more feasibly, it has been suggested that the defect was in her mind, that, with her family's history before her, she regarded marriage itself, the entrusting of her life to any man, as the fate to be feared. But she was the last of her line, and for years it seemed imperative that she marry.

When Elizabeth had been on the throne some three months, she received a deputation from the Privy Council and the House of Commons, come to petition her to marry. In her immediate reply, the Queen spoke vaguely of "marriage with my kingdom". A few days later, her official speech was read in Parliament: she was, she said, grateful for her subjects' concern, but she was determined to remain unmarried, to live to God's service. In the event that she should change her mind, she assured her people that she would give them no cause to complain of her choice of husband, but still, she hoped she might rely on Parliament to help her select some fit person to succeed her, rather than any child of her own. It would be enough for her that at her death "a marble stone should declare that a queen, having reigned such a time, lived and died a virgin".

The first of Elizabeth's many suitors after her accession was none other than her brother-in-law, Philip, now King of Spain, who saw in her (despite her proclaimed loyalty to the reformed English Church) a better potential friend than her cousin Mary, Queen of Scotland, now queen consort of France, who was also claiming the English throne. For the first months of her reign, Elizabeth made polite conversation with the Spanish ambassador on the subject, but once she felt really secure, she was able to refuse the offer. Not that that deterred the Habsburgs: Philip married a French princess (Edward VI's former fiancée Elisabeth), but there were offers on behalf of other members of the Habsburg family, and in the mid-1560s the Queen seemed quite interested in the suit of the King's nephew Charles of Austria. Nor was France dilatory in making a bid for such a useful ally, and proposals and enquiries also flooded in from Scandinavia and Germany. However, though the Queen often said 'maybe', she never once said 'yes'.

There was a body of opinion in the Council that it would be easier to persuade her into a marriage with one of her own subjects, and every unmarried lord from adolescence to dotage seems to have been mooted for the consort's crown. But one of them, Robert Dudley, led the field . . .

Robert Dudley was the son of Edward VI's second Lord Protector, the Duke of Northumberland—he who had attempted to put his daughter-in-law, Jane Grey, on the throne in 1553. Elizabeth had known the Dudley family since childhood, and from the very outset of her reign, when she made him Master of the Horse, she had favoured Robert. Indeed, before her first year was out, it was rumoured that they were lovers, even that she was pregnant by him. But there was one apparently insuperable obstacle to their marriage: Robert Dudley already had a wife. True, she was never seen in his company and was kept in seclusion in the country, and it was said that she was suffering from breast cancer, which must sooner or later kill her—but a wife was a wife, and the Queen was running great risks with her reputation by her obvious infatuation with Dudley.

Then, suddenly, in September 1560, came the news that the lady had been found dead, lying at the foot of a staircase, her neck broken. Immediately everyone thought of murder—a murder that would allow the widower to marry Elizabeth. The Queen at once sent him away from Court, but only a few weeks after his wife's funeral and the inquest (which found a verdict of accidental death), he was back, in as high a place as ever. Nevertheless, there was a good deal of feeling against the marriage now, and though for years Elizabeth and Dudley (whom she created Earl of Leicester) were on the most publicly affectionate terms, it was tacitly agreed that the Queen could not marry a man over whom such a cloud of suspicion would always hang.

Dudley had rivals, of course, among the Queen's courtiers as well as European princes with their proposals in person or by proxy. At home there was the Earl of Sussex, favoured at one time, and Christopher Hatton and Sir William Pickering and various others; the main foreign contender was the French King's brother François (seventeen to Elizabeth's thirty-seven in 1570), who came as near as any man to winning her. His visits to England, in the 1570s, and the love-letters he wrote to Elizabeth from abroad, offer a convincing picture of a courtship, and the Queen certainly encouraged him, with flirtation and affectionate teasing. In 1581 she declared that she would marry François—but (there was always a 'but' with Elizabeth) she left herself escape-routes: there was the matter of her Council's ratification of the marriage, and the Council could be relied on to pick up any hint of doubt on the part of its mistress; there was the problem of François's Catholicism, which he could obviously not forsake lest he be called on to succeed his brother on the French throne. There was always some reason why the marriage could not be celebrated immediately. In the end, the project dwindled, and in 1584 the Frenchman died.

Robert Dudley, Earl of Leicester, died four years later, in Armada year. There can be no doubt that the Queen loved him: even when he married another woman, her own cousin (on her mother's side), she forgave him (though not his countess), and when Elizabeth herself died, and her servants opened a little coffer that had always stood by her bed, they found in it a paper touchingly inscribed "His last letter".

Throughout her reign, Elizabeth I was surrounded by men who professed to worship her, to whom she was the 'Gloriana' of pageantry and poetry. The Queen herself did all she could to fill the role, emphasizing her dual personality of monarch and woman, parading her Court in glittering gowns (which no woman must try to rival) and maintaining every day the pretence that she was served for her beauty and charm as much as for her power. It was a useful pretence, one which bound men to her service, but as she grew older, losing her glowing red hair and many of her teeth, her face chalky white under lead paint, the charade verged on the absurd. As the Queen's personal charms decreased, so her gowns became ever more flamboyant, her jewellery more dazzling—and the ardent professions of her courtiers the more insincere. And yet still, it seems, Elizabeth needed men's adulation and professions of attachment for herself, as much as for her 'image': evading marriage, avoiding any real commitment to a man, she needed to feel that there was one man, among the many, who was peculiarly her own.

In her sixties, that man was the stepson of the late Earl of Leicester, Robert Devereux, Earl of Essex, born in 1567 when she had been on the throne almost a decade. But Essex, to whom she allowed so many liberties, whose misdeeds she pardoned over and over again, damned himself at last by a flagrant act of treason, and in 1601 he was sent to the block.

There is a story that the Queen had once given him a ring, her recognition of the love which she assumed he had for her, and had she received that ring from him while he lay under sentence of death, his life might have been spared. But somewhere on its way to her, the ring fell into the hands of one of his many enemies, who knew its significance and hid it away, and so Elizabeth allowed Essex to die, believing him unrepentant. It was not until January 1603 that she learned the truth, so the story runs, and then she began to die. Two months later she did die, an old, hideous, lonely woman whom real love had always evaded.

Sixteenth-century Scotland

By coincidence, the Scottish royal family dwindled at the same time as that of England, and by 1558, when Elizabeth I was the last Tudor by male descent, in Scotland her cousin Mary stood in the same position in the House of Stewart.* But where Elizabeth died childless, Mary left one son, James, King of Scotland from 1567, and it was he who carried the dynasty into English history, with the union of the crowns in 1603, deriving his claim to the English throne from the marriage of his maternal great-grandfather, James IV of Scotland, and Henry VII's daughter Margaret, in 1503.

James IV was twenty-three, Margaret only eight, when their marriage contract was signed in 1497, but he was content to wait until she should be old enough to marry—content to wait in the arms of his mistress, Margaret Drummond. (Was it only coincidence that she, and her two sisters, died of what was said to be food-poisoning, on the eve of the royal wedding? Two Drummond women had already been queens consort of Scotland, and it was rumoured that James's love for this one might well overcome his desire for alliance with England. The death of the King's mistress, whom some said was already secretly his wife, seemed just too convenient.)

Margaret Tudor was fourteen years old when she was put on the road north in the summer of 1503. She rode in a litter hung with cloth-of-gold embroidered with the royal arms of England, topped with a blue velvet canopy and lined with thick bearskins against the jolting springs. England had never seen anything like her brilliant cavalcade, it was said; the brightly clothed retinue of lords and ladies swelled to around two thousand by the time it reached the border. (How strange it must have seemed to peasant girls, accustomed to unceasing work, rough clothes and certainly never any pampering, to see this wonderfully gowned royal

---

* The House of Stewart until 1567, when James VI used the French form of the name, Stuart, which had been adopted by his father Lord Darnley's immediate forebears.

girl the centre of so much attention, as the procession wound its way along the highroad to Scotland.)

The Scots met their future queen at Lamberton Kirk, just inside the kingdom, to conduct her to James, who was supposedly at Edinburgh. In fact, the King was so eager to meet his bride that he suddenly appeared at Dalkeith to waylay her, and by the time they moved off again, a few days later, she and her bridegroom had spent several hours together, playing cards, he performing for her on the clavichords and lute. When they entered the capital, on 7th August, the Princess was riding pillion behind the King.

The next day, at their wedding in the monastery of Holyrood, Margaret wore a gown of white damask, bordered and lined with crimson velvet, with a gold and pearl collar round her neck and a crown and veil over her long fair hair. James was also in white, a damask figured with gold and lined with sarsenet; his black velvet jacket had sleeves of crimson satin, with a doublet of cloth-of-gold and a pair of scarlet hose.

That evening, after dinner, there was the customary music and dancing, but also, records an English observer, "some good bodies made games of passe-passe [tag] and did very well."[1] The next days passed with the usual wedding round of jousts, balls and feasts, but James found time to have his beard clipped by one of his wife's ladies, because Margaret disliked it. He seemed devoted to her, spending a good deal of time in her company and giving her jewels, while she began to embroider a purse for his money.

The peace with England did not endure, however, and on 9th September 1513 James IV was killed on Flodden Field, where his army was defeated by that of his brother-in-law, Henry VIII.

Now in her mid-twenties, Margaret attempted to rule in the name of her seventeen-month-old son, James V, but the faction-ridden Scottish Council had little respect for her, little trust that she would put loyalty to Scotland before her natural loyalty to England. For years Margaret had to struggle to stay in power; at one point, in 1514, she married Archibald Douglas, Earl of Angus, to gain his clan's support, but that only worsened her situation with the other lords, and over the years even her husband deserted her for her enemies.

The young King James was brought up in an atmosphere of plotting and feuds, and from his adolescence onwards he went from one mistress to another while his ministers—and his mother—attempted to mate him with a suitable princess. Left to himself, James would have married one of his mistresses, Margaret Erskine, but she was married already, and though she obtained a divorce from the Scottish Church courts, James could not persuade officials in Rome to recognize it, or to grant them a dispensation. The Scottish King was not like his uncle Henry of England, who had just taken his Church out of allegiance to Rome for a similar refusal to grant a divorce: James gave up his love and turned to France for a bride.

King François I had only one daughter available, the Princess Madeleine, but she was too young, he argued, and too frail to marry; instead, he gave James his choice between several cousins of the royal House, and in the summer of 1536, on the strength of a portrait and the offer of a dowry of 100,000 crowns, the Scottish King decided on Marie of Vendôme. Since Scotland was "in good peace and rest"[2] (for once), James determined to give himself a holiday, to inspect the bride, and he arrived at the Vendôme Court at St Quentin that September.

The King did not announce himself with the usual trumpetings of majesty but, pretending that he had sent some of his servants on ahead, disguised himself as one of them, thinking to take a look at Marie, "to spy her pulchritude and behaviour unkenned by her."[3] Everyone was deceived but the girl herself. She went to her coffer, took out the portrait of the Scotsman which she had secretly obtained, "passed peartlie to him and took him by the hand and said 'Sir, ye stand over far aside. Therefore, if it please Your Grace, ye may show off yourself to my father or me, and confer and pass the time awhile.' "[4] James should have been impressed by this show of intelligence, but we are told that he was a good deal disappointed by Marie's looks. Still, after a few days with her family, he went on his way to the King's Court, at Lyons, to finalize the contract.

It was only then that he decided to change brides.

The Princess Madeleine is said by one source (the Scots one quoted above) to have fallen in love with him at first sight, begging her father to give her to him; another, rather more realistically, would have it that Madeleine wanted nothing so much as to be a queen. King François and his Council tried to dissuade her—and James, who was probably not the least in love but who saw the better advantage of marrying a king's daughter. James was privately informed that "no succession would come of her body, by reason of her long sickness and that she was not able to travel out of the realm to no other country, which, if she did, she would not have long days,"[5] but in the end everything was arranged, and he even agreed to accept Madeleine with a dowry only half the size of that offered by Vendôme. (Marie was forgotten—the Scots chronicler says that she died of "displeasure", but there is no proof of that.)

The wedding was celebrated on New Year's Day 1537 at the cathedral of Notre Dame, in Paris. (Ironically, the senior prelate presiding was Marie of Vendôme's uncle, Cardinal Bourbon.) Then, says the chronicler, Lindsay of Pittscottie,

> . . . there was never such solemnity nor such nobility seen in France in one day as there was at that time there, for through all France that day there was jousting and running of horses proclaimed, with all other manly exercise, as also skirmishing of ships, through all the coasts and firths; so that in towns, lands, seas, firths, villages, castles and towers there was no man that might have heard for the roar and noise of cannons and other munition, nor scarcely have seen for the vapours thereof.
>
> There was also within the town of Paris cunning 'carveris' and profound necromancers, who by their art caused things to appear which was not, as

follows: fowls flying in the air, spouting fire on others, rivers of water running through the town, and ships fighting thereupon. Their conceits were made to the great wonder of such as tended to the forth-setting and solemnizing of that day, to do the King of Scotland and the King of France, their masters, honour and pleasure.[6]

Because of Madeleine's uncertain health, the couple's journey to Scotland was delayed until May, and their expenses over those months must have been enormous, but generously François defrayed the whole cost—and not only that, he sent his daughter on her way with the first 100,000 *livres* of her dowry and gave her and her ladies the pick of all the materials in his wardrobe for their outfits; in addition, he gave his new son-in-law twenty of his own horses, several suits of gilded armour and two fine ships.

On 19th May 1537 the royal fleet landed at Leith, and when Madeleine stood on the shore, her first act was to kneel and thank God for her safe voyage, scooping up two handfuls of earth and kissing them. But the journey had sorely taxed her strength, and it was decided that she must forego the usual state entry into Edinburgh and that her coronation must be postponed indefinitely. Even though she rested, her old malady (probably tuberculosis) had her in its grip, and on 7th July 1537, less than two months after her arrival in Scotland, the Queen died. She was just over a month short of her seventeenth birthday.

The messengers who took the sad news back to France were also primed with instructions to beg a new bride for James. Without hesitation, François named Marie of Guise, with a dowry of 150,000 *livres* and the honorary status of 'Daughter of France'.

In contrast to Madeleine, Marie was a robust woman, some 6 feet tall, and she had already proved her ability to have children: when her first husband, the Duke of Longueville, had died, just a month before Queen Madeleine, Marie was pregnant, and negotiations for her re-marriage were already well advanced when she gave birth to her second son that August—though, with at least token respect for the two dead spouses, the wedding was not to be until the following summer.

In the meanwhile, Marie received another offer. Over in England, Queen Jane Seymour died that October, and Henry VIII suddenly took a fancy to the widowed Duchess of Longueville, on the strength of a report that she was a fine figure of a woman. There is, however, apparently no substance to the often-told tale that Marie refused Henry because, so she said, she had only one neck—if she had more, she would put one at the English King's disposal. The refusal actually came from King François, on her behalf, with the admonition to Henry that he should be ashamed to ask for the woman who was already pledged to his nephew.

This time, James V made no effort to leave his kingdom to collect a bride but instead sent lords and clergy to bring her to her new home. However, when Marie landed at Crail, in Fife, in June 1538, he did not wait to receive her formally at St Andrews, where he was in residence, but rode out to meet her and conduct her into the city, where they were married on the 12th.

Even that much enthusiasm did not last long. James made no effort to hide his infidelities, and it was not long before the insecurities and fears of his childhood began to show in his character, in what one biographer has termed 'paranoia'.

The Protestantism which was seeping into England had also appeared in Scotland, but James would not follow his uncle Henry's lead: he needed his clergy as a bulwark against his nobles, and when war broke out with England yet again, in 1542, it was the Church on which he relied to rally an army, while the lairds refused to follow their King over the border and ignored the orders of his commander. In November 1542 the Scots suffered a decisive defeat at Solway Moss. James had not been present at the battle, and when he heard the news, he was appalled. On 14th December he died, just a few days after he had received the news that Queen Marie had given birth not to the son for whom he had hoped but to a daughter.

"It cam' wi' a lass, and it will gang wi' a lass," said the dying King, referring to the way in which the crown of Scotland had devolved on the House of Stewart; he was certain that, with threats from England, his lords in virtual anarchy, and ferment in the Scottish Church, no woman could rule.

He was to be proved right. For years, with help from France, Marie of Guise succeeded in holding Scotland together, but the follies of her daughter Mary, after 1561, saw a renewal, an intensification, of all the problems that had beset James V. As it was, when James died, his heiress was only a few days old, and for a time it seemed that Scotland's pledge of the infant Queen in marriage to the only son of Henry of England would stave off further attacks. But that was not to be. As we have seen, not even England's 'Rough Wooing' could keep the Scots true to their promise to deliver Queen Mary to her great-uncle, and in August 1548 the child was despatched to France, with the prospect of marriage with the Dauphin, the future King François II.

It was the best thing that could have happened to her—from a short-term point of view, for she grew up untroubled by the problems of her kingdom. It was only when she returned home, in 1561, that she found her foreign education, her Continental piety, her ignorance of affairs of state and her lack of understanding of the Scots mentality a hazardous handicap to successful rule. As it was, Mary was reared in luxury and ease, amid the French royal family and their courtiers, who indulged and flattered her, and she soon established a dominance over the Dauphin, two years her junior, impressing him with her undoubted beauty as well as by her extra inches in height. François was a weakling, both in health and in character, and Mary's carefree, extrovert, imperious manner awed him even in their childhood.

On 24th April 1558 the sixteen-year-old Queen of Scots, tall, fair, graceful, dressed in a blue velvet gown embroidered with silver lilies and sparkling with jewels, processed to the high altar of Notre Dame Cathedral, in Paris, on the arm of King Henri II, following her bridegroom, led in by the King of Navarre. When their vows had been exchanged, silver trumpets proclaimed the good news to the waiting crowds, who then proceeded to half-kill each other in the scramble for the gold and silver 'largesse'.

That evening, after the banquet, Mary opened the ball with her sister-in-law Elisabeth (Edward VI's former fiancée), and so long was her train that a courtier had to dance behind her, holding it up. Then came the 'disguisings': reciting poets representing the planets, young girls singing an epithalamium, twelve hobby-horses ridden by boy princes, 'chariots' bearing a mixture of pagan and Christian characters and then the *pièce de résistance*, six great ships, "so ingeniously made and led by such great dexterity that one would have said that they floated on water and advanced through waves and swells of water".[7] From the ships issued half a dozen men, including the Kings of France and Navarre and the Dauphin, collecting their ladies from the onlookers and leading them out to dance.

Less than three years later, those golden days had been forgotten. Over in Scotland, Mary's mother died in the summer of 1560, and before the year was out, young King François II of France, Mary's husband, died too, having reigned for a little less than eighteen months.

Mary had been fond of her husband by all accounts, but she was certainly not overcome with grief at his death. Very soon after, she was listening to proposals from Spain for a new marriage, backed with promises (or rather hints) that Spain would realize Mary's claim to the throne of England. Obviously she was now redundant at the French Court, and so, in the summer of 1561, after an absence of thirteen years, she returned to her own kingdom.

In France, Mary had been content to leave policy to her Guise uncles, knowing that they could be relied on to act for her good. Now, in Scotland, her first attempts at statecraft were directed towards keeping control of herself and her powers amid the clan rivalries of her lords, complicated as they now were by religious differences and by English pressure.

Elizabeth of England had, of course, an interest in her cousin's affairs—particularly in her marriage plans, and almost from the outset she made it clear that, if Mary would marry to oblige her, she could well recognize the Scottish Queen as her heiress. The prospect of such a peaceful inheritance was the best way of keeping Mary from allying with Spain, it was thought. Elizabeth even offered Mary her own 'sweet Robin' Dudley—though it is hard to believe that she would ever have allowed him to leave her or that he would have given up his expectations of marrying Elizabeth herself. But Dudley was a Protestant, and Elizabeth had to offer a Catholic suitor also, to make her proposals sound genuine. She had one to hand:

Henry Stuart, Lord Darnley, son of her cousin Margaret Douglas, whose
parents were the late Margaret Tudor and the Earl of Angus. With his
mother's claim to the English throne, as a descendant of Henry VII, and
his father's to the Scottish throne, as Mary's heir presumptive (he was
descended in the female line from James II), Darnley was scarcely inferior
to Mary 'in blood', and the fact that he had been born and brought up in
England would add to their eligibility to rule there. But did the devious
Elizabeth really want Mary to marry Darnley? Certainly, when she
allowed the young man to travel to Scotland, in the spring of 1565, it
seemed that she was in favour of the marriage, but Elizabeth had good
information as to the state of the factions in Scotland, and she knew well
that Darnley's arrival, with its implications, would add to the ferment
there, which could only be to England's advantage.

Mary, who for some time past had been fighting a losing battle against
her lords and their demands on her, looked to Darnley's coming not only
with the interest of a young woman but also with the need of a queen to
have a child to be her heir. Add, on the one hand, Darnley's personal
attraction and, on the other, his dynastic significance, and it is not
surprising that she married him that July.

Despite all her 'fair words' in the past, Elizabeth was furious. She put
Darnley's mother in the Tower, and there was no more talk of Mary and
her new husband being acknowledged heirs to England.

In contrast to her first wedding, Mary's second lacked a good deal in
dignity. In fact, the Queen went through a private ceremony with
Darnley a couple of weeks before the public wedding, on 29th July 1565,
which was performed in the chapel of the Palace of Holyrood. The
English ambassador, an eye-witness, reported to his Queen that Mary
went to her wedding still dressed in mourning for her first husband:

> . . . They kneel together, and many prayers are said over them; she tarrieth
> out the Mass, and he taketh a kiss and leaveth her there, and went to her
> chamber, whither, within a space, she followeth and, being required
> (according to the solemnity) to case off her cares and leave aside these
> sorrowful garments, and give herself to a more pleasant life, after some
> refusal (more, I believe, for manners' sake than grief of heart), she suffereth
> them that stood by, every man that could approach, to take out a pin; and so,
> being committed to her ladies, changed her garments, but went not to bed,
> to signify to the world that it was not lust that moved them to marry but only
> the necessity of her country, not, if God will, to leave it without an heir.[8]

'Lust' there was, in some degree, but in Mary policy and in Darnley
ambition had the first place. Mary seemed only too ready to give her
husband the estates and grants of money that would enhance his
position, but though she was later prevailed on to give him the title of
king, she was cautious as to the powers she should allow him. This was
the basis of the mistrust that grew up between them, the cause for
resentment that drove Darnley into the toils of the unscrupulous lairds
who promised to support him. For a while, it seemed that Darnley had
broken Mary—when he and his friends murdered her Italian secretary

(some said, her lover, though more likely he was a secret agent of the Pope), using the Queen's weakness during her pregnancy to gain the upper hand.

It was a year later, in February 1567, just eight months after the birth of their son, that Darnley himself was assassinated. In the early hours of Monday the 10th, there was a loud explosion in the Kirk o' Field area of Edinburgh, and the citizens who rushed out of their houses to investigate found Darnley's lodgings in ruins, their 'King' lying dead in the garden. But the blast of gunpowder had not killed him—there was no mark of it on his body; he was already dead when it had gone off: he had been strangled.

Whether the Queen was a party to the plot to kill Darnley was debated then and in the years that followed and has been a subject for contention ever since. The chief suspect at the time was one James Hepburn, Earl of Bothwell, a confederate of the Queen since before Rizzio's murder, who had been seen on the streets of Edinburgh at the time of the explosion. Darnley's father, the Earl of Lennox, was obviously convinced that Bothwell was the instigator of his son's death, and he forced Mary to allow him to be brought to trial, but Bothwell was cleared by the court and issued public challenges to his accusers—which none of them cared to take up. Then, moreover, he collected a party of lords and clergy and presented himself to the Queen in the light of a prospective bridegroom.

Here, the web of rumour, legend and accusation obscures the story. Some said that Mary had long been Bothwell's mistress, that she was only too eager to marry him; Mary herself later claimed that she had refused to marry him, still suspecting him of Darnley's murder, and she was also to claim that Bothwell's seizure of her, on 24th April, was an outrage, violence to her royal person; others say that Mary was ready and waiting for him and his small army to strike, deliberately limiting the numbers of her entourage so that there should be no resistance. Whatever was the truth of it, Bothwell took the Queen into his custody, presented her with documentary proof of his supporters' pledges to uphold him in power—and raped her. Having gained a divorce from his wife, the Earl married the Queen on 15th May.

Whatever anyone said of Mary's infatuation with Bothwell, and her complicity in his various treasons, the French ambassador was convinced that she married him against her will. First, there was the matter of the wedding itself—it was performed according to Protestant rites, and Mary had always abhorred the Scottish Reformed Church; then, said Ambassador du Croc, when he visited Mary and Bothwell soon afterwards,

> I noticed something strange in the manner of her and her husband, which she sought to excuse, saying that if she was sad, it was because she wished to be so, and she never wished to rejoice again. All that she wished for was death. Yesterday, whilst she and her husband were together, shut up in their cabinet [private room], she cried out aloud for a knife with which to kill herself. Those who were in the outer chamber heard her.[9]

The English ambassador backed him up. "The Queen was so disdainfully used," he reported home, "that . . . I heard her ask for a knife to stab herself, or else, said she, 'I shall drown myself.' "[10]

Bothwell was not left long in triumph. Despite the care he had taken to collect pledges of support, the forces ranged against him were already gathering. On 5th June he fled south, taking Mary with him, but when an army of his enemies faced his at Carberry Hill a few days later, and his own men melted away, he abandoned the Queen to save himself. In fact, the Earl managed to leave Scotland undetected, but only to meet his doom soon after, when he was captured by Danes and condemned to life-imprisonment for alleged piracy. He died insane in 1578.

Mary, meanwhile, had been captured and imprisoned in the island fortress of Lochleven, and on 24th July she was forced to sign an act of abdication in favour of her year-old son, who now became King James VI. In May the following year, she escaped from her prison and crossed into England, begging protection from her cousin Elizabeth and aid in regaining Scotland, but if Mary had a sincere trust in the English Queen's good will, she was yet again mistaken in character-judgement: there was no way in which Elizabeth could allow Mary to go free, let alone to hazard her own position in England by championing a Catholic queen against her predominantly Protestant subjects, for Mary was still under suspicion of having connived at Darnley's murder, and 'everyone' knew that she had plotted with Spain to dethrone Elizabeth herself.

The story of the last years of the life of Mary, Queen of Scots, is well known: her long imprisonment in England, growing old, losing her looks, creaking with rheumatism, but still wielding the power of a romantic legend to lure young men to hazard life and honour in her service, ever hopeful that someone, Scotsman, Englishman or agent of some friendly foreign power, would find a means of freeing her, restoring her to her throne and avenging the wrongs she had suffered from her many enemies. It was as a result of such a plot—a failure, as were the others—that Elizabeth I was persuaded to sign Mary's death-warrant. For years the English Queen had resisted her ministers' urgent pleas to have the Scottish Queen killed, since alive she would always represent a threat to Elizabeth's person and her kingdom. Reluctantly, she signed Mary's life away—and then, too late, tried to recall the warrant. On 8th February 1587, Mary, Queen of Scots, was beheaded.

Her son, James VI, now twenty years old, made token protest at his mother's death, but in years past he had made no real effort to have her brought to freedom. The powers of Europe condemned the deed, and Spain mounted her Armada the following year using Mary's 'murder' as one pretext for its attempt to overthrow Elizabeth, but the English Queen survived—survived, in fact, another fifteen years without naming her heir, until at last, on her deathbed, she was induced to signify her assent to Mary's son succeeding her on the throne of England.

The Seventeenth Century

'Rational Love'

We have become so accustomed to reckoning the various periods of our history by changes of royal dynasty that it is hard to realize that the lifestyle of a nation does not change overnight at the death of a monarch. The 'Stuart century' took over trends from the 'Tudor century' and developed them, but that is as far as it goes; even the laws which the Stuarts and their Parliaments made only reflect developments in outlook which had their origins years before.

As far as marriage is concerned, the sixteenth century had seen a trend towards indulgence of love-matches, or at least marriages made where a couple seemed most compatible, but the marriage arranged to unite fortunes or titles was by no means dead by the seventeenth century, and there was a perpetual debate between the merits and good results of the two forms. In the 1650s, one Dorothy Osborne wrote,

> . . . I have not faith enough to believe a doctrine that is often preached, which is that, though at first one has no kindness for *them*, yet it will grow strongly after marriage. Let them trust to it that think good; for my part, I am clearly of the opinion (and shall die in't) that as the more one sees and knows a person that one likes, one has still more kindness for them, so on the other side, one is but the more weary of, and the more averse to, an unpleasant humour for having it perpetually by one. And though I easily believe that to marry one for whom we have already some affection will infinitely increase that kindness, yet I shall never be persuaded that marriage has a charm to raise love out of nothing, much less out of dislike.[1]

Dorothy herself wanted to marry for love, but she utterly refused to marry without parental approval, writing to her lover that

> I can never think of disposing myself without my father's consent; and though he has left it more in my power than almost anybody leaves a daughter, yet certainly I were the worst-natured person in the world if his kindness were not a greater tie upon me than any advantage he would have reserved. Besides that, 'tis my duty, from which nothing can ever tempt me, nor could you like it in me if I should do otherwise, 'twould make me unworthy of your esteem.[2]

83

There were many to agree with the Marquess of Halifax, in the 1680s, when he wrote down, in his *Advice to a Daughter*, that young women could not be trusted to choose their own husbands wisely, that "their friends' care and experience are thought safer guides to them than their own fancies".[3] Most parents were, of course, extremely careful in their choice of a husband or wife for their children, and though money or status might be a factor in their choice, morals were also carefully weighed. In 1637 Lady Leicester had to break off negotiations to marry Lord Lovelace to her daughter when she found out his reputation: ". . . I find my lord Lovelace so uncertain and so idle, so much addicted to mean company and so early drawn into debauchery, as it is now my study how to break off with him in such a manner as it may be said that we refused him . . . for though his estate is good, his person pretty enough and his wit much more than ordinary, yet dare I not venture to give Doll to him."[4]

Dorothy Osborne was shocked to see a widow courted only for her money: "She is old and was never handsome and yet is courted a thousand times more than the greatest beauty in the world would be that had not a fortune. We could not eat in quiet for the letters and presents that came in from people that would not have looked upon her when they had met her if she had been left poor."[5] However, the matching of a widow's fortune and household skills with a man's home and protection seemed only sensible, as when the widower Lord Fairfax told his brother in 1646 that

> My solitary condition and want of help in managing household affairs (which I am forced unto) made me think of a gentlewoman for assistance and comfort. Her virtue was the chief thing that drew my affections, which was much commended by the parents and friends of her former husband. . . . She has five children, but provided for in such a manner as I hope will not be burdensome, and her estate (though not great) may be sufficient, by God's blessing, in part to supply the defects of my own towards our maintenance.[6]

With the deathrate still so high in early life, there were many widows and widowers seeking second (and even third) marriages, and to some the power to choose for themselves, without parental supervision, was a temptation to marry for love, or at least because of an attraction. The widowed Mrs Margaret Pulteney informed a cousin that

> My lady Deincourt wrote to me very earnestly about her son, that the match might go forward, but I am so much against it that I will for no conditions in the world hear of it. My mother is for it, for she hears he hath a greater estate than this, which is, I believe, her reason; but for my part I think all the riches in the world without content is nothing—for this liberty I will take to myself, that is, to make choice of one as I affect, as for him I find I cannot. . . . Sure I am not so fond [foolish] as to be in love with any at two days' sight. I hope God will give me power of myself yet. I shall not settle my affections on any till I see some fondness in a man to induce me to it.[7]

Mrs Pulteney was not alone in despising the 'foolishness' of sudden love, a love without anything more than physical attraction as its basis. The Puritan Richard Baxter, in his *Christian Directory* of 1673, remarked that "To say you love, and you know not why, is more beseeming children or mad folks than those that are soberly entering upon a change of life of so great importance to them."[8] Love must be 'rational', he said, "such as you can justify in the severest trial, by the evidence of worth and fitness in the person whom you love".[9] And love must be demonstrated by real kindness and thoughtful concern, not by the foolish kissing and caressing which Dorothy Osborne despised in a certain young husband's conduct to his bride, when she saw an otherwise sensible man "transformed into the direct shape of a great boy newly come from school. To see him wholly taken up with running errands for his wife and teaching her little dog tricks!"[10]

Mrs Lucy Hutchinson's memorial of her husband shows that a woman could appreciate the 'rational' love of an undemonstrative man and find obedience to him no hardship:

> For conjugal affection to his wife, it was such in him as whosoever would draw out a rule of honour, kindness and religion, to be practised in that estate, need no more but exactly draw out his example; never man had a greater passion for a woman nor a more honourable esteem of a wife, yet he was not uxorious nor remitted not that just rule which it was her honour to obey, but managed the reins of government with such prudence and affection that she who would not delight in such honourable and advantageable subjection must have wanted a reasonable soul; he governed by persuasion, which he never employed but to things honourable and profitable for herself; he loved her soul and her honour more than her outside, and yet he had even for her person a constant indulgence, exceeding the common temporary passions of the most uxorious fools.[11]

The marriage service still demanded that a woman promise to obey her husband, and the general opinion was heavily weighted to the proposition that women were so foolish that they needed men to rule them. As Richard Baxter wrote,

> . . . it is no small patience which the natural imbecility of the female sex requireth you to prepare. Except it be very few that are patient and manlike, women are commonly of potent fantasies and tender, passionate, impatient spirits, easily cast into anger or jealousy or discontent, and of weak understandings and therefore unable to reform themselves. They are betwixt a man and a child; some few have more of the man, and many have more of the child; but most are but in a middle state.[12]

Nevertheless, there were limits as to how far a woman must obey an unreasonable man, and even Dan Rogers, a Puritan with the strictest views of woman's duty, released her from obedience to her husband should he suddenly order "removal from present dwelling, upon great change or loss, or to places of ill health, ill neighbours, with loss of Gospel, long voyages by sea to remote plantations or, in the sudden change of trade, by venturing in some new project, lending out or borrowing of great sums".[13]

Returning to the arrangement of a marriage, we have a unique and fascinating glimpse of country life in the 1640s, from the pen of the Yorkshireman Henry Best, who tells of a yeoman's courtship:

> Usually the young man's father, or he himself, writes to the father of the maid to know if he shall be welcome to the house, if he shall have furtherance if he come in such a way or how he liketh of the notion. Then, if he pretend any excuse, only thanking him for his good will, then it is as good as a denial.
>
> If the motion be thought well of, and embraced, then the young man goeth perhaps twice to see how the maid standeth affected. Then, if he see that she be tractable and that her inclination is towards him, then the third time that he visiteth, he perhaps giveth her a 10-shilling piece of gold, or a ring of that price, or perhaps a 20-shilling piece or a ring of that price, then 10 shillings the next time, or the next after that, a pair of gloves of 6, 8 or 10 shillings a pair; and after that, each other time, some conceited toy or novelty of less value. They usually visit every three weeks or a month, and are usually half a year, or very near, from the first going to the conclusion.
>
> So soon as the young folks are agreed and contracted, then the father of the maid carrieth her over to the young man's house to see how they like of all, and there doth the young man's father meet them to treat of a dower, and likewise of a jointure or feoffment for the woman, and then do they also appoint and set down the day of the marriage, which may perhaps be about a fortnight or three weeks after, and in that time do they get made the wedding-clothes and make provision against the wedding dinner, which is usually at the maid's father's. Their use is to buy gloves to give to each of their friends a pair on that day; the man should be at the cost for them, but sometimes the man gives gloves to the men and the woman to the women, or else he to her friends and she to his. They give them that morning when they are almost ready to go to church to be married.
>
> Then so soon as the bride is tired [attired] and that they are ready to go forth, the bridegroom comes and takes her by the hand and saith: "Mistress, I hope you are willing," or else kisseth her before them and then followeth her father out of doors. Then one of the bridegroom his men ushereth the bride and goes foremost, and the rest of the young men usher each of them a maid to church.
>
> The bridegroom and the bride's brothers or friends tend at dinner; he perhaps fetcheth her home to his house a month after, and the portion is paid that morning that she goes away. When the young man comes to fetch away his bride, some of his best friends and young men his neighbours come along with him, and others perhaps meet them in the way, and then there is some jollity at his house. For they perhaps have love-wine ready to give to the company when they light, then a dinner, supper and breakfast next day.[14]

Church weddings, with an invited congregation, followed by feasting and merry-making, were frowned on by the Puritans, who saw matrimony as a solemn business (though that is not to say that there were not loving marriages among them, as for example that of the Hutchinsons, quoted above). Nor would a strict Puritan bridegroom give his wife a ring, for it was seen only as a 'worldly' token of an otherwise spiritual state. When Parliament came to power in the 1640s, the wedding-service from the Book of Common Prayer was first replaced by that from the Puritans' service-book, the Directory; then, in 1652, the new 'Commonwealth' government went further, declaring that all marriages must be made by civil contract only, before a JP rather than a clergyman. There was an outcry against this even from otherwise obedient citizens; others conformed but went through a private wedding-service as well. As one Royalist bride said of her wedding, ". . . if it had not been done more solemnly afterwards by a minister, I should not have believed it lawfully done".[15]

The civil war of the 1640s split the nation as never before or since; no one could stand aloof or remain neutral, but it was in the upper classes where the breach was most apparent, the classes that had the most to lose and gain from the conflict, and even when the war was over and Parliament had won, the nation was still divided.

Dorothy Osborne was the daughter of a Royalist commander who had had far more than his fair share of suffering in the war and its aftermath, and though he was allowed to live quietly under the Commonwealth, he resented the defeat bitterly, so when Dorothy sought to marry one William Temple, whose father had fought against the King and was high in the new government, Sir Peter Osborne was appalled. He had given his daughter the freedom to make her own match, as we have seen, but in the circumstances she could not take advantage of it to do something that would so sadden him. For seven years the young couple loved faithfully, writing to each other frequently, but with little hope of ever marrying. It was only after Osborne's death that they came together, but then they had forty years of marriage before them, before Dorothy died in 1695.

At the Restoration, the old form of wedding-service was reintroduced, and the Puritans' prohibitions on merry-making were lifted. But curiously, by then the upper classes had lost their taste for ostentatious weddings. Even Dorothy Osborne, who was certainly neither Puritan nor miserly, found something distasteful in the thought of publicly parading herself at a wedding, and she told her fiancé that she would not be 'Mrs Bride' in public unless he absolutely insisted.

By the end of the century, anyone with pretensions to taste and 'gentility' thought twice about a public wedding. It was possible to evade even the public calling of the banns by obtaining a licence to marry.

Throughout this period there had been controversy over divorce—as opposed to annulments. The Elizabethan Church had allowed just a couple of divorces *ad vinculo*—that is, permitting re-marriage, but in 1604 a law was passed forbidding the remarriage of any divorced person. For the time being then, the most one could hope for was a divorce *a mensa et thoro*—a separation in which the couple lived apart, with separate financial arrangements. It was only in 1670 that Parliament decreed that a full divorce, with liberty to remarry, could be obtained by the passage of a private Act of Parliament, and very, very few people could afford such a costly procedure. In fact, between 1670 and 1750 there were only seventeen such divorces, though a larger number of couples were freed from

each other by annulments, on the grounds of male impotence or a
partner's non-consent at the time of the wedding.

There were unhappy marriages in plenty throughout the century (the
poet John Milton's among them), where couples might have benefited
from a more sympathetic divorce law, but apparently not as many as one
would expect. The very difficulty of divorce made men and women more
anxious to make a success of their marriages, or at least to find a way of
living with each other's faults without friction. Lord Halifax was a wise
man when he told his daughter that, if women could not love their
husbands, "there remaineth nothing for them to do but to endeavour to
make that easy which falleth to their lot, and by a wise use of everything
they may dislike in a husband, turn that by degrees to be very supportable
which, if neglected, might in time beget an aversion"[16]—excellent advice
to married couples today as then!

The Early Stuarts

At last, with the death of Elizabeth I in 1603, the kingdoms of Scotland
and England were united under one monarch, James VI and I, the first
king of the House of Stuart. And for the first time in more than half a
century, the English people were treated to the sight of a royal *family*,
when James, his wife and their children arrived to inspect their inheritance.

James had married back in 1589, when he was twenty-three years old.
There had been several projects for his marriage when he was a boy, but
by 1585, when he came of age and assumed full powers, the field had
narrowed to two candidates, Catherine of Navarre and Anne of
Denmark. Both were Protestant, which was an essential factor in James's
match, but while Catherine was eight years older than the King, Anne
was eight years his junior, and there was a good deal of debate as to the
relative merits of a mature woman who could give him 'good counsel' and
a young girl whose period of childbearing would be longer. In the end,
James decided in favour of the Danish match, which pleased most of his

people—in fact, when his envoy's departure to Denmark was for some reason postponed, in May 1589, the merchants of Edinburgh rioted for fear of losing the alliance which would be so advantageous to their North Sea trade, and the King had to issue assurances that all was well.

Plans had been made for Anne to marry James at home, by proxy, and then to take ship for Scotland, but though the wedding was duly performed, on 20th August 1589, storms thwarted three attempts by the Danish fleet to put to sea. News reached Scotland that Anne had embarked, but when, weeks later, she still had not arrived, the King was alarmed and ordered public prayers for her safety. When at last he heard that she had been in Oslo all the while, awaiting better weather, he determined to go and bring her home himself.

James had had little to do with women. As a child he had had a governess, the stern and undemonstrative Lady Mar, but then he was put into the care of 'governors' and saw few women, certainly no one to replace his mother; nor was he allowed the company of girls his own age—perhaps from his guardians' fears that he would develop the promiscuous propensities of his recent forebears. So James gave all his affection to the young men who were his companions—a taste he kept for the rest of his life. At the moment, however, he was in love with the unseen bride—or at least so he persuaded himself, and his journey to Scandinavia seemed the epitome of romance.

For the first part of the voyage, the King enjoyed good winds, but on the fifth day storms struck again, and he was forced to put ashore miles from Oslo. Then he had to battle overland through snow to reach the city.

If James had feared that his envoys' praises of Anne's beauty had been merely the usual flattery accorded to princesses, he had a pleasant surprise, for the fifteen-year-old girl was extremely pretty, with an ivory complexion and golden hair.

They were married on 23rd November, and by the time all the festivities were over, it was nearly Christmas. Rather then return to Scotland through the hazardous winter seas, James decided to remain in Scandinavia until the spring, and, travelling overland by sledge, he and Anne passed out of Norway, through Sweden, to Kronborg Castle in Denmark, where her family were waiting to greet them. There they were married yet again, this time by the Lutheran Church to which Anne belonged, and there were more feasts and entertainments. James did not, however, give himself up entirely to pleasure: he attended lectures on theology and medicine at the Copenhagen Academy, took part in religious discussions with the country's leading theologians and spent a good deal of time observing the Danish legal system in practice. He also had some conversations with the Danes regarding witchcraft and convinced himself that the storms his bride had encountered had been raised by Scottish witches who disliked the match: when he returned home, he set a witch-hunt through the kingdom, and when a coven was discovered at North

Berwick, torture was used on the unfortunate women until they confessed to having attempted to sink Anne's ships.

James and Anne had landed at Leith on 1st May 1590, and on the 17th
they were crowned together in Edinburgh. The King was then still in love
with his wife—but not for much longer. He found her frivolous, ignorant,
unwilling (or too stupid) to undertake the theological studies which he
would have delighted to share with her. There was no open breach
between them (though Anne enfuriated him when she was converted to
Catholicism at the turn of the century), but by the time they arrived in
England, in 1603, the couple were little more than casual friends.

By then Anne had borne James five children, and two more were born
in England, but only three, Henry, Elizabeth and Charles, survived the
dangerous childhood illnesses.

Henry, now Prince of Wales, was a paragon: tall, strong, good-looking,
sober and steady, strong-willed but amenable to reason, not studious but
avid for knowledge about the powers and duties of kings, and a keen
apprentice of the martial arts. As he grew up, the young man observed his
father closely and was not always convinced that King James was wise,
especially in his choice of the 'favourites' (some said homosexual lovers)
who always surrounded him.

King James looked first to Spain for his son's bride. He had concluded a
peace with Spain in 1604, and this was to be the seal on the treaty.
Inevitably, however, the problem of religion arose immediately: James
was appalled when Spain demanded the conversion of his heir to
Catholicism. Savoy was less demanding, stipulating only that, if its
princess married Henry, she should be allowed to worship *'privatamente'*
in her own chapel, and France offered much the same terms with the
Princess Christine. The drawback with the French match was that
Christine was only six years old, while Henry was already in his teens, so
she could not give him children for several years. But, as the Prince
reminded his father, if she came over to England while still a child, "there
will be a greater likelihood of converting her to our religion".[1] In fact,
Henry was only quoting King James in this, for some years before, James
had written a book of advice for his heir, the *Basilikon Doron*, in which he
told his son how to choose a wife—and how to treat her. It seems worth
quoting at some length:

> First of all, consider that marriage is the greatest earthly felicity or misery
> that can come to a man, according as it pleaseth God to bless or curse the
> same. Since then, without the blessing of God, ye cannot look for a happy
> success in marriage, ye must be careful both in your preparation for it and in
> the choice and usage of your wife, to procure the same. By your preparation,
> I mean that ye must keep your body clean and unpolluted till ye give it to
> your wife, whom-to only it belongeth. . . .
> I would rathest have you to marry one that were fully of your own
> religion, her rank and other qualities being agreeable to your estates. For
> although, to my great regret, the number of any princes of power and
> account professing our religion be but very small, and that therefore this

advice seems to be the more strait and difficult, yet ye have deeply to weigh and consider upon these doubts . . . disagreement in religion bringeth ever with it disagreement in manners . . . besides the peril of the evil education of your children. . . .

And lastly, remember to choose your wife as I advised you to choose your servants, that she be of a whole and clean race, not subject to the hereditary sicknesses, either of the soul or the body. For if a man will be careful to breed horses and dogs of good kinds, how much more careful should he be for the breed of his own loins? . . .

And for your behaviour to your wife, the scripture can best give you counsel therein. Treat her as your own flesh, command her as her lord, cherish her as your helper, rule her as your pupil and please her in all things reasonable; but teach her not to be curious in things that belong her not. Ye are the head, she is your body. It is your office to command and hers to obey, but yet with such a sweet harmony as she should be as ready to obey as ye to command, as willing to follow as ye to go before, your love being wholly knit unto her and all her affections lovingly bent to follow your will.[2]

Though Prince Henry offered his opinions to his father on the various matches, he admitted that it was the King, and not himself, who must make the final choice; besides, he wrote to James, "Your Majesty may think that my part to play, which is to be in love with any of them, is not yet at hand."[3]

Henry never had his part to play, however, for even while negotiations with France and Savoy were in train, in the autumn of 1612, he contracted typhoid fever and died.

The King was devastated by the loss of this promising youth, but royal mourning was not allowed to overcast, or postpone, the project of the moment, the wedding of his only daughter, Elizabeth, and Frederick, Elector Palatine.

James had sought this Protestant match for Elizabeth to balance the Catholic one planned for Henry. It was extremely popular in England and Scotland—but the Catholic Queen Anne was scathing on the subject, jeering at her daughter's accepting lower rank and calling her 'Goody Palsgrave'. ('Goody' was a contraction of 'Goodwife', the title given to the lowliest women of the kingdom who did not merit that of 'Mistress' even.) Stung to anger, Elizabeth retorted, "I would rather be the Palsgrave's wife than the greatest Papist queen in Christendom!"[4] In fact, when Queen Anne met her prospective son-in-law, who arrived in October 1612, she immediately took a liking to him, and there were no more complaints that her daughter was being 'disparaged' by the match.

There had been no royal wedding in England for nearly seventy years, and never, in all the centuries, in England or Scotland, one that was so magnificent—and expensive. The ceremony itself was staged (on St Valentine's Day 1613) in the chapel of Whitehall Palace, so that it was only the courtiers who saw Elizabeth in her white satin gown, her "crown of refined gold, made imperial by the pearls and diamonds thereupon placed, which were so thick beset that they stood like shining pinnacles upon her amber-coloured hair . . . hanging plaited down over her shoulders to her waist; between every plait a roll or list of gold spangles, pearls, rich stones and diamonds; and withal many diamonds of inestimable value embroidered upon her sleeves".[5]

The Court was also treated to feasts, sports in the Palace tiltyard and interminable classical masques performed by the young lawyers of the Inns of Court, but the citizens of London had their share in the entertainment too, with the fireworks displayed nightly along the Thames. A contemporary account of the spectacles has each description with its maker's name, so that we find, "William Bettis, his invention of such part of the fireworks as were performed by him at the royal celebration, which he contrived in such sort that, if the weather had been rainy or windy, yet his designments should have been accomplished."[6] The "designments" were made to illuminate a wooden castle: "thirteen great fires [seen] to fly to and fro round about the castle, whereby it seemed to be beleagured . . . a flight of great store of rockets" and "buttons" which flew out of the edifice at all angles, "with great cracks, blows and reports in great number"; then finally, rockets which flew up in the shapes of men and women, birds and animals, and one last volley of a hundred 'bangers'.[7] But not all these spectacles were so successful. After one 'battle' between mocked-up galleons on the Thames, the plan to stage another had to be abandoned, since "there were diverse hurt in the former fight, as one lost both his eyes, another both his hands; another one hand, with diverse others maimed and hurt".[8]

Elizabeth and Frederick's story may be quickly told. She found the Rhineland Palatinate far pleasanter than English rumours of German poverty and uncouthness had foretold, and her life might have been pleasant there, but Frederick was tempted to accept the crown of the newly created kingdom of Bohemia, was thereby drawn into war with the Emperor and in the end lost everything. He and Elizabeth went into exile in the Netherlands, and in 1632 he died there, leaving his widow with some dozen children to bring up alone. Then came the Civil War in England and Scotland, and it was not until 1661 that Elizabeth went home—she died a few months later.

With the death of Prince Henry and the departure of Elizabeth, the only one of the royal children left at home was Prince Charles, the new Prince of Wales, aged thirteen. He had little of the virtues, or the strength, of his elder brother.

Nevertheless, he had spirit. In 1623, when negotiations were in train for him to marry the Infanta Maria, daughter of Philip III of Spain, he insisted on going to take delivery of his bride in her own country. King James might have refused his son's request, but when it was joined with that of George Villiers, his current favourite, he could only give in to the two enthusiastic young men.

Spain was much impressed by the Prince's apparent ardour, and the poet Lope de Vega wrote a verse in his honour:

Carlos Stuardo soy,	Charles Stuart I am.
Que, siendo Amor mi guia,	Love has guided me far,
Al cielo d'España voy,	To the Heaven of Spain,
Per ver mi estrella Maria.	To Maria, my star.

An Englishman in Madrid wrote home that "The people here do mightily magnify the gallantry of the journey and cry out that the Prince deserved to have the Infanta thrown into his arms the first night he came."[9]

Philip III, however, had no intention of throwing Maria into her suitor's arms. At first Charles was not even allowed to meet her face to face, only to observe her driving with her family on the Prado. She sat in the 'boot' of the King's coach among other princesses, and a blue ribbon was tied round her arm so that he could recognize her. Maria was fair-haired, with a pink-and-white complexion, but she had the heavy-lidded eyes, thick lips and long chin of the Habsburgs.

Later the couple were allowed to meet, well chaperoned, and the English ambassador acted as their interpreter. But little progress was made, since Maria was tongue-tied with shyness. Charles nevertheless professed himself in love, and one of his attendants prophesied that if he did marry her in Spain, "she will be with child before she gets into England".[10] At one point the Spaniards feared that Charles would not even wait for the wedding, when he leaped the wall of the Infanta's garden and tried to accost her in an orchard—but her screams brought her attendants running, and she was quickly surrounded by ladies in huge farthingales.

Charles had been in Spain over a month when the papal dispensation came which would allow Maria to marry a 'heretic', but then the Pope died, and the girl's father insisted that he must obtain a similar document from the new Pope. It seemed obvious to Charles and Villiers that this was only an excuse to postpone the final arrangements, that the King had no intention of letting Charles have his daughter. So, with polite regrets and vague promises, the two young men set off for home.

Back in England that October, the Prince heard that the second dispensation had come and that a day had been fixed for the proxy wedding in Madrid. But then King James intervened. The enthusiasm with which the nation had welcomed Charles on his return from Spain, realizing that he had come without the Spanish bride, added to warnings of royal ministers, demonstrated how little men's hearts were in the match, how unpopular it, and the King, would be if it transpired. To show that he was not in Spain's pocket, James now demanded that Philip III put pressure on his cousin the Emperor to have Elector Frederick's German lands restored to him. On this the whole business floundered. (A few years later Maria married a future Emperor.)

As usual, France was the second prospect, and here there were no delays or real problems. King Louis XIII's youngest sister, Henrietta Maria, was promised freedom to practise her religion and even to have the care of her children until they were thirteen years old (which would give her a chance to make Catholics of them, even though they would have Anglican chaplains and staff). It would be too much to hope that there would be no further difficulties on the always tricky matter of negotiations: now, France demanded toleration for English Catholics, and James asked Louis for help for his son-in-law in regaining his lands. Then, in the midst of the business, James I died, on 27th March 1625.

The new King, Charles I, made short work of the outstanding problems, primarily by giving a secret agreement to his Catholic subjects' having freedom of worship (which he said he hoped to put into practice in more favourable times), and he had been on the throne less than two months when, on 11th May, Henrietta Maria became his wife in a proxy ceremony at Notre Dame in Paris.

Several queens consort had suffered stormy voyages on the way to England, but Henrietta Maria's ship was tossed for twenty-four hours in the Channel, and when she came ashore, on 12th June, she had to be carried up to Dover Castle and send a message to Charles not to come to her until she had recovered. He arrived on the morning of 13th June, while she was at breakfast. She went out to meet him, knelt at his feet and kissed his hand, but the King raised her up and kissed her several times on the lips. When she caught him staring at her, Henrietta Maria knew why: on his way to Spain, a couple of years earlier, he had visited her brother's Court and caught a glimpse of her; she had been much smaller then; now she lifted her skirts and showed him that she stood on her own feet, without benefit of high heels. Fortunately, she did not grow *too* tall, for her husband was himself only 5 feet 4 inches. Apart from her height, she was a plain, thin, sallow girl, but in the next years her figure improved, her skin cleared and she became graceful and elegant.

Noting that his bride was 'weepy' at their meeting, having parted so recently from her family, he allowed her French lady-in-waiting to ride with them in his coach, and that night, after their wedding at Canterbury, he did her another kindness, when that embarrassing scene 'the bedding' was approaching: elbowing his attendants side, he went alone into her bedchamber and barred the door against them.

Charles's kind concern for his bride was matched by her apparent willingness to accommodate herself to living among Protestants. When, at her first supper with the King, her confessor warned her that she must eat no meat, since it was a Fast Day, she ignored him and shared her husband's dish; when, some days later, one of her ladies asked how she could bear to be the wife of a 'heretic', the Queen replied quickly, "Why not? Was not my father one?"[11] (He was that Henri of Navarre who had been brought up a Protestant but had converted to Rome when he became King of France—"Paris is worth a Mass," he is said to have remarked.)

But these good beginnings soon ended. Charles began to be irritated by his wife's dependence on her French attendants, both the frivolous young women who giggled and chattered with her in her own language and her ever-watchful priests; for her part, Henrietta Maria had taken a strong dislike to George Villiers, Duke of Buckingham, who was always at Charles's side and whom she suspected of speaking badly of her. When the King demanded that her ladies return home, there was a dreadful scene, with Henrietta Maria becoming hysterical. Seeing some of her French people in the courtyard below, she beat on the windowpanes to attract their attention; the glass broke, and blood flowed down her gown. After that, she was not allowed to see any of them, and as soon as could be, they were packed off to France. That incident occurred in the summer of 1626, and it was to be two years before the Queen was rid of her own *bête noire*, Buckingham. She was not alone in hating him, however; there was scarce a man in Parliament (except those in his pay) who could find anything good to say of one who so blatantly ruled the King; but it was not his political enemies but a man with a private grudge who assassinated the Duke, in August 1628. Now the Court had the interesting experience of watching a king and queen fall in love with each other. Relations between them improved immensely after Buckingham's death, and though it had taken Henrietta Maria more than three years before she conceived her first child, now the royal nursery filled quickly.

Unfortunately Charles's relationship with his Parliaments did not improve in the same way, even without the irritant of Buckingham. But that is not a story to be told here—except where it impinges on the next royal wedding.

As the 1640s opened, royal policies and ministers came under ever more violent attacks in Parliament, and so did the King's supposed favour to the Catholics among his subjects—for which Henrietta Maria was blamed. (In fact, though the Queen had gained a good deal of influence over her husband, it was never so much as her enemies supposed.) Now, to show his good faith, Charles agreed to a Protestant match for his eldest daughter, the nine-year-old Mary, Princess Royal. He had once intended to make her Queen of Spain, but that was obviously impossible now, and he was forced to give her to Prince William of Orange, son of a mere Stadholder of Holland. (Formerly even William's proposed marriage to his second daughter, Elizabeth, was regarded as a great 'disparagement' of a princess.)

Mary was ill in bed when her bridegroom arrived, at the end of April 1641. For some days past the little girl had been sitting each day with her parents in a 'box' in Westminster Hall, watching the trial of King Charles's friend the Earl of Strafford. She had taken a bad cold there, and when William arrived, Charles had to apologize to him that her illness had "produced temporary depreciation, her face being much swollen and her complexion yellow. Therefore he feared His Highness would think van Dyck had flattered her in her portrait, but he could still repent and decline her if disappointed".[12] When he had taken a look at Mary, however, the fourteen-year-old Prince gallantly declared that she was even *more* beautiful than in her portrait. The boy acquitted himself well throughout the whole proceedings, and one of the Dutch commissioners reported to

William's father that, "He has pronounced his little speeches with the best grace and with so much courage and goodwill that he has acquired the love of everyone who heard him."[13]

Mary was scarcely recovered when, on 2nd May, she was put through the ordeal of her wedding. It was a real children's affair, for the Princess was led in by her brothers Charles and James, aged ten and eight respectively, and her six bridesmaids were no older than herself. William was wearing a suit of Utrecht velvet, embroidered with silver thread, and his bride wore white silk, also embroidered in silver, "her hair tied up with silver ribands, not dishevelled about her shoulders as in former times used, her head adorned with a garland of pendant pearls".[14]

After the wedding, which had taken place about midday, the royal family dined in public as usual, but there were no real festivities, simply a late-afternoon walk in Hyde Park and then a family supper.

Since Mary was still below the age of consent, it was only a *de futuro* marriage, but by putting the children to bed together that night, her family were making sure that it would be hard for William's family to repudiate if circumstances changed. Of course, it was no real 'bedding', merely a ritual of sitting them in a bed side by side for a matter of less than an hour, and it was all done with the least possible embarrassment to the couple themselves (Charles's Court was far more restrained than others in the past). Nevertheless, there was a good deal of mirth when William, leaving to return to his own room, could not find one of his slippers and discovered that it had somehow found its way round to Mary's side of the bed.

A week later the Earl of Strafford was beheaded, and the royal family was plunged in gloom. William went home soon after.

King Charles had stipulated that his daughter must remain with her family for some years, but by the beginning of 1642 he was so beset by political problems that his need of Dutch support was growing urgent. Thus, on 23rd February the Queen and Princess Mary set sail for Holland, ostensibly to reunite the young couple, in fact as an excuse for Henrietta Maria to broach the subject of aid for Charles and to raise some money on the Crown Jewels.

By the time the Queen returned to England, in February 1643, the nation was in the throes of civil war.

The Later Stuarts

Parliament won the Civil War. King Charles I was captured, imprisoned, tried and, on 30th January 1649, beheaded. The next year the Scots declared for his son, Charles II, and sent an army south to help him defeat the Parliamentary forces in England—only to suffer defeat at the hands of General Cromwell. And that was the end of the monarchy for the time being; the British Isles were to be a republic.

It was a noble ambition; in practice it failed dismally, and for some five years, 1653-8, the republic was under the 'protection' of a virtual dictator, Oliver Cromwell.

The new King (at least in name) had been in exile on the Continent since before his father's death; Queen Henrietta Maria had escaped to France in 1644, and over the years her sons James and Henry and her infant daughter Henrietta Anne were delivered to her by various means, while Princess Mary was still in Holland (her husband had died in 1650, leaving her with an only son, another William of Orange). So the royal family was safe, surrounded by a horde of impecunious Cavaliers, but there was little prospect of a turn in their fortunes.

Charles II found it impossible to interest his French cousins, or any other potentates of Europe, in projects to restore him, so for more than a decade, apart from his brief excursion into Scotland in 1650, England in 1651, he was doomed to enforced idleness. Nor could he find a wife with a fortune to support him or with a family to aid his Cause. His wealthy French cousin Anne Marie Louise, 'la Grande Mademoiselle', turned down his proposal, and so did the ambitious mother of Henrietta Catherine of Orange, who saw no advantage for her family, and many disadvantages, in encouraging the suit of a king without a kingdom.

It was different when Charles was called home in 1660, when the monarchy was restored. Mademoiselle had the pride and good taste not to accept him now, but the Princess of Orange hastened to offer him her daughter Marie (Henrietta Catherine was already married), with un-blushing compliments as to his changed circumstances. Needless to say,

Charles did not accept the proposal.

One of the first results of the restoration of the monarchy, in the personal context of the royal family, was Louis XIV's eagerness to match his brother Philippe and Charles's sister Henrietta Anne, where before, the Princess had been a 'poor relation' at Louis's Court without prospects. Not that her new position was any recompense for the misery of that marriage: Philippe, Duke of Orleans, gave his wife a couple of children, but he was homosexual and offered all his affections to his male lovers—though he did not allow his wife similar freedom to find comfort from a loveless marriage. When she died, in 1670, it was rumoured that he had had her poisoned.

Back in England, one of the King's first priorities was to find himself a wife, and one for his brother James, Duke of York, to ensure the royal succession. But suddenly the news broke that James was already married—or so his 'wife', Anne Hyde, said.

Anne was the daughter of Charles's chief minister during his exile, Edward Hyde, whom the King created Lord Chancellor on his return home. She had been living in Holland for some years, as maid-of-honour to the Princess Mary, and there, so she said, James had courted her and secretly married her, in November 1659. Unfortunately, there was no proof of the marriage—except that she was pregnant.

For a time, James denied that he had ever married Anne, and indeed some of his friends came forward to declare that any one of them could be the father of her child. Chancellor Hyde was appalled at his daughter's condition, but even more so at her apparent attempts to 'entrap' the King's brother, which would, he feared, jeopardize his own position of trust with the King. But Anne was a strong-willed girl, and on 3rd September 1660 she made James go through another secret wedding with her— though this time there were witnesses. But still he did not acknowledge her.

Then, on 22nd October, she gave birth to a son. All through her labour a bishop stood over her, begging her to tell the truth (i.e. deny the marriage), but even in the worst of her pains, Anne never swerved from her story. When she recovered, she was accepted as Duchess of York, and the men who had impugned her honour were only too anxious to beg the forgiveness of the King's sister-in-law.

(Or at least, that is one version of the story. Others have it that King Charles condoned the September 1660 wedding, lest the matter cause a scandal at the very outset of his reign.)

Princess Mary was furious at the presumption of her former maid-of-honour, and Queen Henrietta Maria, who arrived in England that autumn, was not easily brought to accept her daughter-in-law. But Anne proved more than adequate to her new role; the French ambassador reported home that "she upholds with as much courage, cleverness and energy the dignity to which she has been called as if she were of the blood of kings. . .".[1]

Nevertheless, the story has no fairy-tale ending. James was consistently unfaithful to Anne, and all but two of her babies died, but at least she had the satisfaction of converting her husband to Catholicism, which his mother had been trying to do for years without success.

The bride selected for Charles II was the sister of the King of Portugal, the twenty-four-year-old Catherine of Braganza. 'England's oldest ally' was a wealthy nation, mainly from the profits of trade in the Near and Far East, and Charles's subjects were to benefit as well as himself from Catherine's dowry, the ports of Bombay and Tangier.

She disembarked at Portsmouth on 14th May 1662, but it was nearly a week before Charles could leave his Parliament to go and take a look at her. His first impression, an attending gentleman recorded, was that "they had brought him a bat instead of a woman",[2] probably because Catherine was still dressed in the Portuguese style, in a dark, wide-panniered farthingale. Later he overcame his first shock and wrote to Chancellor Hyde that

> . . . her face is not so exact as to be called a beauty, though her eyes are excellent good, and not anything in her face that in the least degree can shame one; on the contrary, she hath as much agreeableness in her looks as ever I saw, and if I have any skill in physiognomy, which I think I have, she must be as good a woman as ever was born. Her conversation, as much as I can perceive, is very good, for she has wit enough and a most agreeable voice. You will wonder to see how well we are acquainted already; in a word, I think myself very happy, for I am confident our two humours will agree very well together.[3]

They were married at Portsmouth, on 21st May, in a very quiet ceremony. The bride wore a rose-coloured dress, with knots of blue ribbon all over it which were later detached and distributed as 'favours'— there was such a scramble for them, and they were cut in so many pieces to share out, that there was nothing left for Catherine herself to keep as a souvenir.

The Court did not know that the couple had gone through another wedding ceremony, performed by a Catholic priest in Catherine's bed-chamber, with only a few of her Portuguese attendants as witnesses. Nevertheless, it was probably not to prevent the secret from leaking out that Charles sent his wife's Portuguese ladies home soon afterwards, rather that they were proving to be even more of a nuisance than foreign retinues usually were: they looked on the free-and-easy ways of the English with contempt, shuddered at the English ladies' 'immodest' dress, were horrified to see men, even noblemen, relieving themselves in public, against the palace walls, and refused point-blank to sleep in any bed which a man had ever used.

Though Charles never really loved his queen, he became very fond of her and was always as kind to her as was in his nature. But he had become a confirmed polygamist over past years, and he made no attempt to reform. Catherine was horrified to find that she must accept his mistress of the moment, Barbara Villiers, as her lady-in-waiting, but her attempt to refuse fell on deaf ears. Over the years she found a way of being polite to her husband's women and at the same time keeping her dignity, but it was infinitely galling to see them presenting the King with numerous bastards while she remained childless.

It was several times rumoured that Charles would divorce Catherine, to remarry and sire an heir, but when the project was proposed to him, he adamantly refused. His brother James would succeed him, he declared, and nothing anyone said against the Duke could ever sway him.

When Duchess Anne died in 1671, and her last remaining son soon afterwards, James was left with only two daughters and so decided to marry again. There was no dearth of candidates. First, there was the Archduchess Claudia Felicitas of Austria, heiress of Innsbruck, extremely beautiful, with black hair and eyes and a transparent complexion. Unfortunately, before this prize could be snapped up, she was promised to the Emperor Leopold. The Earl of Peterborough, who had gone to sue for the Archduchess, had several more ladies on his list: the widowed Duchess of Guise, the heiress of the Duke of Retz, two daughters of the Duke of Elbœuf, a sister of the Emperor, Marianna of Württemberg, Eleanora of Neuberg, an infanta of Spain and two princesses of Modena. For various reasons Peterborough came down in favour of the Italians.

When he arrived in Modena, it was with the intention on surveying the Princess Leonora, for he had heard that her niece Maria Beatrice was intended for the convent. But he was so impressed by the younger princess's beauty that he opened negotiations for her hand at once. The family was delighted, but the girl herself begged to be excused, since she had a real desire to take the veil, and when her mother insisted that she marry James, she cried and screamed for two days, so hysterical that she had to be held down on her bed by force. Perhaps it was exhaustion that made her yield, perhaps it was the letter she received from the Pope requesting her to marry the Duke of York as a sacred duty, for on Saturday 30th September Maria Beatrice repeated her marriage vows at a proxy wedding.

The citizens of Modena, in contrast to the bride, were overjoyed by the event. There was dancing in the streets and the next day a procession to the cathedral for a *Te Deum*; that night the Court feasted and danced.

On Maria Beatrice's fifteenth birthday, 5th October, she left her home and, with her mother, began the long journey to England (a country she had apparently never heard of before Peterborough's arrival). But the news of the wedding travelled before her, and some two weeks later, James was informed that he was already a married man—he sent a note to his daughter Mary that he had provided a "playfellow" for her. She was only four years younger than her stepmother, James twenty-five years older.

When Maria Beatrice landed by boat from her sailing-ship on Dover

Beach, on 21st November, James was there to meet her, and that very night he wedded and 'bedded' her.

Everyone noticed that the bride was still tearful, and at the beginning of January 1674 she was writing home to the Mother Superior of a Modena convent: "I am very well, my dear Mother, God be thanked, but I cannot yet accustom myself to this state of life, from which, as you know, I have always been averse. So I cry much and grieve and am unable to banish melancholy. But this, God be praised, is my cross."[4] As 1674 passed, however, Mary (as the English called her) found new happiness and fell passionately in love with her husband. She gave birth to several children over the next few years, but not one of them managed to live through infancy; like Queen Catherine, Mary had to remain silent while her husband's mistresses gave him healthy sons and daughters.

The Duke's Catholic marriage had caused an outcry in England and Scotland—his wife was reviled as 'the Pope's eldest daughter'. By the end of the decade there were anti-Catholic riots, and Parliament was pressing the King to have his brother excluded from the royal succession. To counter-attack criticism, Charles II had determined that James's elder daughter by Anne Hyde, the Princess Mary of York, must make a Protestant match, and his choice for her was her cousin William III of Orange (the son of the late Princess Mary, the King's sister). James himself would have preferred to see his daughter married in Spain, and he actually wrote a letter of apology to the Pope for allowing her to wed a 'heretic', but he had to agree that Charles was wise in attempting to cool his subjects' tempers.

When Mary was told of her father and uncle's decision, on 21st October 1677, she behaved as her stepmother had four years before: she burst into tears and was not seen dry-eyed for days after. Nevertheless, there she was, just a fortnight later, before a temporary altar in her bedroom, giving her hand and her vows to her cousin William. She wept quietly throughout the ceremony, her stepmother behind her crying in sympathy.

The King tried to raise everyone's spirits by making little jokes, urging the Bishop of London to make haste with the rite, lest the pregnant Duchess of York go into labour and produce a son, who would displace Mary in the royal succession and so disappoint William of his expectations of the crown—her son was born three days later, and William stood godfather to him, but he died in his second month. Then, when William endowed his bride with "all his worldly goods", and put down a handful of gold in token, the King "bid her put all up in her pocket, for 'twas clear gains".[5] Finally, as Charles shut the bed-curtains on the two young people, he cried, "Now, nephew, to your work! Hey! St George for England!"[6]

It would have taken more than her uncle's teasing to make Mary smile that night, more to break William's solemnity any day. The alliance he valued, and the prospect of inheriting the two kingdoms through his wife, but he gave little personal consideration to Mary herself. In the days that followed, one observer wrote, ". . . the Court began to whisper the Prince's sullenness or clownishness, that he took no notice of the Princess at the play and ball, nor came to see her at St James's."[7]

Mary was still crying on the morning of 19th November when the royal family accompanied her and William by barge from Whitehall to Greenwich, to put them on their way to the coast: "The Queen, observing Her Highness to weep as she took leave of Her Majesty, would have comforted her with the consideration of her own condition when she came into England and had never till then seen the King; to whom Her Highness presently said, 'But, madam, you came into England, but I am going out of England!' "[8]

However, her sadness and loneliness soon turned to surprise that she could so enjoy herself in her new home. Holland delighted her from the first, and housekeeping enchanted her. She embroidered, grew exotic plants, visited her poultry-houses and her model dairy, went often to church, chatted interminably with likemindedly houseproud ladies and won and lost large sums at cards—despite the fact that she was heiress to two kingdoms, no one thought to give her a political education, and it was tacitly assumed that she would leave statecraft to her husband when the time came. Another factor in her happiness was that Mary came to love her husband, and though she was made miserable by her failure to give him children, after a couple of miscarriages, and by his taking one of her ladies, Betty Villiers, as his mistress, she found a way of living comfortably with William that was enough for both of them. He was a coldblooded man, at his best in the company of other men, and the only interests the couple shared were their gardens and an eager desire to reign across the sea.

The Princess's sister Anne, three years her junior, was not to be married for love either (though, like Mary, she found it in her marriage). In fact, she always preferred women to men, albeit she was no real lesbian; where Mary had grown out of her adolescent 'crushes' on other girls, however, Anne did not, and one of her friends, Sarah Churchill, was for years the 'power behind the throne' when Anne came to reign.

She had several suitors in her teens, including her cousin George of Hanover and King Charles XI of Sweden, and at one time the poet Lord Mulgrave kept sending her love-letters—the King had him posted to Tangier. Charles II's own choice for his niece was George of Denmark, brother of King Christian V, who made a formal proposal for the Princess in May 1683.

George had visited England in 1670 (when Anne was only five years old, he in his late teens), and he had made a good impression on the Court. Also, he had the distinction of having saved his brother's life, during a recent war with the Swedes. Add to this the fact that he was a Protestant, free from duties at home and thus able to spend the rest of his life (and his considerable fortune) in his wife's country, and it is easy to see why his arrival was hailed with enthusiasm. What Anne thought of her bridegroom is not recorded, but where, as time passed, the Court began to think less of George (who was good-tempered and honest but slow-witted and indolent), she (who was no intellectual herself) settled into a comfortable, placid, affectionate relationship with him. Year after year she suffered miscarriages or gave birth to stillborn babies or to puny ones who soon died; only one of them survived infancy—and he died at the age of eleven in 1700.

Still, while there was hope of Mary and Anne having children, to continue the Protestant dynasty, and while their stepmother did not produce a Catholic son to displace them in the succession, all seemed well. James succeeded his brother Charles in 1685, with apparent good will towards his non-Catholic subjects, and he might have overcome the problems of the next three years if his queen had not produced that dreaded son in June 1688. Now, the fear that Prince James Francis Edward would succeed his father, a Catholic following a Catholic and founding a whole new dynasty of Catholic monarchs, combined with James II's recent political misdeeds, drove the nation to fury and encouraged a few brave spirits to propose to William of Orange that he come over and thwart his father-in-law's evil designs. The affair might have developed into civil war, but, when William landed at Torbay on 5th November 1688, he was greeted as the nation's saviour, while James managed, without too much difficulty (no one wanted another royal martyr), to slip away to France, to join his wife and their baby.

When Parliament offered the crown to William and Mary (jointly), it did so on terms intended to limit the powers of the monarchy (which they accepted) and in the belief that either they or Anne and George would provide heirs to succeed them. When, after Mary's death and that of Anne's son, everyone realized that the Stuart dynasty would soon be extinct in the Protestant line, an Act of Settlement was passed (in 1701) which decreed that, after William's death, and Anne's, their cousins of the House of Hanover (descended from James VI and I's daughter Elizabeth) should come to the throne. In making this settlement, Parliament had passed over several Catholic descendants of James VI and I, including James II's son, declaring that future monarchs must be members of the Church of England and that any member of the royal family who married a Catholic would be automatically barred from the royal succession.

Today it is hard to understand the prejudice against and fear of Catholics that prevailed in England and Scotland at that time—only in Northern Ireland do they still have that potency. But the anti-Catholic Act of Settlement has never been repealed.

The Eighteenth Century

"Marriages Performed Within"

In the eighteenth century, a young man and woman met, were attracted to each other, preferred each other to anyone else and married, just as they do today; the main difference between then and now is that the class system was far more rigid, that money married money, and title title, as a matter of course, and young people had a fine appreciation of what was 'due' to their rank or fortune when they sought a marriage-partner. There were still marriages arranged by parents, but, except in royal families, a young couple were almost invariably given the chance to get to know each other before their wedding, and their right to refuse was widely recognized. In the diaries and letters of the century, there are references to parents forbidding unsuitable matches, to the occasional marriage forced on a young woman by a stern parent, and to sons disinherited for marrying women of whom their families did not approve, but they are recorded as interesting—sometimes shocking—freaks, certainly not as the norm.

The fact that marriages made blatantly for money were so frequently satirized illustrates that they were now generally condemned and becoming unusual. Hogarth's series of pictures *Marriage à la Mode* made a pointed attack on matches that owed more to lawyers' contracts than to a couple's mutual attraction, and Sheridan did the same, with gentler humour, in his play *The Duenna*, in which he has a father tell his son,

> I must confess I had a great affection for your mother's ducats, but that was all, boy. I married her for her fortune, and she took me in obedience to her father, and a very happy couple we were. We never expected any love from one another, and so we were never disappointed. If we grumbled a little now and then, it was soon over, for we were never fond enough to quarrel; and when the good woman died, why, I had as lief she had lived.

And how serious was that famous womanizer Robert Burns when he wrote

Awa' wi your witchcraft o' beauty's alarms!
The slender bit beauty you grasp in your arms!
O gie me the lass that has acres of charms,
O gie me the lass wi' the weel stockit farms!
Then hey for the lass wi' a tocher! . . .
The nice golden guineas for me!

Since most men were now weighing the 'charms' and personalities of prospective wives as well as their financial prospects and status, women's looks and fine manners became a matter of infinite concern to them, and middle- and upper-class female education was directed almost entirely towards their acquisition of showy 'accomplishments' designed to attract the men: girls were taught to play tunes on the pianoforte, to sing prettily and to dance gracefully—and very little else. Even the arts of household management were neglected now, and solid learning was shunned lest it make a girl 'strong-minded' and self-opinionated. "Imbecility in females is a great enhancement of their personal charms," wrote Jane Austen at the end of the century, and most men would agree with her, though Lord Byron, famed as a lover as well as a poet, preferred spirit in a woman to the usual simpering docility:

'Tis true, your budding miss is very charming,
But shy and awkward at first coming out,
So much alarmed that she is quite alarming,
All giggles, blush, half pertness and half pout;
And glancing at Mamma, for fear there's harm in
What you, she, it or they may be about.
The nursery still lisps out in all they utter—
Besides, they always smell of bread and butter.

One new development in matchmaking in the eighteenth century was the proliferation of advertisements for husbands and wives which appeared in the nation's periodicals. Advertisers would describe themselves and then the partner they were seeking; women would name their dowries, and men would put down the jointure they could offer. Men were in the majority of the advertisers, and it may be that women preferred to go to the marriage-bureaux which were springing up in mid-century—'Matrimonial Societies' they were called. Candidates were asked to give a thorough description of themselves—and their finances, and then, rather than listing what they required in a spouse, they would receive a list of members of the Society of the opposite sex, and their income-bracket, with additions as new enquirers came on the Society's list. The choice made, the office would supervise a correspondence between the couple, either of whom could demand a portrait of the other and appoint a representative to investigate claims as to income, character etc. In this way, the agencies insisted, ladies could have the privilege, usually denied them, of making the overture.

This was a point in favour of the advertisements and bureaux, for Britain was rapidly becoming a nation of 'old maids'. In fact, it has been estimated that, where only ten per cent of women were unmarried at fifty in the sixteenth century, the figure was twenty-five per cent in the eighteenth.

Still, most women *expected* to marry, and the 'magic' prediction of future husbands was a widespread practice. There were many means favoured (some still employed—only half jokingly—today), but some of them were thought to give results only if used on St John's Eve, 29th June. For example, a girl must go out after dark to find a stone under a plantain root and put it under her pillow that night, then she would dream of her future husband; the novelist Daniel Defoe was scathing on the number of girls he saw one St John's Eve crawling through the undergrowth—like 'weeders', he said—in search of their stones. Or they might have been looking for a snail, to put on a pewter plate and to trace in its slimy trail the initial of a future bridegroom. More difficult was the making of a cake to put under the pillow—again for dreams: two girls must make the cake, two bake it and two break it in pieces; then a disinterested party must place the fragments under the pillows of all six girls—*but* the whole business must be done in utter silence, not a word to be spoken, or the spell would not work. With six girls together in a kitchen, in a state of excitement and giggling hilarity, such a feat would be a real test of their earnestness.

One rather spine-chilling way of foretelling who a girl would marry was for her to sit alone in her bedchamber by candlelight on Hallowe'en, eating an apple and all the while staring into her mirror; then, it was said, she would see the reflection of her future husband's face, looking over her shoulder.

Some of the old customs, such as scrambling for the bride's ribbons and garters, were disdained now in 'polite society', and 'bedding' was an indelicacy left for the coarsest lower classes—such as the people depicted in Edward Chicken's verses *The Collier's Wedding*, of 1764. Here we find Tommy the collier meeting a lass named Jenny at a country wake; they marry after a brief courtship. After their wedding, the couple are not even allowed to leave the church before their friends' horseplay begins:

Whole troops of colliers swarm around
And seize poor Jenny on the ground,
Put up their hands to loose her garters
And work for pluck about her quarters;
Till ribbons from her legs are torn
And round the church in triumph borne.

Back at their cottage, a cook is preparing a meal—but not fast enough for the hungry guests, who

Play with the plates, drum on the table
And fast as long as they are able,
Then count the number of the knives
And who is there that has not wives;
Some eat the bread, some lick the salt,

Some drink and others find some fault.
Disorder is in every place,
And hungry looks on every face.
In short, they could no longer put
For belly thinks that throat is cut.
They damn and sink and curse the cook
And give her many a frightful look;
They call her bitch and jade and sow—
She says she does what fire can do.

It is a one-roomed cottage, so after the meal, for modesty's sake, the women turn the men outdoors while they undress the bride. The excitement has been too much for Jenny, and she begins to cry, but the old married women tell her,

Come wipe your face, for shame, don't cry!
We all were made with men to lie,
And Tommy, if I guess but right,
Will make you have a merry night.
Be courteous, kind, lie in his arms
And let him rifle all your charms.
If he should rise, do you lie still,
He'll fall again, give him his will.
Lie close and keep your husband warm,
And, as I live, you'll get no harm. [1]

Then the men come back, and with broad jokes and a good deal of noise, Tommy is put in bed with Jenny. The stockings are thrown—and they are left alone.

Such a public wedding was by then shocking to genteel sensibilities and at the end of the century Fanny Burney, the novelist and diarist, wrote:

We have just had a wedding—a public wedding, and very fine it was, I assure you. The bride is Miss Case, daughter of an alderman of Lynn, with a great fortune; the bridegroom Mr Bagg. . . . The walk that leads up to the church was crowded—almost incredibly a prodigious mob indeed—I'm sure I trembled for the bride—oh, what a gauntlet for any woman of delicacy to run! . . . When they had been in the church a quarter of an hour, the bell began to ring merrily, so loud, and the doors opened—we saw them walk down the aisle, the bride and bridegroom first—hand in hand. . . . Well, of all things in the world, I don't suppose anything can be so dreadful as a public wedding—my stars! I should never be able to support it! [2]

Few persons with any pretensions to gentility would then agree to having the banns called, giving their neighbours the news of their intensions and the opportunity to throng church and churchyard, exposing the couple to curiosity and comment. They preferred to obtain a licence, without publicity, and so to be able to go to church in a small, family group.

However, it was not 'delicacy' that prompted some people to go to the even further lengths of marrying in the anonymity of the private chapels of Mayfair and the 'Fleet' wedding-houses of East London. There it was possible to marry without banns or licence, without the parental consent needed by minors, and even with bride (or occasionally groom) too frightened or insensible through drink or drugs to know what was happening. It had begun with a loophole in Church law, with some chapels not under the jurisdiction of a bishop—that accounted for the fashionable St James's, Duke's Place, for example. More notorious were the wedding-houses in the Fleet area of London, staffed by 'rogue' clergy who cared not who they married or when as long as their fee was paid. Back in the seventeenth century, parsons imprisoned for debt in the Fleet prison had earned a few shillings by marrying the inmates to each other; then they married 'visitors' to the prison, and gradually they began to set up business outside the prison's gates, returning for roll-call in the evening. A whole marriage industry developed then, with avaricious, unemployed clergymen (and some frauds) setting up on their own account, though some were salaried by inn-keepers who collected the fees and provided dinner and a bed for the newly-weds. The clergy were liable to a stiff fine if they were caught, but only a few were prosecuted—not enough to deter them, as one Georgian Londoner recalled in later years:

> In walking along the street, in my youth, on the side next this prison, I have often been tempted by the question, "Sir, will you be pleased to walk in and be married?" Along this most lawless space was hung up a frequent sign of a male and female hand conjoined, with 'Marriages Performed Within' written beneath. A dirty fellow invited you in. The parson was seen walking before his shop, a squalid, profligate figure, clad in a tattered plain night-gown with a fiery face and ready to couple you for a dram of gin or a roll of tobacco.[3]

None of them cared if their clients had been married before, or if one of the parties was unwilling, or under age, or even insane, and many an heiress lost her fortune to an adventurer by a 'marriage by abduction', while it was even known for men to be dragged in dead-drunk, to wake up and find themselves married. All classes used the Fleet clergy (and their brethren in the more salubrious Mayfair chapels 'up West')—from thieves and prostitutes to dukes.

By mid-century the situation had become so shocking that a Bill for regulating marriages was introduced in Parliament to end it once and for all. Lord Hardwicke proposed that only Anglican church weddings should be legally binding (with special provision for Jews and Quakers, but for no other Nonconformists), with obligatory calling of banns on three consecutive Sundays in a parish church or public chapel, or purchase of a licence; that all weddings must be recorded in the church register; that they must take place by daylight, with the church door open so that anyone might enter, to watch or to object; that no one under twenty-one might marry without the consent of parent or guardian—if anyone lied about his/her age, the marriage would be null; and that clergy found evading the law should be liable to fourteen years' transportation to a penal colony.

Somewhat surprisingly, there was a good deal of opposition to the Hardwicke Bill, even from 'respectable' persons who would not have dreamed of contracting an irregular marriage. Minors would be totally subjected to the power of parents or guardians, it was said, notably where there was a financial interest to keep them single as long as possible; one objector said there would be more loveless marriages than of recent years and that English society would become as adulterous as that on the Continent, where husbands and wives notoriously sought love outside marriage; a philanthropist suggested that the poor would be the hardest hit, for marriage would be too expensive for them (even without the cost of a licence, the parson and the clerk would still expect their fee), and thus there would be more 'living in sin', more bastards, even more infanticide of unwanted babies.

Despite the opposition, the Bill was passed in 1753, to come into effect in March 1754. But it applied only to England and Wales; Scotland, the Isle of Man and the Channel Islands had their own legal systems. Thus anyone bent on evading the law had only to cross the sea or border to marry by any of the old forms. The Isle of Man rejected such a ploy by passing its own, similar Act in 1757, and the frequent hold-ups of boats to the Channel Islands in bad weather deterred all but a few eloping couples, so Scotland became their haven. Thus began the legend of Gretna Green—a legend in that there never was a blacksmith to marry runaways over his forge, but true in that, since Gretna Green is only some 9 miles from the border, it really was the goal for many young couples.

The story of the Earl of Westmorland and the banker's daughter Sarah Child is typical of the history of elopements in which the father gave chase. Child had refused to allow Sarah to marry the impoverished Earl, since he was so obviously after her money, but she either loved Westmorland or hankered to be a countess, for one night she drugged her governess into sleep and joined him in a coach in which they were to make for Scotland. Child overtook them at Hesketh-in-the-Forest and shot the lead-horse of Westmorland's team, but the postillion cut the dead horse's traces, and the couple drove on and made the border. The banker never forgave Sarah, and he cut her out of his Will, but he did leave money to her daughter, on condition that she take the name 'Sarah Child'. Fortunately he did not live to see his grand-daughter follow her mother's path to Gretna Green, to become the wife of the Earl of Jersey.

If it was still comparatively easy to marry, divorce was still extremely difficult to obtain, by those private Acts of Parliament instituted in the previous century: there were sixty divorces between 1715 and 1775, seventy-four between 1775 and 1800. Of these, the vast majority were at the husband's instigation, for it was far more difficult for a woman to win a case based on her husband's adultery, with male infidelity so prevalent and so lightly regarded. The double standard also prevailed, at least in the first quarter of the century, when the desperate resorted to murder to rid themselves of a spouse: a man was hanged, as for any other murder, but a

Leaving home after the wedding: the embarkation of James VI and I's daughter Elizabeth and her husband, Frederick, Elector Palatine, by Adam Willaerts. The couple took ship from Margate on 25th April 1613 on their way to Frederick's German domains.

Charles I's daughter Mary and her bridegroom, Prince William of Orange —a painting from the studio of van Dyck.

The future King James II with his first wife, Anne Hyde, whom he had married secretly abroad.

The wedding of James 'III' ('The Old Pretender') and Princess Maria Clementina Sobieska at Montefiascone in Italy on 3rd September 1719.

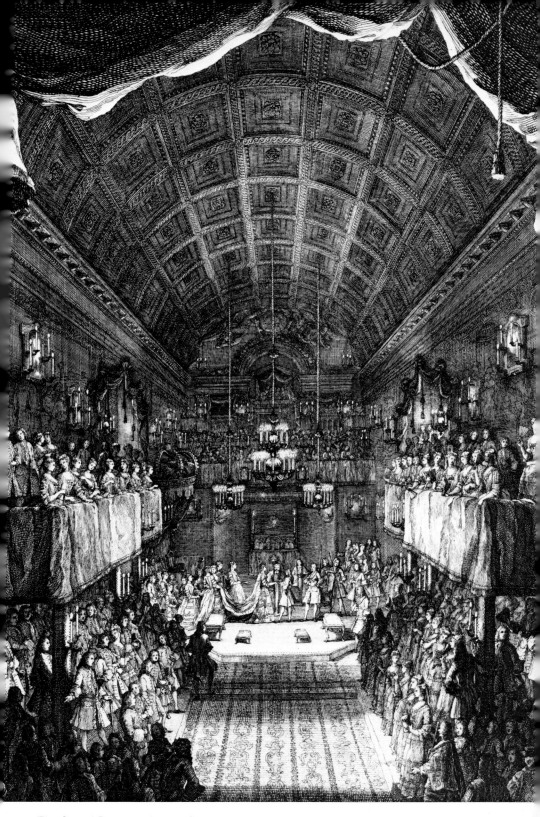

The Chapel Royal, St James's Palace, was the scene for the wedding of George II's daughter
Anne, Princess Royal, and William IV of Orange on 25th March 1734.

'Wife and No Wife': a contemporary cartoon on the wedding of the future King George IV and Mrs Fitzherbert. The politician Charles James Fox, asleep left, was not present at the wedding and in fact denied in Parliament that it had ever taken place.

The wedding of the future King George IV and Caroline of Brunswick on 8th April 1795.

Princess Charlotte's wedding-dress: white satin covered with silver lace.

'The Homburg Waltz': a cartoon of the royal family celebrating the wedding of Princess Elizabeth and the Landgrave of Hesse-Homburg in April 1818.

A scene from Hogarth's satire *The Rake's Progress*: the Rake is marrying a rich old woman (a typical 'Smithfield wedding').

'The Penny Wedding' by David Wilkie, 1818. Guests contributed a penny each to the cost of the food and drink.

'The Wedding Morning', by John H. Bacon, 1892.

'The Toast of the Bride', by Stanhope A. Forbes, 1889.

The wedding of Queen Victoria and Prince Albert at the Chapel Royal on 10th February 1840.

woman was burned at the stake, since her killing of her 'lord' was regarded as 'petty treason', scarcely less heinous than treason against her king; the last woman burned was Catherine Hayes, at Tyburn, in 1726. Nor, though one reads of cases of wife-selling (as in Thomas Hardy's novel *The Mayor of Casterbridge*), does one ever hear of a woman selling her husband.

While law and convention subjected a woman to her husband's will, while a man automatically took possession of his wife's money, while a husband could obtain divorce for adultery far more easily than could a wronged wife, and while almost the whole of society accepted this state of affairs, there were some women who were beginning to rebel, to point out the injustice of the system, such as Mary Wollstonecraft with her remarkable (and remarkably courageous) *Vindication of the Rights of Women*, of 1792. But the future 'battle of the sexes' meant nothing to the majority. As the century opened, two great women novelists, Fanny Burney and Jane Austen, were providing far more popular reading-matter for women (and for many men), with heroines ranging from the 'bread-and-butter miss' to the despised 'old maid'—but all with one thing in common: the great object of their lives is to marry the men they love.

The Early Hanoverians—and the Last of the Stuarts

George I, King of Great Britain and Ireland—as the nation had been called since the Act of Union in 1707—came from Hanover to take possession of his inheritance in September 1714, a month after the death of his cousin Queen Anne. With him came his only son, another George, now entitled Prince of Wales, and a month later his daughter-in-law, Caroline of Anspach, arrived with her small daughters—her son, Frederick Lewis, having been left at home, for a German education.

Children, parents and grandfather—a charming picture, or so George I's subjects may have thought at first glance. It was only later that other opinions began to permeate the kingdom, based on stories that cast a very different light on the family.

Why was there no queen? someone might ask. There was, but she would never come to Britain. Sophia Dorothea of Celle, who had married George in 1682, had been in prison for twenty years, having been caught out in adultery and condemned to live out the rest of her life in seclusion; she died in 1726. Nor was the King a kindly, loving father, and his subjects watched his relations with his son deteriorate rapidly after their arrival in Britain, when he saw how popular the Prince and his clever wife were making themselves while he, the King, was slighted or ignored.

However, it was not the private personality of George I which drove some of his subjects into rebellion in 1715, merely the 'fact' of the King, of his taking the throne that 'by rights' belonged to James II's son, now in his mid-twenties and calling himself 'James III'. But the rising was an ill-managed affair, and though James put in an appearance, when he saw the strength of the opposition and the rapid disintegration of his own forces he speedily returned to safety on the Continent, leaving disappointed 'Jacobites' to their doom of prison or the block.

But Stuarts had been in exile before, and James could feasibly liken his own plight to that of his uncle Charles II who, after years of apparently hopeless exile, had been welcomed home. It might not come in his own lifetime, but perhaps in that of his son . . . and so James determined to marry.

It was Charles Wogan, a Jacobite officer in exile, who discovered the Sobieska princesses, grand-daughters of a former King of Poland, and interested James in them. Besides the fact that their father was very rich, they had the advantage of being cousins, though their mother, of the Emperor Charles VI, and the youngest of them, the sixteen-year-old Maria Clementina, was the god-daughter of the Pope. Clementina was a charming girl, Wogan reported, petite and lively, with light brown hair and black eyes, and she was perfectly amenable to marrying a man she had never seen and to becoming queen of a realm she was not certain ever to visit.

Although Prince Sobieski gave his consent to the match, however, it soon appeared that the Emperor would never countenance it: when George I heard of James's plans, he immediately put pressure on Charles VI to forbid it; it was even said that George offered to increase Clementina's already considerable dowry by £10,000 if she would marry anyone but James. However, Sobieski was not to be threatened or bribed, and in the summer of 1718 he offered to send Clementina to James in Italy.

But Italy was hundreds of miles from the Sobieskis' home, near Prague, across a vast stretch of imperial territory, and the Emperor was not fooled by the family's pretence of sending the girl and her mother off on a pilgrimage to the Italian shrine of Loreto. When the two princesses reached Innsbruck, they were arrested and held in custody there. Pope Clement demanded his god-daughter's immediate release, and her mother's sister, the Dowager Empress, begged her son to let them go free, but to no avail.

Then Charles Wogan, who had initiated the match, suggested to James a plan for rescuing his bride, a plan which James whole-heartedly endorsed . . .

Innsbruck was still lying under snow that April of 1719 when a small party of foreign travellers entered it and settled at an inn, and the night of 27th April was moonless and bitter cold when two of them, a man and a girl, passed silently through the streets and slipped into the Schloss Ambras where Clementina and her mother were being held. The princesses had found a means of corresponding with the outside world, and of receiving letters secretly, so they were on the alert. Clementina was ready, dressed in several layers of warm clothes, and she had taken the precaution of writing a note addressed to her mother, telling her of the escape, so that the elder Princess would not be suspected of conniving at it, for she was to be left behind, to delay their captors' knowledge of the escape. The plan was for a young French maid, Jeanneton, the girl who had come to the Schloss with Wogan, to stay with the Princess Sobieska and to substitute for Clementina, lying in her bed as if she was ill.

It was one in the morning when Clementina safely gained the inn where the other members of the company were waiting; by two they were on the road, and as the last hours of the night passed, they put more and more miles between themselves and Innsbruck. Then came the first delay, when the Princess suddenly realized that her jewels were missing, valuable family jewels and those James had sent her, which were Stuart heirlooms. One of Wogan's friends, Lucas O'Toole, was sent back to search for them at the inn, and miraculously there they were, still lying behind a door, where they had been dropped in the haste of departure. He rejoined the party without mishap, but before long he was off again, this time with one John Misset for company, to see how the land lay ahead.

It was as well that they took this precaution, for the alarm had already been raised in Innsbruck. (It was the Princess Sobieska's fault, for not following instructions; instead of putting Jeanneton in her daughter's bed, she had locked her in a cupboard out of harm's way.) Now imperial agents were being despatched to cover all the roads into Italy, to try to overtake the party. So it was that, when O'Toole and Misset were resting in an Alpine inn, they were joined by one of the couriers. Fortunately he took them for foreign merchants and accepted a glass of wine from them—then another, and another, and when he was quite drunk and had passed out, it was an easy matter for them to destroy his despatches. Then they put him to bed, poured brandy down his throat and left; when he came round, twenty-four hours later, it was too late to give chase—even if he could with such a hang-over.

The Princess's companions had their problems too. On the way down from the Brenner Pass, the coach hit a tree-stump and veered over the edge of the road, with a precipice below it; twice, later on, axles broke; but by the afternoon of 29th April the last imperial garrison was behind them, and a couple of days later they reached Bologna and safety. There, on 9th May, Clementina went through a proxy wedding, and on 15th May she entered Rome.

James, meanwhile, had been in Spain, for not even the arrival of his bride could outweigh the importance of an offer of military aid from the Spanish king, and it was not until 2nd September that he met Clementina, at the little town of Montefiascone, near Viterbo. The next day they were married at the cathedral there.

By then, Princess Sobieska had been released, and she and her husband had been sent by the Emperor into 'exile' at Passau; Jeanneton too had been allowed to go free, and in the end she found her way back to the Jacobites, to take service with Mrs Misset again. There were knighthoods for three of the rescue-party, a baronetcy for Wogan—but fine titles buy no bread, and James was far too poor (royally speaking) to offer any more practical reward.

For a while, the royal marriage seemed a success. Clementina gave James a son, Charles Edward, in December 1720, and then another, Henry Benedict, in 1725, but soon she found that life with a 'pretending' king had nothing to offer her. James was still only thirty-two years old when he married, but already he had the silent patience of an old man, the melancholy of one who knows he has had his one chance and failed, and he was totally incapable of understanding Clementina's high spirits and of coping with her impatience and quick temper. After the birth of her second son, she departed for a convent, and when she did return, a few years later, she was changed: once she had enjoyed 'society' more than he; now she was even more pious than her husband and spent all her time in prayer and philanthropy; like him, she had accepted defeat. She died in 1735.

Ten years later, James made another attempt to gain his throne, this time sending his son Charles Edward to represent him, but though 'Bonnie Prince Charlie's' exploits made him the subject of endless historical legends, they brought the Stuarts no nearer to restoration. When James died, in 1766, there were few left to hail his son as 'King Charles III' and to toast 'the King over the water'.

In 1772 Charles married a German princess, Louise of Stolberg-Gedern, twenty years old to his fifty-one, innocent and too naïve to stand up to the cynical, sadistic roué which this 'Prince Charming' had by then become. They had no children, and with the death of Charles Edward in 1788, and that of his brother, Cardinal York, in 1807, the royal House of Stuart at last came to its end.

Back in Britain, the Jacobite uprisings of 1715 and 1745 had been only brief alarms. By 1745 George I had been dead some eighteen years, and his son, George II, was, if not popular, at least secure.

Despite his good will towards the British, George II was still basically German, and when it came time to find a bride for his eldest son,

Frederick Lewis, Prince of Wales, the prime qualification—apart, of course, from religion—was that she be German too. (There was no way that the King would countenance his son's marriage to Lady Diana Spencer, whom her grandmother, the Dowager Duchess of Marlborough, offered the Prince, along with a £100,000 dowry, once he realized it involved the Prince's political involvement with Diana's Whig relations.)

When Augusta of Saxe-Gotha arrived in London, in April 1736, to marry Frederick Lewis, she was only seventeen years old, away from home for the first time in her life, understanding no English and obviously terrified. But the wedding had been arranged for that very evening, and so she was put into her wedding-dress and marched to the altar, not understanding a word of the service.

> I told her to look at me, and I would make a sign when she ought to kneel [recounted Queen Caroline later]. She clutched at my skirt and said, "For heaven's sake, please don't leave me," but Griff [the Prince of Wales] bawled in her ear, making her repeat the marriage sentences. She did not want to let go of my skirt. After the service, she and her husband knelt to ask the King's and my blessing, which the King bestowed most benignly, and she, poor creature, just as one has seen in plays—she was sick. . . .[1]

Despite her real sympathy for the girl, Queen Caroline could still see the humour of the 'bedding': her son wore a nightcap like a 'grenadier's bonnet', she said. She thought the marriage would be a success: "As far as one can judge, her husband is perfectly pleased with her." For her part, Caroline had no complaint: "She is the best creature in the world. One puts up with her insipidity because of her goodness." Still, there were obvious defects in the Princess's upbringing, and "I could scold the old Duchess of Gotha for not having given the poor, good child a better education," the Queen declared.[2]

The King and Queen loathed their eldest son, and for his part he did everything he could to annoy them, worst of all adopting the policies of 'Opposition' politicans and openly denouncing his father's ministers. With some wisdom, Augusta followed her husband with docility, though she never did anything of her own volition to worsen relations with his parents.

Frederick Lewis's sister Anne, the eldest of the princesses, was a good daughter and was really loved by both parents. They were apparently heart-broken when they had had to part with her at her marriage, two years earlier.

Originally Anne had been intended for King Louis XV of France, until the inevitable demand from the French that she turn Catholic. Then there came a proposal on behalf of William IV of Orange (second cousin of the late King), and though George thought such a match a 'disparagement' of his eldest daughter, he was persuaded that nothing could be so popular in the country. As for the Princess, when she was given the chance of refusing William, and though she was warned that he was deformed and ugly, she declared that she would marry a baboon if he offered for her—probably reckoning that any marriage was better than none, especially when her brother, whom she hated, should succeed their father on the throne. Even when she saw just how much like a baboon William was, she kept her resolution.

Court opinion as to his physical defects was divided. One courtier, Lord Hervey, wrote that, "The Prince of Orange's figure, besides his being almost a dwarf, was as much deformed as it was possible for a human creature to be; his face was not bad, his countenance sensible, but his breath was more offensive than it is possible for those who have not been offended by it to imagine."[3] Lord Chesterfield, on the other hand, recorded that, ". . . I think he has extreme good parts. He is perfectly well bred and civil to everybody and with an ease and freedom that is seldom acquired but by a long knowledge of the world. His face is handsome; his shape is not so advantageous as could be wished, though not near so bad as I had heard represented."[4]

When William appeared in his nightshirt on the wedding night, Lord Hervey remarked that "he looked behind as if he had no head, and before as if he had no back and no legs", but when Queen Caroline told him the next day that she pitied her daughter for having to go to bed with such a "monster", Hervey said comfortingly, "Oh, madam, in half a year all persons are alike; the figure of the body one's married to, like the prospect of the place one lives at, grows so familiar to one's eyes that one looks at it mechanically, without regarding either the beauties or deformities that strike a stranger." Still, Caroline thought, "One may, and I believe one does, grow blind at last, but you must allow, my dear Lord Hervey, there is a great difference, as long as one sees, in the manner of one's growing blind."[5]

Princess Anne's wedding was the first in the royal family to be celebrated in Britain since that of Queen Anne, back in 1683, and it was suitably celebrated, at George II's expense—which exonerated him, so he thought, from adding anything to the generous £80,000 awarded his daughter by Parliament. (This represented twice the amount of any dowry of earlier years, but then it did not come directly from the public purse: it was raised from the sale of land on St Christopher's Island in the South Atlantic.)

William of Orange arrived in London in November 1733 and was to have married Anne almost straight away, but on the day before his wedding he went to worship in London's Dutch Church, which was packed to capacity with Dutch merchants and many citizens eager to see the bridegroom, and coming out from that crowd and heat into a bitter winter day, he caught a chill which developed swiftly into pneumonia. For days he was thought to be dying, but he recovered at last, and then he went off to Bath to take the healing waters of the Roman spring. So it was 25th March before the wedding took place.

In the days that followed, it was noticed that the Princess was paying court to her husband, rather than *vice versa*, behaving, so Hervey said, "as if he had been an Adonis"—she "addressed everything she said to him and applauded everything he said to anybody else".[6]

As had been predicted, the match did prove popular in the country, for the Prince had a good deal of personal appeal for those who could remember King William III. In recent years, George II had been jealous of his eldest son's popularity; now both King and Prince of Wales were chagrined by the applause that William was winning away from both of them. It was for the loss of Anne, rather than her husband, that the King wept, when the couple left for Holland six weeks after the wedding.

Less than two months later, the Princess was home again. It was not that she and William had disagreed, but he was away at war, and Anne was pregnant and longing for home. Without a word to any of her Dutch attendants, who would have tried to prevent her leaving, she had just taken flight, and she arrived at Kensington Palace, where her parents were staying, in the middle of the night of 2nd June. Everyone advised her to go home, and William demanded her return when he heard the news, but it was October before the Princess was put on the road to Harwich, to take ship, and while she was passing a night at Colchester, on the way, she took it into her head not to leave after all. So suddenly, on 22nd October, she appeared in London again. But she had only a month's respite before her now exasperated father sent her off once more. This time, she actually put to sea, but when her ship sailed into a smart wind, she threatened to go into convulsions, and the frightened master had to put back to port. This time the King forbade her to return to London, and she was directed to avoid the capital on her way to Dover, to take the shorter crossing to Calais. Never, he said, was she to return home uninvited (not surprising, for her visit had cost him £20,000 for her upkeep and that of her staff). So at last the Princess went back to Holland, and there she stayed—until 1737, when her mother died. Even then, when she came home again, to 'comfort' her father, the King packed her off to Bath straight away.

When Frederick Lewis, Prince of Wales, died in 1751, his widow professed the utmost respect for her father-in-law, George II, but in private she did everything she could to keep up the family quarrel, always warning her son, the new Prince of Wales, against his grandfather. Thus, when the King suggested that his new heir marry Sophie Caroline of Brunswick-Wolfenbuttel, Augusta put up her own niece, Frederica of Saxe-Gotha, as a rival. Left to himself, Prince George would have had neither, for in 1759 he fell in love with a fourteen-year-old Irish girl, Lady Sarah Lennox. But George was a conscientious young man and was readily brought to appreciate the importance of his marrying yet another German princess. When he came to the throne, in October 1760, at the age of twenty-two, he saw it his duty to make a speedy marriage.

There was no shortage of candidates, at least on paper. Princesses of practically every German duchy, principality and kingdom were examined and appraised, over the next few months, but gradually the deformed, ugly, eccentric, immoral and ignorant were eliminated, leaving the sixteen-year-old Charlotte of Mecklenburg-Strelitz as 'front runner'. Even though George III was still hankering after Lady Sarah, he put in his bid for Charlotte and was immediately accepted.

Though Princess Charlotte was no older than Princess Augusta had been when she came over to marry George's father, she had a great deal more composure. While her ship tossed on the North Sea in the traditional 'bride's gale', and her English ladies were feeling unwell, the future Queen was playing a harpsichord, reputedly teaching herself 'God save the King'. There was only one moment of panic: when, on 8th September, she caught her first glimpse of the Palace, she "grew frightened and turned pale", according to the Duchess of Hamilton, one of the ladies who attended her. When the elder woman smiled, the Princess said, "My dear Duchess, you may laugh, you have been married twice, but it is no joke to me!"[7] Her lips trembled as the coach drew up, but Charlotte gathered her courage, and when the King himself opened the garden gate to her, she knelt to him prettily.

Like Augusta before her, Charlotte was to be married the very evening of her arrival, and after supper she was put into her wedding-dress— which she had not seen until that moment. It was, recorded the Duchess of Northumberland,

> . . . a silver tissue, stiffen-bodied gown, embroidered and trimmed with silver, on her head a little cap of purple velvet quite covered with diamonds, a diamond aigrette in form of a crown, three dropt-diamond ear-rings, diamond necklace, diamond sprigs of flowers on her sleeves and, to clasp the back of her robe, a diamond stomacher; her purple velvet mantle was laced with gold and lined with ermine. It was fastened on the shoulders with large tassels of pearls.[8]

Despite the fact that Charlotte had ten maids-of-honour to carry her train, it was so heavy, said one observer, that as the evening passed, it dragged down the neck of her gown, so that "the spectators knew as much of her upper half as the King himself".[9] But that was all they were to see of Charlotte's *déshabille*, for she was to be the first queen in centuries not to appear in a nightdress to be 'bedded' beside her bridegroom before the whole Court. It was George III himself who put an end to the old custom, to spare his bride, and who had their coronation put off until 22nd September so she could recover her "bashfulness", as he said. From the outset George was always concerned for Charlotte's well-being and to secure her affection, which the girl herself much appreciated. Both of them put real effort into making their marriage a success—an effort which was rewarded by their becoming a byword for domestic happiness, a model for every well-meaning couple in the kingdom.

The Later Hanoverians

Queen Charlotte produced her first child, the future George IV, on 12th August 1762, when she had been married just over eleven months. Twenty-one years later, she gave birth to her last child, her fifteenth. Over that period (before the King's illness, which was diagnosed as madness), the royal couple established a reputation for marital respectability and mutual devotion in marked contrast to the behaviour, habits and lifestyle of other monarchs in Europe. It was unfortunate that, when their eldest son entered manhood, he should spoil the image which George and Charlotte had so carefully created.

But even before the younger generation was grown up, the marriages of the King's brothers and sisters, in the decade after his own, warned him that he could not rely on the decorum of his family.

In 1765, when Princess Caroline Matilda was only thirteen years old, George betrothed her to the heir of the King of Denmark, two years her senior, who was the son of her aunt Louisa. Caroline Matilda was told that she need not leave home for several years, until she had grown up, but when the King of Denmark died in 1766, her departure was arranged immediately. The girl was in a pitiful state when she entered the Great Council Chamber of St James's Palace for her proxy wedding—as an avidly observing Duchess reported: "Before she set out in the procession, she cried so much that she was near falling into fits. Her brother the Duke of Gloucester, who led her, was so shocked at seeing her in such a situation that he looked as pale as death and as if he was ready to faint away."[1]

There was to be no reassurance for the girl's fears when she reached Denmark. The French envoy was soon reporting to his master that she had "produced hardly any impression on the King's heart; but had she been even more amiable, she would have experienced the same fate, for how could she please a man who seriously believed that it is not good form for a husband to love his wife?"[2] Christian VII of Denmark was only seventeen when he received his bride, but since childhood he had shown tastes for 'low company' and the bottle; his debaucheries, added to a hereditary disease, had so enfeebled him as to make him appear almost imbecilic at times.

When Caroline Matilda realized the sort of man she was coupled with, what sort of life she was condemned to lead, it was no wonder that she turned to one who offered something more than sympathy. But while she might have managed to continue in Denmark with a lover kept discreetly in the boudoir, the Queen used what influence she had to advance him in politics, so that the whole nation could see that she and Struensee (formerly a Court physician) were using the King's inadequacies to mask their own growing power. For a time the couple controlled the situation, but every politician has his enemies, and Struensee's had ample ammunition against him: in 1772 he was arrested, later executed, and Caroline Matilda was sent into exile in Germany, never to see her children again (her husband was no loss), never to return to Denmark. She died in 1775, still in her early twenties.

George III had been appalled at his sister's crime and her unhappy fate, but, after all, she was out of his power. Not so his brothers. In November 1771 the Duke of Cumberland informed the King that he had been secretly married for three months to the Honourable Mrs Anne Horton, a widow who was a couple of years his senior. Cumberland knew what George's reaction would be, so he did not even dare break the news by word of mouth: he handed the King a letter and stood by anxiously while he read it. In view of the rapidly increasing younger generation of the royal family, Cumberland's marriage could hardly affect the royal succession; no, it was the *lèse majesté* that struck the King—far more deeply than seems reasonable now, but at the time the Duke's misdemeanour caused a real scandal. George offered his brother the chance to repudiate his duchess, but he refused, and the couple found it prudent to go abroad until the furore died down.

The King now determined not to give any other member of his family a chance of so shaming him, and he himself instigated the entry of the Royal Marriage Bill into parliamentary legislation that same year. Under its terms, it would be illegal for any member of the royal family (except, of course, the children of British princesses who had married foreigners) to marry without royal permission; princes and princesses over the age of twenty-five might do so only by giving the Privy Council twelve months' notice of the proposed marriage, and even then not if it objected. The Bill also declared null and void any marriage made in contravention of its terms.

It was the latter clause in the Bill (enacted in 1772) that drew a confession from the Duke of Gloucester that he had been privately married to Maria, Lady Waldegrave, for the past six years; now, he said, his wife was pregnant with their first child. There was no proof that a wedding had ever taken place, for it had not been recorded and the clergyman who had performed the ceremony had since died, but Gloucester would not take advantage of this to cast off his wife. When George III refused to recognize the marriage and receive the Duchess, the couple still continued to live together openly, and Maria used her new title without royal approval. It was some years before the Gloucesters and their children were accepted into the family circle.

As far as the heir to the throne, the future George IV, was concerned, the Royal Marriage Act might never have existed, for in 1785 he did just what his father had intended to prevent—he made a secret marriage with a commoner, as his uncles had done. In fact, it was *because* of the Act that he felt able to do so, knowing that the marriage was null and void from the very moment it was contracted. If it had been legal, it would have cost him his future throne, for his bride, Maria Fitzherbert, was a Catholic, and under the terms of the Act of Settlement, any member of the royal family marrying a Catholic automatically forfeited his place in the royal succession. But marriage was the only means of inducing Maria to sleep with the Prince (as many other women had over the past few years), and the Prince must always have his way, so marriage it was—a secret marriage, so secret that, when rumours of it were circulated, even his best friend could stand up in Parliament and deny it.

Not that it was easy to persuade Maria even to marriage: she had firmly repulsed all George's early advances, and when, in July 1784, he staged a suicide attempt in the best romantic tradition of the day, though she did come running, she brought a chaperone with her. For a moment, she weakened and agreed to become his wife, but the very next day she fled abroad. George could not follow her (he would need his father's permission to leave the country), but he did pursue her with letters, dozens of letters, some of them twenty, thirty pages long, full of passionate appeals, threatening to renounce everything for love of her, offering to disappear with her into the depths of America.

When Maria did give in, in December 1785, the wedding was performed in her own London house, her father and uncle the only witnesses, with a clergyman brought up from the Fleet prison to undertake the ceremony (in return for payment of his debts and the promise of a bishopric when George became king).

The twice-widowed Mrs Fitzherbert was no conventional beauty, but she had soft, dark eyes, a curvaceous figure and the gentlest of manners. Content to seem to be the Prince's mistress, knowing—or at least believing—that she was his wife, she graced his London house and seaside retreat as well as any princess, placed some curbs on his extravagance and gluttony and held his affection for nearly a decade. Then, unfortunately, his eyes began to wander, and they lighted on Lady Jersey, a self-seeking sophisticate who demanded more than a discreet liaison behind Maria's back. When George left his 'wife', she made no open complaint, certainly never contemplating blackmailing him by producing evidence of their marriage; nor did she come forward when, that same year, the King refused to ask Parliament to pay the Prince's debts (£375,000) unless he married.

In consultation, the King and his son agreed to send a proposal to Caroline of Brunswick, daughter of George III's sister Augusta, who, on paper, was suitably qualified. Too late it was discovered that, though she was attractive in a rather blowsy way, she lacked manners, self-restraint, education and—according to the man sent to bring her over—any idea of personal hygiene. It was even put about, when the Princess proved so unsatisfactory, that the Prince's mistress, Lady Jersey, had chosen her for him (having heard 'initimate' reports of Caroline's person and personality) so that she would not be ousted by his wife.

Lord Malmesbury, sent to Germany to collect the Princess, did his best to see some good in her, but everyone at the Brunswick Court seemed bent on warning him that she must be treated carefully if she was to be a success. Her father the Duke admitted that "She is *not bad*, but she has no judgement—she has been brought up strictly, and it was necessary,"[3] and even the Duke's mistress took Malmesbury aside to advise him that Caroline must be "closely curbed", that George must make her respect him as well as love him—"Without this she will assuredly go astray."[4] Even so, it must have been hard for the Englishman to believe one report, that the Princess was so 'free with her favours' to young men that, when she danced with any of them, a lady had to follow her round the room, lest Caroline initiate a *risqué* conversation that might lead to worse. Malmesbury gave the Princess plenty of good advice during their journey to England (he even ventured to mention her personal cleanliness—to some effect, for she appeared the next day, "well washed all over", so he said), but when they arrived at Greenwich, on 5th April 1795, she passed out of his control.

Lady Jersey had been appointed the Princess's chief lady-in-waiting, and she was determined to show the upper hand from the outset: when the Princess disembarked, it was to find that the ladies who were to attend her to London had not yet arrived—Lady Jersey had made them all late. When she did appear, she made such a fuss about Caroline's supposedly 'unsuitable' clothes that she made the girl more nervous than she had been, which, with Caroline, made her even more noisy and 'giggly' than she was under normal circumstances.

The Prince of Wales was nervous too—and disappointed when he viewed his bride. "Harris," he gasped, turning to Lord Malmesbury, "I am not well. Pray get me a glass of brandy."[5] As he left her, Caroline exclaimed, "My God! Is the Prince always like that? I find him very fat and nothing like as handsome as his portrait."[6] But Caroline was not so 'sensitive' as her bridegroom; besides, she had come to marry the most eligible man in Europe and would not be put off by such a little thing as his portly figure; by dinnertime, Malmesbury (who had already had to excuse himself to George for bringing her by reminding him that he had had a definite commission, not dependent on Caroline's personal

charms) noticed that she was at her very worst, "flippant, rattling, affect-
ing raillery and wit and throwing out coarse vulgar hints" about Lady
Jersey's relations with the bridegroom.[7] George himself was "disgusted",
he noticed.

When the couple were married, three days later, Malmesbury observed
that "The Prince was very civil and gracious, but I thought I could
perceive he was not quite sincere and certainly unhappy; as a proof of it,
he had manifestly had recourse to wine or spirits."[8]

"Judge what it is to have a drunken husband on one's wedding day,"
Caroline told a lady-in-waiting years later, "and one who spent the
greater part of his bridal night under the grate where he fell and where I
left him."[9] There were some who said that, after the first few nights of
marriage, George never shared Caroline's bed again. But those nights
were used to effect, for nine months less one day after the wedding, the
Princess gave birth to a child, a daughter, who was named Charlotte for
her paternal grandmother.

> . . . After I lay in [Caroline said years later in the thick German accent she
> never lost]—*je vous jure*, 'tis true; upon my honour, upon my soul 'tis true—I
> received a message. . . to tell me I never was to have de great honour of
> inhabiting de same room wid my husband again. I said very well—but as my
> memory was short, I begged to have dis polite message in writing from him.
> I had it—and vas free—I left Carlton House and went to Charlton. Oh how
> happy I was! Everybody blamed me, but I never repented me of dis step.
> What I have suffered![10]

Caroline's memory had telescoped events somewhat, but certainly she
had suffered in those few months with her husband: the Prince insulted
her, his mistress insulted her, even the Queen withheld any kind word
that might have helped her (she had summed up Caroline from the start);
together they combined to keep Caroline friendless, since the Court did
not dare offer sympathy with the Prince looking on. George III alone had
some kindness for his niece/daughter-in-law, and when his son
proposed the separation, he tried to persuade him to keep up appearances
at least, by continuing to live in the same house as his wife. But the Prince
of Wales utterly refused to compromise, and on 30th April 1796 he gave
Caroline that "piece of writing" for which she had asked, in which he
wrote of their incompatibility and the only escape—separation, and
promised her that never in the future—not even if their only child were to
die—would he expect her to return to him.

In his own unhappiness, George's thoughts had turned away from
Lady Jersey to "the wife of my heart and soul", Maria Fitzherbert. Three
days after the birth of his daughter, he had written his Will, in which he
cut off his wife with the proverbial shilling and left everything else to
Maria. But now she refused to return to him—at least until he threatened
to tell his father about their 'marriage', to give up everything to be hers
again. Even though this weakened her resolve, Maria agreed to return to
her 'husband' only on one condition: that the Pope be informed of their

marriage and himself confirm it. That took time, but by the summer of 1800 Rome had agreed that George was truly her husband (not recognizing the validity of the Royal Marriage Act), so they came together again.

The reconciliation was not permanent, however. By the time George became Regent of the kingdom in February 1811 (when his father was at last judged incapable, after intermittent periods of madness), he was the lover of Lady Hertford and completely under her sway. Five months later, Maria wrote to him that she was withdrawing from his life for ever.

The Princess of Wales, in the meantime, had been pursuing love on her own account, so careless of her reputation that in 1806 the King had been forced to institute what was called 'the Delicate Enquiry', mainly to find out the truth of a rumour that she had had another child, not her husband's. Though Caroline had been indiscreet, however, she had had no more children, but this turn of events only served to alienate her still further from the royal family.

The Princess Charlotte, who was allowed to see her mother only at infrequent intervals, grew up wholeheartedly faithful to Caroline, hated her repressive grandmother and treated her father with considerable mistrust. She had the wilfulness of both parents, the brusque, careless manners of her mother in abundance, but she was a good-hearted girl, always conscious that she was destined one day to be a queen.

In the early teens of the new century, the question of his daughter's marriage troubled the Prince Regent considerably, but in yet another William of Orange he found what he thought could be the ideal match: admittedly William was an unattractive young man, with sallow skin and spindly legs, but he was Protestant, not unintelligent, had served creditably under the Duke of Wellington in Spain and had spent two years at Oxford University—and besides, the Dutch connection was always popular in Britain. Charlotte took a look at William and labelled him 'Frog', but she allowed herself to become engaged to him, without much enthusiasm, towards the end of 1813. It was only later that she realized that he intended to take her to live in Holland—a plan which she was convinced her father had had in mind all the time, to rid himself of her because she was becoming his rival for national popularity. This so enfuriated Charlotte—and worried her, since it would mean her losing contact with the kingdom one day to be hers—that when her fiancé returned to England the following spring, she broke off the engagement.

There was a good deal of speculation at the time that the Princess had discarded her fiancé not only for policy, and one lady attached to the Court surmised that "she wants to get a look at another prince or two before she makes her choice of a husband".[11] There were a good many princes in London then, for the festivities marking the end of the Napoleonic Wars, so Charlotte had a fine opportunity to survey potential husbands. One of them, Augustus of Prussia (a thoroughly disreputable young man but very handsome), was her own fancy, and that June they contrived to meet secretly—but not secretly enough: when her father heard of it, he ordered her off to Windsor, to lodge in the castle grounds, there to see no one but her grandmother and to be guarded by ladies replacing those who had been so lax as to let her loose with Augustus.

At his wit's end with such a daughter, the Regent was brought to agree when Charlotte named another bridegroom, one with no real 'black' against his name—apart from the fact that there was absolutely no profit or prestige in a match with so minor a prince as this Leopold of Saxe-Coburg-Saalfeld, the impecunious younger brother of a German duke. Leopold was a personable young man, obviously intelligent beyond the norm of princes, prudent and discreet, and Charlotte was given no time to seek out his faults. They became engaged in January 1816, married that May.

The wedding was celebrated at Carlton House, the Prince Regent's London residence, in the presence of all the bride's family—except her mother. Charlotte wore a silver gown, with a wreath of roses in her hair, and she was in the highest of spirits: when Leopold vowed to endow her with 'all his wordly goods', she laughed aloud at the absurdity of it.

In fact, he was just what she needed, a man with no responsibilities but to keep her company and make her happy. More important, he began to 'tame' her, subduing her hilarity to propriety, showing her how to consider someone other than herself and beginning, at least, to coach her for her future role as queen. Unfortunately, his efforts were wasted. Soon after the Princess had given birth to a dead child, in November 1817, she died.

Charlotte's death was not only a grief to her family but brought with it the serious problem of replacing her in the royal succession. As things stood, not one of George III's surviving offspring had a legitimate child who could take the crown in the next generation. Unless some of them did something about it soon (for they were all middle-aged by then), the royal House of Hanover would become extinct over the next half-century, and the British Crown might ultimately pass to—of all people—the Brunswicks, the children of George III's sister Augusta, with the Princess of Wales, Caroline, among them.

Three of the Regent's brothers were married by the time of Charlotte's death. York had married Frederica of Prussia in 1791, but since they had had no children in all those years, there seemed little likelihood of their providing the new heir. Cumberland had married in 1814, taking as his wife his maternal cousin Frederica of Mecklenburg-Strelitz (twice widowed and with a sinister reputation); they too were childless to date. A third brother, the Duke of Sussex, had put himself out of the running by marrying without royal permission, so that the union was void under the terms of the Royal Marriage Act, and his two children were thereby ineligible to succeed to the throne.

That left the Dukes of Clarence, Kent and Cambridge, and all their sisters save the eldest, who had been married to the King of Württemberg for the past couple of decades without producing a child, and Mary, who had married her cousin Gloucester in 1816 but, at forty, was unlikely to have children now. Queen Charlotte had always been loth to part with her daughters, and the princes who offered for them were quickly discouraged. Three of the princesses had had love-affairs with courtiers— whom, of course, they had no hope of marrying with royal permission, and one of them, Amelia, had had an illegitimate child. Amelia had died young, but the rest were left to serve as extra ladies-in-waiting to their mother, never off duty, and by then Queen Charlotte had become an imperious matriarch demanding complete docility and obedience. Now she put up a fight against the forty-eight-year-old Elizabeth's marriage to Frederick of Hesse-Homburg (forty-nine-years old, a widower, enormously fat), but the Princess was determined to have a home of her own—if not the child so necessary to Britain, and she had her way. There was, of course, no child of the marriage, but at least the occasion had given one of the housebound royal sisters her release.

Clarence and Kent had thought of marriage before Princess Charlotte's death, mainly as a means of gaining a parliamentary grant towards the liquidation of their debts. They were both of them domestically inclined anyway: Clarence had been faithful for twenty-odd years to his actress mistress Dorothy Jordan, who had given him ten children, and Kent had lived for nigh on thirty years with a Frenchwoman, Julie de St Laurent; but where Clarence, the elder, had parted from his mistress some years previously, Kent had to break the news to his that he was about to leave her for a princess. (Not for either of the dukes the *insouciance* of their brother George, who had had no intention of parting with his mistress when he found a bride!)

William of Clarence, a bluff naval officer with quarterdeck language and no social graces, made something of a fool of himself during his search for a bride, proposing indiscriminately—or so it seems—to British heiresses before a suitable German princess was picked out for him. The poor girl, half his age, was brought over to London and presented to her bridegroom with little ceremony, in full knowledge that she was merely to be 'breeding-stock'. But fortunately Princess Adelaide of Saxe-Meiningen was a sensible young woman, Clarence a kindly man—it was not his fault that his eldest bastard broke his leg the day after the wedding and had to be nursed by his new stepmother, and that the rest of the 'Fitzclarences' turned their home into a bear-garden.

William and Adelaide shared their wedding with the Duke of Kent and his bride, Victoire of Saxe-Coburg. She was the sister of the widowed Prince Leopold, who, with Princess Charlotte, had begun to arrange the match some years before. Then, Victoire had hesitated to accept Kent's proposal, for she was a widow, the guardian of her young son's principality in Germany, and had ties there which were hard to break, but now, in 1818, she agreed to marry Edward of Kent, and after a Lutheran ceremony in Coburg and the Anglican rite in England, the couple set up house in Kensington Palace.

At about the same time, the youngest of the three Dukes, Adolphus of Cambridge, married the Princess Augusta of Hesse-Cassel, and almost simultaneously the three new Duchesses and the Duchess of Cumberland became pregnant. Augusta gave birth to a son on 26th March 1819, Adelaide had a daughter the following day, on 24th May Victoire also produced a daughter, and the same month Frederica had a son. The Clarence baby would have had precedence, had it lived, but it survived birth only by a few hours, so the child of the next of the dukes in seniority, Kent, stood eventually to inherit the throne. Her name was Victoria.

At the time of her birth, she stood fifth in the royal succession, but the death of her father and her grandfather, George III, within days of each other, in January 1820, advanced her; and in 1828 the Duke of York died too, so that only William of Clarence stood between George IV and Victoria of Kent.

At one time, however, it seemed that the little Princess might lose her chance of the throne, when her uncle George seemed to be casting round for a second wife. His first, Caroline of Brunswick, had died in 1821—though only after completing her scandalous career by attempting to gain her place as Queen Consort by trying to enter Westminster Abbey during her husband's coronation, following his unsuccessful bid to divorce her. The divorce case had been the most unpleasant business, with a full-scale 'trial' of Caroline's morals in Parliament, in which bedroom evidence was produced for the edification of the newspaper-reading public of the nation. Never in the annals of British royal marriages had a monarch and his consort so openly 'washed their dirty linen in public'—though in fact, it was all Caroline's 'dirty linen' (her flagrant adulteries on the Continent over the past few years), while George himself came out virtually unscathed—except as regards public opinion. However, the 'trial' had broken down, Caroline's storming of the Abbey had failed, and, before she could do anything worse, she had died—so George IV was free, if he liked, to seek a new wife.

It was not until 1826 that he showed any signs of doing so—and even then he did not put much effort into the project. The object of his attentions was close at hand: the Princess Feodora of Leiningen, daughter of the Duchess of Kent's first marriage, and thus Victoria's half-sister. She was a pretty adolescent of the 'bread-and-butter-miss' type, not sufficiently ambitious to set out to 'fascinate' the King intentionally. Her mother was ambitious enough for the whole family, but her ambitions were not set in that direction: the widowed Duchess was determined that her Victoria should be Queen Regnant, and Feodora was not allowed to upset her plans by becoming Queen Consort and mothering a brood of children who would replace Victoria in the royal succession. So Feodora was packed off to Germany, till George's fancy for her should evaporate, and she was soon married to a German princeling.

Thereafter there was no talk of the King's marrying again. He settled down comfortably with his elderly mistresses, and in 1830 he died.

In December 1820 Adelaide of Clarence had given birth to another daughter, but the child lived only four months to vex the Duchess of Kent's plans, and thereafter Victoria was safe in the royal succession as far as the Clarences were concerned. The reign of William IV came and went, from 1830 to 1837, and so Victoria became queen, the last monarch of the House of Hanover.

The Nineteenth Century

'Lie Back and Think of England'

In 1897, one Mrs Humphry wrote a little handbook entitled *Manners for Women*, aimed at supplying socially aspiring ladies with the information they required on personal conduct and the organization of social functions. Several of her chapters were devoted to the responsibilities of a bride's mother, taking her from the etiquette of announcing her daughter's engagement through the despatch of invitations to the wedding, the instruction of caterers and the control of the family's servants ("They are so anxious to be of use in every way that they incline to neglect their own special department, and the amount of chatter that goes on is something stupendous. If the mistress gets excited too, everything will go to pieces"[1]); then there was the decoration of the church, and packing for the bride (". . . the bride cannot always collect her thoughts sufficiently to apply them to this matter"[2]) and even the choice of horses to take the girl to church—"The fact is that a smart pair of greys has been found to attract much notice, with the consequence that an undesirable crowd frequently assembles at the bride's house. This gathering is mainly composed of nurse-girls in charge of perambulators, and butchers' boys with material for sundry dinners of the vicinity on their wooden trays, to say nothing of fishmongers' wares, whose proximity is not always pleasant."[3]

It was all a dreadful chore, Mrs Humphry decided, and for the bride's father a dreadful expense. Add to the cost of the once-worn wedding-gown that of a full trousseau, of lingerie and corsetry, tailor-made suits and coats and capes, day-gowns and evening-gowns, hats and bonnets and shoes and gloves, and all the minutiae of the Victorian woman's complex attire—to say nothing of jewellery, and any father might be harassed at the expense of 'marrying off' a daughter.

The trousseau was not, of course, designed only for the dazzling of the new husband: a bride now had her honeymoon trip to consider. In the eighteenth century many couples had spent the first months of marriage in visiting relations, but, as the new century opened, it became fashionable to spend the first few days or weeks (even months, if the Continent were the object) at a hotel at some scenic spot—often Brighton or the Lake District.

This departure for anonymity far from family and friends was designed partly to spare the couple the embarrassment of appearing after the 'wedding-night'—modesty about such things had been increasing for years. On the other hand, since engaged couples were so strictly chaperoned, so that now weeks of each other's company, unadulterated, might come as rather a shock, it very sensibly became the custom for the bride's sister, or one of her friends, to accompany the newly-weds on their honeymoon. The practice is mentioned in Jane Austen's novel *Mansfield Park* and in the mid-century in George Eliot's *Middlemarch*, but by the last couple of decades of the century it had completely died out.

In the meantime, how many girls were given 'the facts of life' by their newly married sisters—facts which, we are told, so many mothers were too shy to reveal? 'We are told' . . . many historians of the period would have us believe a great many things about Victorian sexuality which cannot be proved, since the Victorians were so reticent about speaking of, even writing of, sexual relations. Prudish they were, at least in mixed company (some women even refused to be examined naked by a male doctor), but just because they lacked today's frankness about sex does not mean that all Victorian women found sexual relations not only unspeakable but unspeakably unpleasant, or that all Victorian men looked upon 'good' women as 'above all that', regarded marital sex as only for 'the procreation of children' and resorted to prostitutes for pleasure. (The fact that reliable statistics prove that there were far more brothels in Victorian Britain than there are today does not mean that there were more than in past, reputedly 'sexually healthier' centuries for which no statistics are available.) It is the Victorians' reticence in mentioning sex which gives the impression that they were ashamed of their own sexuality, a silence which we might equate with today's reticence on the subjects of religion and death, on which the Victorians spoke uninhibitedly.

The 'white' wedding, the expensive catering, the weeks of preparation, the careful observance of etiquette through the whole proceedings, the honeymoon—and, in the last decades of the century, the presence of a photographer at the wedding, were signs that a family had some means, money to spare over and above the budget for daily living. Accounts of weddings at the lowest end of the social scale show a very different picture. There was, for example, the Essex navvy who married a Luton straw-plaiter in the 1850s, on his savings of £4.15s: they had what he recalled as a 'quiet' wedding, but his friends did muster a drum and an old tin kettle to give them "the rough music". When another straw-plaiter, Lucy 'M.', married a farm-labourer, Will Luck, in December 1867, with the rain pouring down and slushy snow making the roads treacherous, there was no money for a wedding-party, and after the ceremony she and her bridegroom went to the hotel where his brother worked as an ostler, dried their clothes by the fire in his harness-room and had a bite to eat there before setting off for their cottage (rent: 2 shillings a week).[4]

Where there was even a little money to spare though, everyone would try to put on some degree of style for a wedding. In the 1830s, the famous chronicler of English rural life Mary Russell Mitford wrote of the wedding of a publican's daughter and a shoemaker:

> The bride was equipped in muslin and satin . . . the bridemaidens were only less smart than the bride; and the bridegroom was 'point device in his accoutrements' and as munificent as a nabob. Cakes flew about the village; plum-puddings were abundant; and strong beer, aye, even mine host's best double X, was profusely distributed. There was all manner of eating and drinking, with singing, fiddling and dancing between, and in the evening, to crown all, there was Mr Moon the conjurer.

The girl who could not expect a father to provide a trousseau would, as like as not, sew a stock of at least underwear and household linen ready for marriage, sometimes starting in her early teens before there was any man in prospect. But some of those trousseaux must have lain in bottom drawers for years, for there was real caution now, on the part of the poor and especially in the middle classes, not to marry until there was sufficient money saved to set up house, and an income that could be relied on. Some trousseaux would never be used, for in 1851 women out-numbered men by half a million, and fifty years later they were in the majority by nearly 1½ million. (In 1897 Mrs Humphry headed one of her chapters 'Brides Two a Penny'.)

The superfluity was most noticeable in the middle classes, partly due to the despatch of so many young men to the colonies, partly because of the strength of class divisions: a 'gentlewoman', however poor, would lose her status by marrying 'beneath' her, even where there was money. Her plight is perhaps best brought home in a letter written to the advice column of a women's magazine as late as the 1890s:

> I am that social 'pariah' a Dissenter and belong to a poor dissenting church, the male society of which consists entirely of dockyard labourers, mechanics and petty tradesmen. They are honest, decent but uneducated men, and their tastes, ideas and habits are such that anything like social intercourse between us would be only uncomfortable, unequal and strained. Other opportunities for meeting, on equal terms, men who would be considered to belong to my own class, I have absolutely none.[5]

The problem of these 'extra' women was solved partly by their taking the only 'genteel' employment available to them, as governesses or teachers in schools, ladies' companions or nurses (after the mid-century), where they would be housed as well as paid; but for the majority it was necessity rather than choice that put them to work, and many preferred to become dependent on male relatives who accepted the obligation to provide for them. Thus, if the Victorian spinster was to be pitied, so was the brother who had to support her, whose own chance of marriage might have to be postponed until he could find the means to keep a wife as well.

Family obligations were deeply felt by the Victorians, and if real affection did not inspire a man to take care of an unmarried sister (or a penniless widow or an orphan), then public opinion would certainly prompt him to remember his duty.

A married woman, unless widowed without means, had found a safe haven; she might have to bear poverty, but she would know that her husband would do everything in his power to prevent her having to work to supplement the family income. Prejudice against married women working was strongly entrenched even in the 'lower-middle' and artisan class: a farmer's wife, and the wife of a man who kept a shop, living above the premises, might see little hardship in taking on a share of the work (and it was generally agreed that the farmer's wife could count 'egg money' and the profits of other market produce as her own), but then these women were working at home, not out in the world unprotected. The wife of a carpenter or a clerk, a postman or a plumber, would expect to be kept by her husband, her province the household and the children, and if her husband, through illness or laziness or drunkenness, failed to provide for them, and she had to take in washing or go out 'charring', she would certainly not count it a pleasure.

The economic dependence of women on their husbands in the nineteenth century, as for so many centuries past, which is seen today as such a hardship, such a restraint on their personalities, was in fact the aim and goal of the vast majority of women—though they might not admit as much. We look back and wonder how so many women could have been content to obey their husbands in everything, disobeying them at the risk of forfeiting the financial support which men alone could give (and, indeed, how so many men could have committed themselves to marriage without the safeguard of a potential second income to fall back on in hard times). In fact, the only Victorian women who seem to have complained were those who had inherited money, who had to hand over their own fortunes to a husband to have it doled out to them at his whim. It was this small minority who were catered for in the Married Women's Property Act of 1870, and in subsequent legislation, which has only since the Second World War expanded to anything like real financial equality between husband and wife.

The Victorian legislators did a good deal towards delineating the married state as we know it today. The first Act of any real significance was that of 1836, which laid down the rule, once and for all, that weddings must be performed only in a recognized place of worship or in a registrar's office, at the same time demanding the recording of the marriage in a national register. Scotland, with its own civil legal system, was not covered by the Act; there, the age-old vows de praesenti were still admitted as legal.

In the first half of the century, divorce was possible only by Act of Parliament, as it had been since the seventeenth century, and, as before, it was the 'innocent' husband who was generally the petitioner; only four divorces were awarded to women between 1800 and 1850, and then not on the plea of a husband's adultery alone—it had to be exacerbated by his desertion, sodomy etc. One limit on the total of divorces was the fact that they were still expensive—costing at a minimum £700, sometimes running into thousands. The Matrimonial Causes Act of 1857 took divorces out of Parliamentary jurisdiction and into a new system of courts, but apart from that, there was little new: the wife had still to prove offences worse than adultery on the part of the husband, while the husband had only to prove that his wife had been unfaithful—which 'society' regarded as far more heinous than a husband's infidelity. The Act did result in an increased, and rapidly increasing, number of divorces (about 150 a year in the 1860s, nearly six hundred a year in the 1890s), but it was still obvious that their cost was the major factor in limiting them even thus far.

A considerable factor contributing to the Matrimonial Causes Act of 1878 was public concern about facts brought to light of the ill-treatment of working-class wives by their husbands, against whom they had no legal protection; this Act allowed magistrates' courts to grant legal separations, with maintenance and the custody of children under ten, to women assaulted by their husbands. More Acts followed: in 1886, for example, magistrates were empowered to serve maintenance-orders on husbands who had deserted their wives or refused to support them. By the end of the century, some eight thousand separation orders were being issued every year, witness to the fact that judicial separation was so much cheaper than divorce.

In the middle classes, matrimonial misdemeanors voiced in public were looked upon with horror, the parties involved with disdain. At the highest level of society, divorced women were not received at Court; further down the social scale, they would be ostracized by erstwhile friends—and not only from 'moral snobbery': there was a real repugnance towards marital 'crimes'. By the end of the century, though the middle class, careful of its gentility, was still closing ranks against marital offenders, the aristocracy was far more tolerant—but then the aristocrats were by now 'demeaning' themselves so far as to marry actresses and American heiresses, to the horror of those bastions of the class system a couple of social notches below them.

Many historians of the nineteenth century have been tempted into acceptance of the stereotyped Victorian marriage—the wife a 'clinging vine', the husband a stern and domineering 'lord and master', and unfortunately that view is still widely accepted today. Yet from a reading of the memoirs of Victorian men and women, and from their fiction (the novels of Mrs Henry Wood, Mrs Humphrey Ward and Charlotte M. Yonge, as well as the works of Dickens, Eliot, the Brontës, Trollope and Hardy), a picture emerges of a wide spectrum of marriages from which it would be as hard to estimate an average as it is from today's. If there were clinging vines and domestic tyrants, there were also termagant wives and timid husbands; if there were homes in which couples lived together on sufferance, merely to keep up a front of respectability, there were also homes in which there was at least as much affection and understanding as there is today. If there ever was that legendary Victorian wife who forced herself to 'lie back and think of England' when her husband demanded his conjugal rights, how many more women were there who embraced their husbands with real enthusiasm and loving response?

Victoria and Albert

Some historians have held that Victoria was marked down to marry her cousin Albert even when they were in their cradles; certainly by the time they were in their early teens their mutual uncle, Leopold of Saxe-Coburg (Princess Charlotte's widower and, since 1831, King of the Belgians), had formed his plan to match them. It was he who superintended Albert's education, preparing him for partnership in ruling Britain even while he tutored Victoria for her future crown.

It seems that Victoria knew of Leopold's plan when she was still in her early teens, some years before Albert himself realized his destiny, but even to the last moment she was determined to reject him if he did not suit her, and it was only her sudden, overwhelming love for him, when they met for the second time in 1839, that decided their future.

Their first meeting had occurred in 1836, and it was under rather embarrassing circumstances, for Leopold had sent Albert and his brother Ernest over to London at the same time as Victoria's paternal uncle, King William IV, had invited Princes William and Alexander of Orange to meet her, with a view to her marriage. The King was furious when he learned that Leopold was setting up a rival, but nothing he could say could prevent their coming, and it was galling to him to find Victoria disdaining the Oranges and enthusing about Albert's perfection.

Nevertheless, when, a year later, Victoria succeeded William IV on the throne, she did not rush into marriage with her cousin. Apart from the fact that she was revelling in her liberation from years of firm repression under his mother's regime at Kensington, there were too many male admirers to be enjoyed for her to settle with just one man. There were young courtiers, always ready to ride with her, dance with her, fill her leisure hours, and the fatherly Lord Melbourne, the Prime Minister, for *tête-à-têtes* solemn and frivolous, as well as an influx of young princes from all points of Europe to woo her. So, though Victoria was in the mood for 'dalliance', she was not minded to commit herself to marriage yet awhile. When her uncle Leopold pressed her to invite Albert for another visit, she agreed, but she firmly declared that she could not commit herself to marriage.

For his part, Albert was only too ready to step down, if Victoria did not want him, so awed was he by the prospect of a lifetime in a foreign country with never a day to call his own. But Albert had a mighty conscience and a real conviction that he could 'do good in the world', if called to it, and so, while admitting his fears to his uncle, he pledged himself to a career as the Queen's husband if she wanted him; all he asked was that the suspense should soon be over, for he could not face perhaps years of indecision while Victoria enjoyed her 'salad days'.

However, from the moment Victoria set eyes on him, entering Windsor Castle on 10th October 1839, all her doubts fled. "It was with some emotion that I beheld Albert, who is beautiful," she wrote in her diary that day.[1] Just five days later, the Prince was summoned to her 'closet', to hear her propose to him.

> After a few minutes I said to him that I thought he must be aware why I wished him to come, and that it would make me too happy if he would consent to what I wished (namely, to marry me).
>
> There was no hesitation on his part, but the offer was received with the greatest demonstration of kindness and affection. He is perfection in every way—in beauty, in everything. I told him I was quite unworthy of him. He said he would be very happy to spend his life with me. How I will strive to make him feel as little as possible the great sacrifice he has made![2]

Victoria did not keep that last resolution very long, however. When Albert had returned to Germany, and the announcement of their forth-coming wedding had been made to her subjects, she set about arranging Albert's future, and every letter he received from her over the next few months must have made the young man miserable: Victoria listed his new attendants; Victoria told him they could have only a couple of days' honeymoon because of the calls of duty on her time; Victoria explained that Parliament could never be brought to give him a British title, that he must be content with being made up to 'Royal Highness'; Albert was merely being 'difficult' when he voiced any wish of his own. But when he arrived for the wedding, the following February, she was so delighted, so affectionate, that all their recent problems were put aside.

On the morning of their wedding (a morning of pelting rain and high winds), the Queen wrote a note to her bridegroom:

Dearest . . . how are you today, and have you slept well? I have rested very well and feel very comfortable today. What weather! I believe, however, the rain will cease.

Send one word when you, my most dearly beloved bridegroom, will be ready.

Thy ever-faithful
Victoria R.[3]

The gown she had chosen was pure white, unshaded by any of the silver lace or embroidery which had characterized royal wedding-dresses of the past century. It was of satin, trimmed with Honiton lace, with a veil of the same held in place by a wreath of orange-flowers and some unobtrusive diamond-headed pins. She wore a diamond necklace and ear-rings and, the only colour, a sapphire brooch which had been Albert's wedding-gift to her.

At 12.30 Victoria drove from Buckingham Palace to the Chapel Royal, St James's, with her mother and her Mistress of the Robes, and on her arrival she took the arm of her uncle the Duke of Sussex, who was to 'give her away'. Albert was there already, having entered to the tune of 'See the Conquering Hero Come', and Victoria's arrival was heralded by a fanfare of trumpets. Behind her came a dozen bridesmaids, the daughters of peers, dressed in white with white-rose wreaths and carrying her long train. One of them, Lady Wilhelmina Stanhope, gives us an eye-witness account of the ceremony:

Her Majesty was quite calm and composed. When Prince Albert was asked whether he would take this woman for his wife, she turned full round and looked into his face as he replied, "I will." Her own responses were given in the same clear, musical tone of voice with which she read her speeches in the House of Lords, and in much the same manner. . . .

The Queen gave her hand to her husband, who led her back through the rooms (where her reception was enthusiastic) to the Throne Room, where the royal family, the Coburgs etc signed their names in the Registry Book. . . .

After this, she took her departure down the back stairs, at the foot of which I consigned the train to Prince Albert's care, who seemed a little nervous about getting into the carriage with a lady with a tail 6 yards long and voluminous in proportion.[4]

Those carriage-rides to and from the Chapel Royal, and the couple's drive from London to Windsor, were the only chance Victoria's subjects had to see anything of the wedding, but the streets were full of cheering crowds, and, after all, she was only away three days on honeymoon before her work called her back to the Palace.

Then, the Queen was as busy as ever, Albert unemployed—and not enjoying the experience. He found that he was expected to be ready at a moment's notice to go to his wife, to be petted, to play the piano to her, to read aloud, and the only share of her work he was allotted was blotting her signature on the state papers she had signed. Victoria, on the other hand, was delighted with marriage, with its intimacies as well as with parading Albert before the Court, and she wrote excitedly in her diary of his putting on her stockings for her and of her fascination with his performance at shaving, an operation she had never seen before. And almost immediately it became clear that Albert had fulfilled the main function of a royal consort: Victoria was pregnant. Just nine months and eleven days after their wedding, her first child was born, a girl, another Victoria.

If the nation was satisfied with Albert and Victoria's promptness in giving them an heir, the Queen herself was furious at being 'caught' so soon. She hated the discomfort of her 'condition' and the lassitude it induced, but even more she disliked the inquisitive stares that followed her everywhere. She was disgusted when she found that, even before the first baby had been christened, the second was on the way. For the next few months, Victoria was at her worst, sulky, rebellious, impossible to please, always ready to burst into noisy tears or temper—at one point she even dashed a cup of tea into her husband's face. His patience with her was sometimes calming, sometimes only the more enfuriating.

However, while the Queen was laid low with her pregnancies, the Prince demonstrated to her his talent for tactful dealings with her ministers and his ability to make précis of the complicated documents which absorbed so much of her time. Soon, the harness was adjusted to suit them both, and with every year that passed, Albert found himself allowed to pull more weight in his wife's government duties. At home, too, she came to accord him complete mastery of the household and the prime responsibility for the upbringing of their children, which he saw not only as a pleasure but as a sacred duty.

It is to Victoria's credit, however, that of the nine children to whom she gave birth between 1840 and 1857, all were reared safely; the youngest boy, Leopold, was tainted with a dangerous blood-disease, haemophilia, and he was always a worry to his parents, but by careful treatment he lived to manhood. In order of birth there was Victoria, Princess Royal (born 1840), Albert Edward, Prince of Wales (1841), Alice (1843), Alfred (1844), Helena (1846), Louise (1848), Arthur (1850), Leopold (1853) and Beatrice (1857).

Pressure on the eldest boy, 'Bertie', because of his future as king, marred his childhood, for Albert saw in his son weaknesses that must be eradicated before they could spoil his character, and year after year the father fought the son's indolence, his lack of interest in his studies, an inclination to quarrel and to resent correction, faults that were only accentuated by the diligence and docility of his elder sister. 'Vicky' was always Albert's favourite, and she was the most like him of all the children.

Though Albert applied himself earnestly to Britain and its interests, he was, as he said, "a true Coburg and Gotha man", with an avid interest in German affairs. The nation was then still fragmented in numerous kingdoms, duchies and principalities, and it was the great wish of Albert's life to see it united, preferably under Prussia, the strongest of the

Protestant kingdoms. Anxious to gain influence in the founding of the new Germany, Albert planned to have his eldest daughter married to the eventual heir to the Prussian crown, Prince Frederick William, and he was delighted when their first meeting, when Vicky was ten, 'Fritz' twenty, produced a friendship between them. Vicky was still only fourteen when the Prussian Prince came again, but he came with his parents' permission to propose to her and quickly gained Albert and Victoria's blessing too.

The royal family were then on holiday at Balmoral, in Scotland, and Fritz found a chance to speak to Vicky in a few moments alone while they were riding behind the main party. He began by saying that he hoped to see her soon in Prussia, then that he would like her to stay there forever. She blushed; was she annoyed, he asked—"Oh no!"—at which he put out his hand and shook hers and begged to be allowed to tell her parents. But Vicky insisted on keeping that pleasure for herself. That evening she entered her parents' room eager to tell the news. Had she always loved Fritz, her mother asked. Always! Vicky exclaimed. And then there were kisses and embraces, and Fritz came in and there were more. It was all the best possible blending of policy and love.

Since Vicky was still so young (and since Albert had plans to intensify her education to fit her for a place in German political life), the wedding was not to be until January 1858, by which time the Princess would be seventeen. In the years in between, Vicky never wavered. Even at the wedding, when her mother admitted to being more nervous than she had been at her own (and when she trembled so much while one of the photographs was being taken that her figure comes out a blur), still Vicky was perfectly composed, a tiny, childlike figure in a huge crinoline of white moire antique, flounced with Honiton lace and wreathed with orange-flowers and myrtle.

There had been a little unpleasantness with the Prussian royal family, who had wanted the wedding to be over in Germany, but Queen Victoria had been adamant that her daughter must be married at home. In fact, Vicky found her welcome in Prussia not as warm as it might have been. She found herself mistrusted, as a foreigner, and discovered that her position was to be nothing more than ornamental. Her husband appreciated the intellect which everyone else seemed to condemn, and he did his best to stand between her and the worst criticism, but he was out from dawn till late at night with the army, and Vicky was left to make polite conversation with German ladies who, for the most part, looked upon her with suspicion. Even the birth of her first child, in 1859, did not put her right in the eyes of the Court and the royal family, for it was a difficult labour and during the delivery the child's left arm was so twisted that it was to be virtually useless.

Vicky's was to be the last royal marriage in Britain made for political ends. When her parents came to seek a bride for her brother Bertie, towards the end of the 1850s, they knew that, with his already pro-

nounced tastes, he must have beauty in his bride, whatever her homeland and status might be. But beauty was in short supply among the
in-bred princesses of Protestant Europe. One after another was written
off, and at last Victoria and Albert had to admit that the only feasible
candidate was the Princess Alexandra of Schleswig-Holstein-Sonder-
burg-Glucksburg, despite the fact that, with her father heir to the Danish
throne, and with Prussia casting a greedy eye on Danish territories, the
alliance had political perils. But Alexandra was a beauty, there was no
denying that, and her character was blameless, her education good—for a
princess. So in September 1861 Vicky contrived an 'accidental' meeting
between her brother and Alexandra, while they were sightseeing in the
cathedral at Speyer, and Bertie came away from it obviously attracted.

That did not, however, prevent his having an affaire, that autumn,
with a young actress, Nellie Clifden. When Albert found out, he was
appalled. The Prince Consort had suffered a good deal over his son's
misdemeanours, and now, with this new blow, coming at a time when he
was already exhausted from overwork and grieving from a series of
family deaths, he was shattered. Early in December, he admitted that he
felt ill, and the royal physicians were summoned. It was typhoid, not
always a killer but, with the Prince's low state of health and apparent lack
of will to live, now swift and fatal. He died on 14th December.

For a time Victoria's family, ministers and servants feared for her
sanity. She would weep wildly, sit silent and withdrawn, alternate her
moods of despair and self-possession until no one knew what to expect of
her. Sometimes she would mourn over the happy times in the past,
sometimes over the many, many occasions when she had hurt her
husband and annoyed him. Even the sight of her children was too much
for her, and the Prince of Wales, whom to a great extent she blamed for
'worrying' Albert into his grave, gave her feelings of deep revulsion. She
longed to die too, she said, in the worst moments, though at others she
would resolve to live on, to serve her country and bring up her children.
She would be as Albert would wish her to be.

One solace to the Queen, and her intermediary with the ministers she
refused to meet, was her second daughter, Princess Alice, a calm, quiet
girl of seventeen. So useful was Alice to her mother at that time that
Victoria might have been tempted to keep the girl with her permanently,
to act as a buffer between her and the difficulties of widowed life, but
Albert had decreed that Alice was to marry, and Victoria could not begin
her new life by flouting his will.

Back in February 1860, yet another Prince of Orange had been brought
over to Britain as a potential bridegroom—but, like his two predecessors,
he was to be rejected. At one point, when Alice heard that her younger
sister Helena would have him if she would not, she declared that "she
should die no other death than her sister being preferred to her and that
she wanted to be Queen of Holland",[5] but 'Citron', as the family called
him, was so shy, giving such an impression of rudeness and utter

indifference, that even Alice could find no good in him, and in the end neither princess took advantage of the offer. A few months later, the older, more sophisticated Prince Louis of Hesse-Darmstadt had more success. Victoria and Albert liked him, and Alice was enthusiastic. She indiscreetly told a girl-friend that, "when they parted, [they] exchanged pocket-handkerchiefs, which were quite in a sop with their tears, and she wears night and day a little miniature of him tied with a bit of velvet which she fears won't last as she is always rubbing it."[6]

And so now, with Alice anxious to marry Louis, Victoria roused herself sufficiently from her grief to plan a quiet wedding for them, at Osborne House on the Isle of Wight, the house which Albert had planned, built and hallowed and to which Victoria had retired in the first months of widowhood. Even then, with just the family, bridesmaids and a few courtiers present at the ceremony (in the State Dining-Room), the Queen could not bear to be stared at, and she sat in a corner, shielded by her sons, while the wedding was in progress.

Like Vicky's marriage, Alice's was perfectly happy, even though she too had her troubles over in Germany—hers were comparative poverty and the irksome ritual of a tiny but etiquette-ridden Court.

Both Alice and Vicky returned home to witness the wedding of the Prince of Wales in 1863. Alexandra had been told of the Prince's 'fall from grace', but it had not overly shocked her, and they had become engaged in Belgium, under the supervision of the now septuagenarian King Leopold, in the autumn of 1862. Alexandra was obviously in love with Bertie (she told one of his sisters: "You perhaps think I like marrying your brother for his position, but if he was a cowboy I should love him just the same and would marry no one else"[7]), and Bertie seemed so too, though, given as he was to brief enthusiasms, his pessimistic mother was not convinced on that point.

Alexandra and her parents landed at Queenborough on 7th March 1863, and three days later she and Bertie were married at St George's Chapel, Windsor. Besides the royal family, the chapel was crowded with peers and peeresses, ministers and foreign dignitaries, too avid for all the sights for Queen Victoria to brave them: she sat high above the body of the church, in a little balcony-room known as 'Catherine of Aragon's Closet', which had a fine view of the whole proceedings (though she did miss the moment when her Prussian grandson, 'Willy', bit one of his young uncles on the leg, when they tried to restrain the child from rushing after a Scottish dirk from his costume, which he had thrown across the floor).

Bertie entered first, wearing Garter robes, and then, to the strains of Handel's Processional March, Alexandra, on her father's arm and followed by eight bridesmaids, swept down the aisle. Her wedding-dress was a vast crinoline of white satin covered with lace, tulle 'bouffants' and wreaths of flowers—so many wreaths that guests were left with the strong impression that there was too much 'greenery' hung round her.

For a while, the Prince of Wales was a devoted husband, and there is no doubt that he had a real affection for his wife as long as he lived, but, like his Hanoverian forebears and like at least half the Coburg men, he was not naturally monogamous; at first discreetly, then with cool heedlessness of family and public opinion, he took one mistress after another—as well as enjoying the varied sexual amenities of foreign capitals and resorts. Alexandra, occupied with her children, wisely made no open complaint against her husband's habits and only now and then sought relief from London gossip in long holidays with her Danish relations.

Her Danish relations . . . that was the real disadvantage of the match. When, in November 1863, the old King of Denmark died and Alexandra's father succeeded him as Christian IX, Prussia laid claims to the formerly Danish duchies of Schleswig and Holstein, and a couple of months later the two kingdoms were at war. With letters from Vicky on the one hand, furious that Britain would not support Prussia, and with Bertie and 'Alix' fulminating on behalf of Denmark, Queen Victoria had to lay a ban on mention of the disputed duchies in her hearing. But it went deeper than that: Vicky's Fritz was in the Prussian army, even then invading Schleswig-Holstein, and Alix was becoming frantic for the safety of her family. In her distress, the Princess of Wales gave birth prematurely to her first child, Albert Victor, in January 1864. However, the war was brief, and no member of the royal families of Prussia and Denmark was killed.

In view of the situation, Queen Victoria might have been wiser to have put aside her hopes for her third daughter, Helena, marrying Prince Christian of Schleswig-Holstein, for he was the younger brother of the main candidate for the duchies, against Alexandra's father. But Victoria had set her heart on having at least one daughter remain with her, and since Christian had no commitments abroad, he could spend his life, with Helena, in attendance on his mother-in-law. Helena had seen him a couple of times before he was invited to Britain in the autumn of 1865, and though he was fifteen years her senior, and seemed even older, she seemed quite content in her mother's choice.

Their wedding, in the royal chapel at Windsor, was celebrated on 5th July 1866, and, like Alice's, it was overshadowed by gloom—but for a different reason. A few weeks before, Prussia had gone to war with Austria: now, Vicky's Fritz was in the army that opposed Alice's Louis, who, like many South German princes, had chosen the Austrian side. In Berlin, Vicky was praying for her husband's safety and grieving for one of her sons, who had died of meningitis in June; at Darmstadt, Alice was forced to send her two daughters to her mother, as the war came nearer, and when she gave birth to another child, early in July, she did not know if her husband was dead or alive. With the pro-Austrian Christian arrived for the wedding, and with Bertie and Alix violently anti-Prussian, the Queen's household was prone to unpleasant silences on certain matters.

Of course the fear, the wounds, the deaths, were borne by those on the battlefield, by the poor, by those whose homes and land were devastated by the two armies, but that cannot discount the suffering of the princesses safe at home but racked by uncertainty. Nor could it diminish the impression left in Queen Victoria's mind that foreign marriages, made for political alliance or for personal feeling, were more trouble than they were worth. Five of her children remained unmarried, and in the years to come she would neither try to influence any of them to marry in the interests of Britain's foreign policy nor look upon foreign matches for love without doubt as to their outcome. On the other hand, of course, she would not admit that Albert, in marrying Vicky to Fritz to cement Anglo-Prussian relations, had made a mistake. It was not until 1914 that that became clear, when Victoria's children and grandchildren learned the pain of a royal caste divided against itself.

The Later Victorians

In view of Queen Victoria's anguish on behalf of her children in the European wars of the 1860s, her encouragement of her daughter Louise to marry not a foreign prince but a Scottish nobleman, John Campbell, Marquess of Lorne, should cause no surprise. "Times have changed," the Queen wrote to the Prince of Wales when he showed signs of objecting, "great foreign alliances are looked on as causes of trouble and anxiety and are of no good. What could be more painful than the position in which our family were placed during the wars with Denmark, and between Prussia and Austria? Every family feeling was rent asunder, and we were powerless."[1]

In 1868 it had been rumoured that Princess Louise was to marry either the Crown Prince of Denmark or the perennial William of Orange, and in 1869 her sister Vicky championed her husband's cousin Adalbert of Prussia, but that same autumn the Queen was superintending Lorne's wooing of Louise, and when he proposed to her, her mother gave enthusiastic approval.

Abroad, and especially in Prussia, there was a good deal of resentment at the Queen's 'condescension', for the British aristocracy was looked upon as far below even the most minor Continental princes, despite the fact that most of them had a good deal more money and equally ancient pedigrees. In Britain, however, the match was generally popular, and *The Times* asked its readers to agree that the marriage was "in harmony with the principle of life Her Majesty has prescribed for herself". "The Queen," it continued, "has preferred the happiness of her daughter to a pedantic adherence to traditional principles of state policy. . . ." It pointed out that

> . . . a new stage in the development of the functions of the Crown has been reached. The jealousy that was at one time felt at alliances of subjects and persons of the blood royal was due to fear that members of the family of the subject thus honoured might obtain a dangerous influence in the councils of state, or even foment intrigue affecting the succession. The supremacy of the House of Commons has completely destroyed the force of these apprehensions.[2]

(Even so, when, two decades later, the widower Prime Minister Lord Rosebery showed signs of wanting to marry Princess Victoria of Wales, that was felt to be taking the 'new stage' too far, and the idea was quickly scotched. Nor, probably, would such a marriage be approved today.)

Though Princess Louise had had more freedom than her elder sisters in choosing a husband, ironically she found less happiness in marriage than they. As Marchioness of Lorne, later Duchess of Argyll, she was seen apart from her husband more and more as the years passed, and though there was never an open breach between them, not even a formal separation, it was generally agreed that they were happier apart.

When the search for a bride for Prince Alfred had begun, back in the 1860s, there was no thought of scanning the British peerage for her, even though the choice of Protestant princesses seemed to the Queen discouragingly narrow. 'Affie' was turning out to be so much like his elder brother, so obviously a prey to sexual temptations, that Victoria saw marriage as the only means of 'saving' him. So she was more amenable than she might have been when she found out that her son had set his heart on marrying the Grand Duchess Marie of Russia, of whose nation, family, Court and religion she had deep mistrust.

As to religion, Marie's being of the Orthodox Church was no bar to her marriage, as it would have been had she been a Catholic, but it did add weight to the Tsar's insistence that his daughter be married in her own country. Victoria could not, of course, attempt the journey to Russia herself in the depths of winter (the wedding was in January 1874), but Vicky, Fritz and Prince Arthur did, to 'support' Affie.

There were, in fact, two weddings. The first, in the Imperial Chapel of the Winter Palace of St Petersburg, was performed according to Orthodox tradition, with the full ritual of 'wedding crowns' and the couple's procession round the altar, holding lighted candles, with the incense, the chanting, the mystery of the ancient rites; the second, immediately afterwards, was the Anglican service, conducted by the Dean of Westminster.

While St Petersburg was celebrating, with bells pealing out for days over the city, and with the Court and their foreign visitors regaled with dinners, balls, concerts and moonlight sleigh-rides, back in Britain, in Alfred's duchy of Edinburgh, a great bonfire was lit on 'Arthur's Seat' above the Scottish capital, to mark the day.

The Queen was not much impressed by her new daughter-in-law's looks when they met, and Marie was certainly haughty and somewhat disdainful of the comparative informality of the British Court, but the marriage proved reasonably successful. There were four daughters, whom Marie brought up sensibly, and one son, who died young; Affie's extra-marital affaires were handled discreetly, and in 1893 his wife's ambitions were satisfied when he succeeded his uncle Ernest as Duke of Saxe-Coburg-Gotha.

In contrast to his two elder brothers, Prince Arthur, Duke of Connaught, gave his mother no cause for concern or complaint. His army career suited him, and his personal life was comparatively virtuous. The Queen was disappointed when he chose to marry a Prussian princess of one of the junior lines, for Vicky's experiences had given her a new wariness of the Prussians, but Arthur's Louise proved as well behaved, as well intentioned and, it must be admitted, as dull as her model husband.

The youngest of the Queen's sons, Leopold—the prince who suffered from haemophilia—was less satisfactory. The doctors insisted that he must live very quietly, very carefully, for the least abrasion of the skin could lead to uncontrollable bleeding, and any jar or bruise might cause internal bleeding that could kill him, but Leopold would not settle for invalidism and often enfuriated (and worried) his mother with his gratuitous risks. In April 1882 he married a very minor German princess, Helen of Waldeck, but just two years later, while she was carrying her second child, one of his accidents at last proved fatal.

Leopold was the second of Victoria's children to die: Princess Alice had been carried off by diphtheria back in 1878, leaving several children whom the Queen mothered as her own. In 1884 she went to Darmstadt to attend the wedding of the eldest, another Victoria, to Prince Louis of Battenberg—and encountered more than she had expected. First, only hours after the wedding, the bride's father secretly married his mistress— but not secretly enough: even before the wedding party had left for home, Victoria had got wind of the marriage, and she immediately demanded that it be annulled. It was.

Then there arose a problem not so easily solved, for at Darmstadt her youngest daughter, Beatrice, had met Prince Henry of Battenberg, brother of her niece's bridegroom, and had 'formed an attachment to him', as the Victorians would say. Victoria had been determined that this last daughter should have no distractions from home duties, and she had managed to keep Beatrice single into her middle twenties: now the Queen was appalled at the thought of losing her, of being 'alone', but nothing she could say could dissuade Beatrice from wanting to marry her 'Liko', and even when the Queen refused to speak to her—for some two months, the Princess remained adamant. With tact, but firmly, the family took Beatrice's side, and in the end Victoria was brought to consent to the marriage. After all, Liko was as landless, as free of responsibilities, as Christian had been when he was brought over to marry Helena, and he seemed only too glad to exchange comparative poverty and an aimless life on the Continent for one of security, comfort and a by-no-means arduous career in Britain.

In fact, that very obscurity of the Battenbergs which was so acceptable to Victoria's schemes was a dreadful stumbling-block to acceptance of the marriage abroad, notably in Berlin. Vicky's parents-in-law were even more shocked than they had been in 1870, when Louise married Lorne, for the Battenbergs were the products of a morganatic marriage—that is, a marriage between a prince and a commoner, in which the offspring could not inherit their father's rank. One of Victoria's reasons for staging her daughter's wedding at the parish church of Whippingham, on the Isle of Wight (near Osborne House), was that it was so small that she would have an excuse not to invite the Prussians, but apart from that, the island was very dear to her, with its associations with Albert.

After the wedding, on 23rd July 1885, the Queen wrote in her diary:

A happier-looking couple could seldom be seen kneeling at the altar together. It was very touching. I stood very close to my dear child, who looked very sweet, pure and calm. Though I stood for the ninth time near a child and for the fifth time near a daughter, at the altar, I think I never felt more deeply than I did on this occasion, though full of confidence. When the Blessing had been given, I tenderly embraced my darling 'Baby'.[3]

Beatrice gave birth to the first of her four children in 1886, her last in 1891, making up the number of Queen Victoria's grandchildren to its final thirty-nine (though some died in infancy); but by then the Queen already had several great-grandchildren, the eldest of them just entering her teens, so there was a confusing overlapping of generations as well as a large crowd of young people to be brought together at the family reunions.

In the late-nineteenth century, the old royal way of marrying for policy was at last dying out, on the Continent as well as in Britain, but with young princes and princesses meeting so often, it was inevitable that they should—if not fall in love—at least attract each other sufficiently to marry, and so preserve the royal caste into the twentieth century. It scarcely seemed necessary for any of them to marry outside their own circle, so numerous were the royal, ducal and princely Houses of Europe in that period—though marriages were still only very rarely made across the chasm between Catholic and Protestant.

Queen Victoria thoroughly enjoyed the business of marrying off her grandchildren, always with an eye to their happiness rather than their aggrandisement. Only in Prussia was her influence over marriage negligible.

In 1871, Prussia had been victorious in war with France, and in the triumphant aftermath Prince Albert's dream of a united Germany had been fulfilled, with the creation of the German Empire and the King of Prussia becoming the first 'Kaiser', William I. But William and his Chancellor, Bismarck, had no thought of establishing the empire on the comparatively democratic lines which Albert had advocated, and while they distrusted Vicky's Fritz for his 'advanced' political ideas, they distrusted her more, as the chief influence on him. Worse, Bismarck convinced Vicky's eldest son of the error—and dangers—of his parents' political stance, setting him firmly against them. When Vicky's father-in-law died in 1888, and her Fritz became Kaiser, he was already suffering from cancer of the throat and had no time to set in train the reforms on which he and his wife had set their hearts, before his death some three months later. William II, from the very outset of his reign, showed his mother that she had no place in his political life and, while he evinced the utmost affection and respect for his British grandmother, he left her perfectly aware just how ineffective her influence over him would be if ever their nations' interests conflicted.

Back in the 1870s, Vicky and Fritz had taken their daughter 'Moretta's' part against the old Kaiser and 'Willy', when she fell in love with Alexander of Battenberg. A part of the opposition came, as we have seen, from the family's lowly status in Germany, but partly from Alexander's acceptance in 1879 of the principality of Bulgaria, under Russian patronage, for Germany was already looking suspiciously at Russian influence in the Balkans. Moretta's grandfather the Kaiser forbade her absolutely to marry 'Sandro' of Battenberg, and Queen Victoria was powerless to intervene.

Another family which, like the Battenbergs, dared not expect fine marriages within Germany was that of Teck, descended from the morganatic marriage of a member of the royal House of Württemberg. Just as there had been some horror when Victoria's daughter Beatrice married Henry of Battenberg, so there was when her grandson Albert Victor, second in line to the British throne, became engaged to Mary of Teck in 1891. The fact that Albert Victor—'Eddy', Duke of Clarence, was a thoroughly disreputable young man, and 'May' a fine, dignified, well principled, well educated young woman, did not even up their inequality of rank in certain eyes. But Queen Victoria did not share German prejudices. To her, May was an ideal match for Eddy, one of those valiant girls who would take on, and improve, a less than perfect bridegroom. In fact, May and Eddy were distantly related, her mother being Victoria's cousin Mary of Cambridge, and since the Princess had been born, and partly brought up, in Britain, the match was scarcely regarded as a new link with Germany by Victoria's subjects.

The engagement was announced on 6th December 1891, the wedding-day set for 27th February 1892, but on 7th January, the day before his twenty-ninth birthday, Eddy took a chill—which led to influenza—to pneumonia—to death. At his funeral May's wedding-wreath of orange-blossom lay on his coffin.

Had Eddy lived, had May failed to improve both his morals and his sense of duty, what would the British monarchy have become? Certainly Eddy had shown no aptitude or taste for anything but extravagance and debauchery. As it was, his place in the royal succession was taken by his brother George, Duke of York, a young sailor of exemplary character and diligence.

In the days after Eddy's death, May and George had been together a good deal. Add her pitiful situation and his solicitude to the fine sense of duty (and of history) inbred in both of them, and the inevitable happened: on 3rd May 1893 they became engaged.

The original wedding had been planned to take place in St George's Chapel, Windsor, like most of its recent predecessors, but since the Chapel had been used for Eddy's funeral, no one could think it appropriate now, so it had to be the Chapel Royal at St James's Palace. (There was still no thought of using Westminster Abbey; centuries had passed since a royal wedding there.) Londoners were delighted with the choice.

By the 1890s there was an intensity of feeling for, and interest in, the royal family unprecedented in the monarchy's centuries of history. Queen Victoria had been on the throne nearly sixty years, and many of her subjects had managed to ascribe political and social developments of that period and Britain's ever-advancing prosperity to her very rule; every schoolchild knew the story of her life, and magazines and newspapers frequently carried news and pictures of members of the royal family, to satisfy an ever more avid curiosity about their lives. Now, some of the women's magazines produced a 'royal wedding number', with details of the trousseau May was collecting for her wedding (her second trousseau in as many years); visitors crowded into London's Imperial Institute for a glimpse of the royal wedding-gifts, the first to be put on public display, and were rewarded with the sight of *objets d'art*, plate, china, glass, napery and jewellery to the tune of £300,000. Spectators were thick on the ground on the morning of the wedding, thronging the route of the bridal procession, along Constitution Hill, Piccadilly and St James's Street, which were garlanded with flowers strung between 'Venetian masts'.

Before Victoria left for the ceremony, the bride was brought in to see her. "Her dress was very simple," the Queen wrote in her diary, "of white satin with a silver design of roses, shamrocks, thistles and orange-flowers interwoven. On her head she had a small wreath of orange-flowers, myrtle and white heather, surmounted by a diamond necklace I gave her, which can also be worn as a diadem, and her mother's wedding-veil."[4] The dress was "simple"? Not to modern tastes. The material, a satin brocade, had been specially woven, with its national emblems—and 'true-love knots'—in silver; the bodice was cut perfectly to fit May's fashionable hour-glass figure; the front of the skirt was left open to reveal a plain satin 'slip' beneath it, but the overskirt was lavishly festooned with lace and sprays of orange-blossoms. Only the wedding-veil was on a modest scale: the long silk veil interwoven with may-blossom which had been prepared for her wedding to Eddy had been put aside, as too sad in its associations, and its replacement, the Duchess of Teck's veil, was little more than a short lace scarf.

The ceremony over, there was another royal wedding 'first': Queen Victoria led George and May onto the central balcony of Buckingham Palace and presented them to the cheering crowds. But even then the throng did not disperse: when the couple drove out of the Palace, showered with rice by wedding-guests, more cheers met them, and on down the Mall, with its garlands and triumphal arches, through the City of London to Liverpool Street Station (especially cleaned up and hung with flags for the occasion)—and so away, to Sandringham, the Prince of Wales's Norfolk estate, for the honeymoon.

A few months later, George wrote to May:

> You know by this time that I never do anything by halves; when I asked you to marry me, I was very fond of you but not very much in love with you, but I saw in *you* the person I was capable of loving most deeply, if you only returned that love. . . . I have tried to understand you and to know you, and with the happy result that I know now that I do *love* you, darling girl, with all my *heart*, and am simply *devoted* to you. . . . I *adore you, sweet May.* I can't say more than that.[6]

The future King George V was always to find it difficult to "say more than that", to express his emotions at any time, and May was equally reticent, but it was a love that endured, one that enabled them to support each other through a world war and dismal days of recession.

Of George's three sisters, daughters of the Prince of Wales, one was already married before him. This was Louise, the eldest, who, like the aunt for whom she was named, married a Scotsman. Alexander Duff, Earl of Fife (created Duke at his marriage), was forty years old, to her twenty-two, when they married in July 1889—in the little chapel of Buckingham Palace, at the shy bride's particular request. But Queen Victoria was not the only royal mother to grudge daughters their husbands, wanting to keep them with her: Alexandra, Princess of Wales, was the same—with far less excuse. Louise had gone, and Princess Maud escaped at the age of twenty-six, when she married her mother's nephew Charles of Denmark, later King of Norway, but the third of the Wales princesses, Victoria, had to bear the brunt of her mother's possessiveness until Alexandra's death in 1925, when she, Victoria, was in her late fifties.

Queen Victoria had no objection to the marriage of first cousins—where the families were healthy (she had not realized the extent to which haemophilia was being transmitted through her daughters). In 1888 Vicky's son Henry married Alice's Irene, and six years later Affie's daughter Victoria Melita married Alice's Ernest Louis. This was the famous 'Coburg wedding', for by then Affie was ensconced in his father's childhood home as Duke of Saxe-Coburg-Gotha, and it was the occasion for one of the largest of family reunions. In Britain, the illustrated magazines carried pictures of the couple and the festivities, and they detailed the gowns and jewels of the ladies with as much zest as if the ceremony had been performed at home.

In fact, the wedding was somewhat overshadowed by the announcement, the next day, of the engagement of the bridegroom's sister 'Alicky' and the bride's Russian cousin Nicholas, the Tsarevitch (prompted partly, some said, by Alicky's unwillingness to remain at home, 'playing second fiddle' to her new sister-in-law). It was a real love-match, but it was worse-fated than any arranged marriage could be, for though the couple were supremely happy in each other, not only did Alicky bring haemophilia in her blood, transmitting it to her only son, but her meddling in Russian government and her infatuation with the powers of the 'mad monk' Rasputin were to prove important factors contributing to her husband's overthrow in 1917 and the murder of both of them, and their five children, in 1918.

For the most part, the marriages which were made under the benign eye of Queen Victoria were happy ones—and why should they not be happy? After all, counting up the royal and imperial families of Europe, and the ducal, grand ducal and princely Houses, and remembering the size of families in those days, there was a broad network comprising every shade of personality and temperament in which princes and princesses could make the choice of marriage-partner. So frequent, so large, were 'gatherings of the clans' in the late-nineteenth century, at the spas and seaside resorts of the Continent as well as in the palaces, that young people had the chance to meet at least as many others as any modern teenager does in the course of a year, and with the security of common background and expectations. Even in the past couple of decades, royal marriages have resulted from meetings at 'international' weddings and jubilees: that of ex-King Constantine of Greece and the Danish Princess Anne Marie, for example, and of his sister Sofia and the present King of Spain.

Equally, of course, there were unhappy marriages, though far fewer than one might expect. There was the Coburg couple, Victoria Melita and her cousin/husband 'Ernie', for example: they were just incompatible, with no shared interests, no tolerance of each other's faults, no understanding of each other's needs, and they divorced in 1901, some years after they had separated. Another failure was the marriage of Princess Helena's daughter Marie Louise and Aribert of Anhalt, which was annulled (by his father, according to an ancient prerogative of his title) in December 1900. In her autobiography, Princess Marie Louise was restrained in her account of the break-down of her marriage, confessing that some of the blame was hers that it had not worked, but a lady-in-waiting to the Queen, Marie Mallet, heard the inside story:

Her Prince Aribert has made up his mind to divorce her on the pretext that she is too fond of England and has no children; he has no real cause and does not even attempt to trump up one. He has squandered all her money, i.e. her allowance from England, her jewels etc, and has now seized her despatch-boxes and broken open her locked drawers. Princess Thora [her sister] says all he will find are letters from her calling the Germans pigs and brutes, but I fear that will strengthen his case. It appears that every rotten little German principality can make its own 'Haus' laws and can issue edicts for divorce and re-marriage with the greatest possible ease. I call it horrible and thank my stars I am not 'Made in Germany'.[6]

Maybe Queen Victoria called it 'horrible' too, for she telegraphed her grand-daughter to come home.

The Queen died in January 1901. She was eighty-one years old and had reigned for sixty-three years. Three of her nine children had died before her (Affie, Leopold and Alice), and Vicky would die before the year was out; but her grandchildren were numerous and mainly thriving, every year increasing the number of her great-grandchildren—who were themselves marrying as the new century opened. 'The Grandmother of Europe', Victoria was called in her last years, when her descendants were to be found in so many palaces on the Continent. (Grand-daughters of the Queen became Queens Consort of Spain, Romania, Greece and Norway, one was Crown Princess of Sweden; some were in Russia, many were ensconced in the greater or lesser Houses of Germany.) At the time it was a matter for pride, and her subjects could be forgiven for believing that it would be unthinkable for the cousins ever to go to war against each other. But statesmen did not trust to royal alliances now: even in the early years of the new century there were mutterings about a conflict with Germany looming ahead.

When war did break out, in 1918, Queen Victoria's descendants sublimated family feeling in an upsurge of patriotism, cousin arming against cousin, even brothers and sisters finding themselves enemies. Britain's King George V allied with his cousin (through their mothers) Tsar Nicholas II against his cousin the Kaiser, and in their wake trailed other cousins, following the lead of the Great Powers into four years of European war.

Thus, for the exalted, as well as for the 'common man', the First World War was a ghastly tragedy. The emperors, kings, dukes and princes were not the ones who rotted in trenches, burned alive in shot-down planes and drowned in icy seas: that was the lot of those 'bound to obey', their subjects, sent to fight and die for a cause that few understood, but even the most bellicose of rulers—even the Kaiser, whose 'war-mongering' has been blamed by so many for the outbreak of war—felt the anguish of a royal caste divided against itself. The men and women in the palaces of Europe may have been immune from the privations suffered by their subjects, but they were not immune from the anguish of calling brothers and cousins 'the enemy'.

Once upon a time kings had supported each other against rebellious subjects. Now, at the end of the war, there was no one to shore up the crumbling Russian Empire and to save its Tsar from death, or to raise a voice for the Kaiser when he was dethroned after his defeat, the German dukes and princes falling with him as the Republic was established. Other monarchies never really recovered and were left weak, easily overthrown in years to come.

In the face of the horrors of war and this tremendous political upheaval, it seems a derisory footnote to say that the new age saw the end of the royal marriage system as it had existed for centuries, a system that Britain was among the first to discard—but it was so. Nations had come to trust to the council-tables of politicians, not to the beds of kings, for policies of peace and international understanding.

The Twentieth Century

'For As Long As Ye Both Shall Love'

'Love, love, love,' chant the singers of the late-twentieth century. 'Love is all you need.' Love is an obsession, the search for it begun in the early teens; by the age of twenty, one young man in ten is married, more than a third of all girls. Today, love equates to happiness, the happiness of the individual is god, and where love—or marriage—turns sour, the search is resumed until the happy state is again achieved.

For the vast majority, however, marriages result from an accidental meeting rather than a conscious search for a mate, but though some people meet future marriage-partners at school or at work, they are far more likely to do so at dances, clubs or public houses, where they are 'dressed to kill'—to attract members of the opposite sex. Young Conservative Clubs have a high reputation as marriage-marts, and so have Young Farmers' Clubs in the country, while in the suburbs of towns and cities, the ubiquitous youth clubs of post-war years fostered marriages in plenty. One North London club, attached to a Methodist church, opened in 1964 with a nucleus of about forty members, from whom emerged four marriages and a constant interchange over weeks and months of that 'pair-bonding' that so interests modern sociologists. Far removed from the experts' jargon, there is a whole new vocabulary of mating: a boy and girl 'go out' together; after a few weeks they are 'going steady'—though the old word 'courting' is still used in the north.

'Going to bed' is often the next development. Now that so many young people live in their own flats and bed-sitting-rooms, their freedom to entertain privately, without parental supervision, has enlarged considerably, and so has their freedom for sexual relations in comfort rather than on park-benches and in cars. Advances in effective contraception in the past half century were designed originally for controlling the number of children of married couples, but the various contraceptive devices and pills have long since been diverted to the use of the unmarried too, though not so completely as to prevent all unwanted births: sixty per cent of teenaged brides are pregnant on their wedding-day. But in fact, while some couples marry when a child is already on the way, others 'regularize their union' specifically to have children, once they are reasonably sure that they can 'be happy' together for the rest of their lives.

Even in those circumstances, there is likely to be pressure on them to go through a traditional-style wedding—a 'white wedding', even if the bride's white gown can no longer be taken to connote her virginity. Frequently it is the parents, rather than the couple themselves, who insist on the traditional 'pomp and circumstance', especially if the bride's mother was herself a war-bride, denied the 'trimmings' by war-time austerity and shortage of money. The fact that the wedding may take place in a registrar's office by no means rules out the other traditional elements: it is now quite common for a bride to appear in wedding-gown and veil at a registrar's office and for the party to go on to a home or hotel reception, where once that type of ceremony was for those who could not afford 'anything better'—or for the few atheists who could not bring themselves to use church, chapel or synagogue.

English law offers a choice of banns or licence for marriage, but they take several weeks to come into effect, as a deterrent to those spur-of-the-moment weddings so common in the United States. Until 1929, boys could marry at fourteen, girls at twelve (or even earlier if they continued together after those ages), but in that year the age for both was raised to sixteen, so that, with the age of majority still at twenty-one, though it was legal to marry in the late teens, parental permission had to be given. This spurred many eager (or desperate) young people to take advantage of Scotland's more lenient laws, though even then, they had to establish two weeks' residence north of the border before the wedding, which gave parents the opportunity to give chase. In 1969 the age of majority was fixed at eighteen, so now there are only two years in which young people must have parents' permission before they can marry.

As to the wedding itself, the law requires only that a certain basic vow be exchanged, that assurances are given that no legal impediment to the marriage exists, that there are two witnesses, that the door is left open to allow anyone to enter and state an impediment which the couple have ignored or of which they are ignorant, and, of course, that the couple and their witnesses sign the register. A wedding must also take place in a registrar's office or a recognized place of worship (unlike in America, where there have been weddings in planes, under water and in television studios), but sometimes the formal wedding is supplemented by another, more personal ceremony elsewhere: among 'witches', for example, acting out age-old cult rites, or between members of other unorthodox sects, who read from sacred books or recite poetry about love, eternity and alien gods. Since homosexuality between consenting adults has been permitted by law, there has been a spate of homosexual weddings—not, of course, according to the law, which does not recognize them, but a solemn pledge of devotion and fidelity which is honoured at least as often as those between heterosexual couples.

The wedding of the future King Edward VII and Alexandra of Denmark in St George's Chapel, Windsor, on 10th March 1863.

Winterhalter's painting of the wedding of Victoria, Princess Royal, and Prince Frederick William of Prussia, 25th January 1858.

The wedding, at Osborne House, of Queen Victoria's daughter Alice and Prince Louis of Hesse-Darmstadt, on 1st July 1862.

The wedding of the future King George V and Mary of Teck at the Chapel Royal, St James's, on 6th July 1893.

A picture-postcard souvenir of the wedding of Princess Alexandra, Duchess of Fife (niece of Edward VII), and Prince Arthur of Connaught, her cousin (son of Queen Victoria's third son), in 1913. Her bridesmaids were (from top right, clockwise) Princess Mary (George V's daughter), Princess May of Teck (Queen Mary's niece), Princess Patricia of Connaught (the bridegroom's sister) and Princess Maud of Fife (the bride's sister).

The Duke of Windsor (the former King Edward VIII) and his bride, formerly Mrs Simpson, after their wedding at the *château* of Candé on 3rd June 1937.

Opposite: Albert, Duke of York (the future King George VI), and his bride, Lady Elizabeth Bowes-Lyon, kneel before the high altar of Westminster Abbey, during their wedding-service, on 26th April 1923.

HRH the Princess Elizabeth (now Her Majesty Queen Elizabeth II) with HRH Prince Philip, Duke of Edinburgh, on their wedding-day, 20th November 1947.

Princess Margaret curtsies to her sister the Queen, and her bridegroom, Antony Armstrong-Jones, bows, at the end of their wedding ceremony on 6th May 1960.

Sir William Worsley leads his daughter Katharine to the altar in York Minster where she married the Duke of Kent on 8th June 1961. Note the television cameras at top right.

Princess Anne and her husband, Mark Phillips, in procession down the aisle of Westminster Abbey after their wedding, on 14th November 1973, followed by Prince Edward and Lady Sarah Armstrong-Jones.

An innovation of the 1960s, a situation now established and increasing, is the intermarriage of racial groups. Since the influx of West Indian and Asian families into the United Kingdom, second-generation 'immigrants' have been mixing ever more freely with indigenous young people, not only at school and work but in social contexts too, and though the arranged marriages of Moslems still continue (amid perennial controversy), inter-racial marriages are by no means uncommon—though most of them have to be celebrated in registrars' offices, so deep is the prejudice between religions.

Weddings are still family occasions, a survival of the time and class in which family alliance had real meaning. There is still the custom of the bride's father (or a senior male relative) 'giving the bride away', and surprisingly few modern brides see this as signifying, as it does, the handing-over of responsibility for her from father to husband, from one family to another. (In 1972, it was still so rare for a bride to see this as a denial of her independence that a case could attract newspaper attention.) Weddings still bring together, from all parts of the country, relations who may never see each other between the family's weddings and funerals, and who are invited just because they are family, not from any real desire on anyone's part for their presence. And in a church (though not in the sex-divided synagogue or in the often cramped registrar's office), the bride's and groom's families are still rigidly separated, seated by ushers after a murmured enquiry as to 'which side'. In a popular sociologists' record of family life in the mid-century, *Family and Kinship in East London*, a working-class wedding-reception, at the bride's home, is strictly for family:

> The thirty-two guests squeezed down at the cramped tables for the wedding-breakfast of ham and tongue, salad and pickles, trifle and jelly, washed down with ale and Guiness. The heat became greater, the faces more flushed and the talk louder. After an hour, the meal and toasts over, the telegrams read, the trestle-tables were cleared and stacked away. Sylvia and Harry [the bride and groom] concentrated on trying to bring the two families together. . . . Harry took off his jacket and carried a tray of drinks around the by now smoky room. Before long he anxiously asked his wife's grandmother, who was sitting close to the fire, "It's going very well, isn't it, Gran? Everybody's mucking in, I mean, you can't tell which side is which, can you?"[1]

In mid-evening the party moved over to the local pub, where they were joined by some of the bride and groom's workmates, and at closing-time friends joined family at the bride's parents' home for last drinks and the remains of the feast.

The social levellers of money and education have contributed to the standardization of weddings in this century, so that it needs a connoisseur to tell the difference in quality between the bridal-gowns of a princess and a working-class girl (there were any number of imitations of Princess Anne's wedding-gown in the months after her wedding, cheap approximations of its custom-made material and thousand-pearl trimming), or between the various grades of champagne and sparkling wines offered at receptions. Magazines for brides (such as *Wedding-Day* and *Bride*) have replaced the old books of etiquette in providing information on how to organize the ceremony and reception, and in every issue there are pictures of fashionable wedding-gowns (with, of couse, the names of the shops that provide them), menus, outlines of the now ubiquitous 'present lists' and page after page of advertisements for everything a bride could require for her 'great day', her trousseau and her new home. (Bridegrooms are not catered for; it is scarcely their place to do anything but say 'I will' and arrange the honeymoon.)

Today's 'traditional' weddings combine elements picked up over the centuries—even relics from the Roman Empire two thousand years ago. There may, first of all, be a formal engagement, with the gift of a ring from fiancé to fiancée, though without the exchange of vows that used to go with it. (Engagements are no longer binding, and since 1970 jilted fiancées have not had the recourse of the breach-of-promise suit, although it had become rare long before officially abolished.) On the morning of the wedding-day, it is now customary to issue carnation buttonholes to guests, the modern equivalent of the old favours and bridal gloves. In this late-twentieth century, a bride in a floral print or pastel-shaded gown no longer causes raised eyebrows (some have been married in jeans, others in 'unisex' uniformity with the bridegroom), but white still dominates the scene, and while many wear hats, the veil is still common. As to the bridegroom's 'morning suit', still often seen, that is only an imitation of upper-class dress over the past century, as is the hiring of the Rolls Royce to take the bride to church and then the newly-weds to the reception.

The wedding-cake, or biscuits, once broken over the couple's head, has turned into the paper confetti so much disliked by church-forecourt sweepers, and the cake now appears, as it has since Victorian times, as the centrepiece of the so-called wedding-breakfast—usually a lunch, high tea or early-evening dinner. The custom of keeping the top, smallest tier of a multi-tiered cake to be the christening-cake of the couple's first child seems to be a twentieth-century addition to wedding customs.

Toasting the bride and groom, the speeches of the father and the best man, and the reading of telegrams, give an opportunity for jokes, rarely subtle or original, about the 'pleasures to come', and the age-old temptation to horseplay now centres on stuffing confetti into 'going-away' suitcases and attaching tin cans and old shoes to the couple's car. When the couple leave the reception, the bride may give her bouquet to her mother, perhaps to preserve some petals for her as a keepsake, but many still toss theirs into the group of bridesmaids: whoever catches it, the superstition goes, will be the next bride (rather like the old stocking-throwing game, in reverse).

With so many honeymoons now being spent abroad, weddings are frequently timed for mid-morning, to give bride and groom the chance to enjoy at least part of the reception before they rush away to catch a plane which will deliver them at their destination in time for the wedding-night, though others spend their first night of marriage in a local hotel and journey on the next day. Many grooms refuse to reveal the destination, simply because some bridegrooms' male friends have in the past pre-pared elaborate practical jokes, to ensure the honeymooners' embarrass-ment at hotels where they had hoped for anonymity.

The fact that so many modern weddings incorporate some, if not all, of these traditional elements, that so many weddings seem exactly the same, whatever the personality of bride and groom, may seem surpris-ing, but, as one wedding-arranger recently pointed out, without the slightest trace of sarcasm, the old customs are so dear, so glamorous, that few brides reject them for *"mere individualism"* on their 'one great day'. During the Second World War, when there was little spare cash available, and anyway no shops full of bridal-gowns and veils to spend it in, and when food-rationing was so strict that even iced cakes were banned, brides went to extraordinary lengths to create some semblance of the traditional wedding. Gowns were passed round among friends (bride-grooms wore their uniforms), bridesmaids would appear in made-over evening-dresses, with no regard to the group's uniformity, and even though it was illegal to give away clothing-coupons, friends would club theirs together to give the bride at least a small trousseau, while the gift of a pair of the new nylon stockings was much appreciated. As to the cake, it might be a plain sponge, concocted with powdered egg and several people's ration of sugar—there were none of the fruit ingredients for the traditional 'brown' cake; but many confectioners recouped their war-losses by hiring out replicas of wedding-cakes, a cardboard shell with white decoration, some two or three tiers high, which could be used for adorning the table. Many war-wedding photographs show bride and groom beside one of these mock cakes.

The words 'for as long as ye both shall live', included in the wedding-service of most Christian denominations, are often satirized today as 'for as long as ye both shall love', and certainly the recent incidence of divorce reveals that far fewer marriages are for life than ever before: twelve marriages in every thousand now end in divorce each year. Half the divorces of today are granted within the first ten years of marriage, and statistics show that the younger the couple when they marry, the more likely they are to divorce—not that the experience of one unhappy marriage seems to be a deterrent to chancing a second: in one in six weddings today, one party is already divorced; in half of these, both parties have been married before.

The law of divorce has changed drastically in this century. In 1923 Parliament enacted that women might petition for divorce on the same grounds as men, that is, adultery without the exacerbating circumstances demanded before; in 1937 a new Matrimonial Causes Act allowed mental cruelty, desertion and prolonged insanity as pleas for divorce; in 1949 provision for legal aid was granted more widely than ever before, putting divorce within the means of thousands of people who could not have afforded it without assistance. Many who took advantage of this were the couples who had married in the Second World War, or immediately after it, though even before 1949 thousands had already ended hasty marriages, or marriages over-strained by the husband's long absence abroad: there were some sixty thousand divorces in 1947 (compared with fewer than four thousand back in 1931), a number not surpassed until the 1970s.

The 1969/1974 Acts caused a new 'high', largely by allowing couples to be divorced in an undefended suit after two years apart, though with the stipulation that a real attempt at reconciliation must be made, and be seen to be made. (This 'divorce by consent' also means that in many divorces neither party can be accounted 'guilty' as they are in suits involving adultery and desertion.) Even so, though the annual divorce rate is unprecedented (a million divorces between 1970 and 1980), it has not reached the proportions prophesied by opponents of the liberalization of the divorce laws who envisaged marital breakdown running at the same rate as weddings.

Catholic couples, or a Catholic and non-Catholic married in a Catholic church, must submit to ecclesiastical restraints on the dissolution of their marriage far more daunting and lengthy than those in the civil courts. It *is* possible to obtain an annulment (never a divorce as such) from the Catholic Church, but many Catholics prefer to turn to civil law, if not to seek divorce (which their Church does not recognize) then to apply for a judicial separation, which makes formal provision for a dependent wife and children but does not allow the couple to remarry.

In recent years, the Anglican Church, once adamant against permitting the remarriage in church of even an innocent party, has accepted the 'thin end of the wedge' in certain cases, though it is left to the conscience of individual clergy, under episcopal advice. In Methodism, for example, among the Nonconformist Churches, ministers are under instruction not to marry anyone adjudged the guilty party in a divorce, but where there has been a 'divorce by consent', without a judgement of any guilt, they have the latitude to perform a church wedding for a divorcé, after consultation with church officials.

The ease with which a divorce is obtained in Britain in the 1980s has been regarded with disapproval not only in Christian circles but by many people who suspect that more marriages could be made to 'work' if only couples did not give up trying so soon, if only the reasonable expectations of affection and companionship were not so much overwhelmed by the impossible expectation of maintaining forever that state of passionate love in which marriage usually begins. There is an argument that divorce is only a recognition that a marriage has already broken down, that it is a release from a situation already found intolerable and that 'painless' divorce is a modern blessing; others say that, if divorce were more difficult to obtain, those who expect too much in marriage and seek divorce when disappointed would be more liable to settle for something less than perfection, not to divorce and seek it elsewhere.

A feature characteristic of twentieth-century marriages is the increased equality of husband and wife, not only in law but in the sharing of decision-making and responsibility as regards money, home and children, partly because in so many marriages the wife brings home a second income, 'earning' the right to share the powers formerly the prerogative of the male bread-winner. The twentieth century has also brought married couples a new form of decision-making: how many children to have. Until this century, the only effective birth-controls were abstinence and coitus interruptus, with a little help from rudimentary male contraceptives, and it was not only Catholics who regarded contraception as a perversion of God's plan for mankind. The 1920s saw the introduction of new contraceptives and of more widespread professional advice on limiting the size of families, and thereafter the birth-rate dropped—only to suffer the shock of the 'post-war bulge'. By the 1960s the female contraceptive pill was widely available, and in the 1970s abortion became legal, but the vasectomy operation for men has still not been found an acceptable alternative.

And the marriage of the future? Will women develop their 'liberation' so far as to take the initiative in proposing marriage to men? Will there be so many divorces that the law will be changed to allow marriage-licences to be issued for five or ten years, with the option of renewal or automatic divorce at the end of the period? Will the institution of marriage survive at all, or will it break down as the pressures of respectability, religion and financial dependence continue to reduce? In that case, will there be total sexual promiscuity, with a woman bringing up children maintained by their several fathers, the men contributing portions of their income to the various mothers of their offspring—or even taking custody of the children themselves? Will there be so many inter-racial marriages that the population of Britain will be neither 'white' nor 'black' but something in between? Will there be such overcrowding on this planet that governments will license marriages for those who agree not to have children and special ones for those allowed to breed? At the furthest stretch of the imagination, will scientists discover human life in space, contact it, meet it and begin inter-stellar marriages?

The House of Windsor

In 1917 King George V made the declaration that he and his family would no longer be known as 'the House of Saxe-Coburg-Gotha' but as 'the House of Windsor'. It was only a gesture, a renunciation of nominal ties with Germany long after the real break had been made, but, added to the family's untiring share in the war-effort, it proved to the British people the dynasty's identification with the nation, the sacrifice of family ties to the nation's interests.

After the war, the British royal family did not, of course, cut themselves off from the Continental monarchs—there were, after all, the allies and the neutrals, even if traditional German links had been severed, but in most countries—certainly in Britain—monarchy was ceasing to function as the policy-maker, so a king's close friendship with one monarch, dislike of another, was irrelevant to the nation's foreign policy. Abroad, royal families might maintain their elite status by intermarrying, but in Britain that concept had lost its significance too: of George V's four younger children, three married at home in the next two decades, and the one who did marry a foreigner did so wholly for love, without the slightest thought of making an alliance or mating with blood royal.

Back in Queen Victoria's reign, scarcely a month had gone by without a visit from some foreign 'cousin' or other, and the British royal family and their princely visitors would form a group above, apart from, the resident Court. Victoria's eldest son, Edward VII, however, preferred the company of the British aristocracy, and while he was Prince of Wales, even more when he was King, there began a 'levelling-off' between royalty and nobility. Then came George V, never entirely at ease with foreigners, and since his children were aged between nine and twenty when the First World War broke out, they had little experience of earlier international gatherings where cross-frontier friendships (and enmities) and marriages had been made, and so during and after the war their contemporaries in the 'native' nobility were their natural companions.

After the war, the Prince of Wales threw himself joyfully into the social round of the 'bright young things', who scandalized their elders with their night-clubs, bathing-parties and fast-car jaunts. George V was heard to dread the day when one of his sons presented him with a social butterfly for a daughter-in-law, one of those brash young people with their cock-tails and chain-smoking and jazz who so offended his more-Victorian-than-the-Victorians sense of decorum. But as the years passed, the Prince of Wales showed no sign of meaning to marry, and the 'intendeds' his brothers and sisters brought home were not in the least brash.

Princess Mary's bridegroom was not even young: in 1922, at twenty-four, she married the thirty-nine-year-old Viscount Lascelles. Once she had said that she would like to marry someone like her grandfather, Edward VII, but apart from the fact that Lascelles looked old enough to be a grandfather, he was nothing like that latter-day 'merry monarch': tall, thin, heavily moustached, with 'tired' eyes, and, in his photographs, an invariably glum expression, he was neither a Prince Charming nor even a young girl's idea of the fascinating roué which Edward VII had been all his life. Then there was Prince 'Bertie's' choice: anything less like a social butterfly than Elizabeth Bowes-Lyon would be hard to imagine. She was softly feminine, quiet, 'gently spoken' as it was said, calm and self-possessed, where other debutantes of the era were fashionably flat-chested, generally shrill, frenetic in their search for 'fun'. Nor was she one to snap up the chance of a royal marriage: twice she refused Bertie, before she could steel herself to a lifetime in the public eye—how public she could not then guess. Like Elizabeth, Prince Henry's bride came from an old Scottish family, one with the distinction of a 'treble-barrelled' name— . Alice Montagu-Douglas-Scott, and also like her sister-in-law, Alice was far more at home on a grouse-moor and in a tranquil drawing-room than in a night-club or cinema; at thirty-four she had matured far beyond the 'jazz age'.

Prince George was the odd-man-out, with his marriage, in 1934, to Princess Marina of Greece—'of Greece' but scarcely 'from Greece', for her parents had been established in Paris since they went into exile after the deposition of the Greek king in the early 1920s. Nevertheless, Marina was truly cosmopolitan, with relations throughout the Balkans, in Denmark and among the Russian émigré community, and it was while she was staying in Yugoslavia, in a chalet in the Julian Alps, that Prince George (later Duke of Kent) came to propose to her. In the Press sensation that followed, some stressed her romantic foreignness, her sophistication, her culture, her many languages, her leadership of fashion; others offered the homelier facts that she had had a British nanny and, from habits of childhood, always said her prayers in English; all emphasized her perfect, classic beauty; no one suggested that the match was made for anything but love, certainly not that it would make any difference to Britain's relations with Greece, for better or for worse.

Of the four royal brides of the 1920s and 1930s, Princess Marina could not fail but be the most distinguished, shimmering in her wedding-gown of white and silver brocade, lined with silver lamé (from the House of Molyneux), rising tall and slender from the sheath-like dress with its sweeping train and crowned with a fringe tiara. In contrast, eleven years earlier, Elizabeth Bowes-Lyon had suffered from the fashions of the period that flattered very few: she wore a sack-like dress of silk crêpe (by Madame Handley-Seymour of New Bond Street), with a lace veil clamped firmly over her forehead; her eight bridesmaids wore floral head-dresses much resembling earphones, only slightly more attractive than Princess Mary's attendants, in limp veils.

Every royal wedding of the era seems to have been a 'first' in some way. Princess Mary became the first daughter of a sovereign to wed an English-man (as opposed to a Scotsman) since Henry VII's daughter Mary married Charles Brandon, Duke of Suffolk, and the first since the Middle Ages to marry in Westminster Abbey (though not the first princess: that distinction went to George V's cousin Patricia of Connaught, married there in 1919). Elizabeth Bowes-Lyon was the first royal bride (*legal* royal bride: discount Mrs Fitzherbert and the brides of George III's brothers) to be married from a house in a numbered street. George and Marina were the first royal couple to have their wedding ceremony broadcast on the radio—a concession by the Chapter of Westminster Abbey eleven years after they had refused it when Albert of York married Elizabeth Bowes-Lyon. In contrast, the Gloucesters' wedding was a 'last'—the last royal wedding so far this century to be celebrated in Buckingham Palace chapel. It had been planned, like its recent predecessors, for the Abbey, but the bride's father, the Duke of Buccleuch, died suddenly a few weeks before the wedding date, and there was an understandable desire for privacy.

In the first two of this series of weddings, memories of the recent war were still fresh, and the royal brides paid their tribute to the war-dead when Princess Mary halted her carriage returning from Westminster to offer her bouquet at the Cenotaph and when Elizabeth Bowes-Lyon laid her flowers on the Tomb of the Unknown Warrier as she entered the Abbey.

While the immense size of Westminster Abbey allowed the seating of more guests than ever before during the ceremony, the long drive to and from the Palace brought out record crowds to line the route. With each wedding, the fervour grew—even for the Gloucester wedding, when all the public could see was the future Duchess driving in the Glass Coach from her Mayfair home to the Palace, and then the traditional appearance on the central balcony. But all these weddings seemed to be the prelude to one that would eclipse them all—the wedding of Edward, Prince of Wales.

By 1935, however, when the last of his brothers married, the Press was no longer rumouring the Prince's marriage to this or that princess, this or that titled lady of the British aristocracy. Indeed, though the Press avidly followed the Prince on his world travels, it was singularly reticent about his 'love life'. Not so the foreign papers: there the names of Mrs Dudley

Ward and Thelma, Lady Furness, were well known—and their implications, and by the mid-1930s there was a new name, a new face seen regularly in the photographs of the Prince's entourage, that of Mrs Ernest Simpson.

Wallis Simpson was American, in her thirties, divorced from a first husband and married to a second, a wealthy businessman, Ernest Simpson, with whom she had entered London 'society' some years before, where her elegance and wit had readily found her a niche. As a friend of Lady Furness, Wallis had been introduced into the Prince of Wales's coterie of fast-living sophisticates, and when Lady Furness went off to America on holiday late in 1933, it was Wallis whom she put in charge of the Prince—largely to keep him from returning to her rival, Mrs Dudley Ward. So it was with some shock and horror that she found, on her return, that her protégée, Mrs Simpson, was now engrossing all the Prince's attention and that she had suddenly become *persona non grata* in his private life. Thereafter, Mrs Simpson was seen everywhere with 'David' (the name used instead of the formal 'Edward' among his family and friends), his hostess at Fort Belvedere, his country retreat, invited as his companion when he visited friends—and as often as not with her husband in tow, the perfect chaperone. Occasionally the Simpsons figured on the Prince's invitation-list for Court functions: at a royal reception, at the Kent wedding in 1934 and once at a State Ball, but never in any intimate gathering of the royal family. George V and Queen Mary had never approved of their eldest son's relations with the 'fast set', and the rumours that reached them of their son's involvement with a series of married women had always been a source of both bewilderment and concern. For some time past, the King had been meaning to 'have it out' with the Prince, but talk about emotions had never come easily to him, and when George V died, in January 1936, it had all been left unsaid.

Others were regarding the new King Edward VIII with concern as the first months of his reign unfolded. There was the King's Mediterranean cruise, with Mrs Simpson among his guests, hounded from port to port by foreign reporters and photographers. Though the British Press lords had made a compact not to publicize the royal romance, Britons coming home from the Continent, or from America, that summer, brought strange stories about their king from the foreign Press, and if they now caught wind of the Simpson divorce, they could form their own conclusions as to the news that was about to break at home.

With the coming of autumn, the crisis approached, for the King was now determined to marry Wallis Simpson.

The great dilemma was that she had been twice divorced, that the Anglican Church did not recognize, and would not perform, the re-marriage of divorcés (even the 'innocent party') and that the King was Head of the Anglican Church. Even if they married only in a civil ceremony, Wallis would still be queen—a queen to be crowned alongside her husband in a ceremony planned for the spring of 1937, to be crowned by the Anglican Primate as though the Church countenanced their marriage. There was talk in the royal clique of a morganatic marriage such as kings and princes had made on the Continent when their brides were commoners, and whereby wives did not share their husbands' titles, nor their children inherit them. But such a marriage was without legal precedent in Britain—and anyway, that would still leave Edward VIII to be crowned by a Church whose rules he had flouted. He could, of course, wait until after the coronation to marry Mrs Simpson, but in that case the intention would be as heinous as the deed—and underhand to boot. All these ideas were tossed around in November 1936, between the King's friends, his ministers and the Press barons 'in the know'—and of course, between David and Wallis themselves. Time and again, Mrs Simpson offered to 'withdraw', to leave Britain for ever rather than see the King ruin his life, damn himself in the eyes of the Church, lose all respect in the country. But, as she later recalled in her autobiography, ". . . he insisted that he needed me, and as a woman in love I was prepared to go through rivers of woe, seas of despair and oceans of agony for him".[1]

The pressures on both of them were enormous. Mrs Simpson was besieged in her London house by reporters, once the news broke in Britain, and her mail contained abusive and even threatening letters. At the same time, the King was almost daily undergoing painful interviews with members of the government and the Church, at one moment hopeful of a solution to the problem, at others plunged into despair. Through it all his mother maintained a stance of rigid, frigid, disdainful opposition to his plans, of condemnation of a love that could threaten duty.

The word 'abdication' had been spoken. As each day passed, the King and his ministers became more accustomed to the idea, his brother Bertie, the Duke of York, more appalled at the fate awaiting him. Diffident, often morose, a prey to intense anxiety whenever he had to speak in public even (because of a speech impediment never wholly cured), the Duke of York lived in a nightmare of suspense while the King's marriage was being debated, while he waited for the news that he must succeed his brother on the throne.

On 2nd December 1936 the subjects of King Edward VIII learned that he and Mrs Simpson were to marry, that he was 'to go'.

On the morning of 10th December the King signed the Instrument of Abdication, and that evening he broadcast to the nation, telling his people what he had done and explaining that ". . . I have found it impossible to carry the heavy burden of responsibility and discharge my duties as king as I would wish to do, without the help and support of the woman I love."[2]

Even today, many remember the furore the Abdication caused: women quarrelling in shop-queues, men defending Mrs Simpson's good name or reviling her in public-house brawls. It was a long while before Edward VIII was forgotten—or forgiven. But he was gone. In the early hours of the morning after the Abdication he sailed for France.

On 3rd June 1937 they were married at the château of Candé—married, after all, according to the Anglican rite, for a Darlington clergyman who felt strongly that this must be done had braved public opinion and the probable repercussions on his career to cross the Channel to perform the ceremony. Still, there was a small, quiet party of faithful friends to wish the Duke and Duchess of Windsor well.

On the day of his brother Bertie's coronation, as King George VI, the former King had said to Mrs Simpson: "You must have no regrets—I have none. This much I know: what I know of happiness is for ever associated with you."[3] So did they live happily ever after, the couple for whom it was 'all for love and the world well lost'? They said so—forty years later they said so, after years of exile from Britain, after the Duke had been denied an active part in the Second World War when he had offered his services to his brother and the nation, after the Duchess had been snubbed time and again. It was only when the former King died, in 1972, that his wife could stand among the royal family, at his funeral at Windsor, and be seen by the nation as part of them—just briefly, before she returned to their home in Paris. By then the nation had come to accord her and the late Duke a strange sort of respect for the love that had cost them both so dear, a love that had made a ring worth more to them than a crown.

Mountbatten-Windsor

"She won't give her heart lightly," Queen Mary once said of her grand-daughter, the future Queen Elizabeth II, "but when she does, it will be for always. It does sometimes happen that one falls in love early, and it lasts for ever. Elizabeth seems to me that kind of girl."[1]

If the majority of royal biographers are to be believed, that is exactly what happened: Elizabeth fell in love at thirteen, they say, and has since proved that an adolescent attachment can mature into the love of which marriages are made. Not that her marriage was in any way arranged for her, or that her future husband was ever presented to her as someone suitable and potentially lovable (as Albert was to Victoria): rather that she had the good fortune to come across not only a man who could return her love but one who had all the qualities necessary to face up to the challenge of a royal marriage.

They may have met in early childhood, but the first meeting that the royal couple themselves remember was in July 1939, when Elizabeth was thirteen, Philip eighteen, when the royal family visited the Royal Naval College at Dartmouth where he was a cadet. Being detailed as escort to two little girls, Elizabeth and her sister Margaret, aged nine, might not be a chore to the taste of every young man, but by all accounts he gave them a fine time, and when the royal yacht left Dartmouth harbour, followed into the open sea by cadets in a flotilla of college craft, one remained in the yacht's wake long after the others had turned back: Philip, rowing manfully alone until from the royal yacht he seemed just a speck on the waves.

Perhaps, if life had continued as normal for the royal family, the incident might have faded more easily from the Princess's mind, but only a few weeks later the Second World War broke out, and for years afterwards she and her sister were left in safety and seclusion at Windsor Castle. In other circumstances, Elizabeth would have had a gay social life, mainly among the 'scions of the nobility' from whom she could be expected choose a husband; as it was, they were all off at the war, and the only young men she met were those of the intimate family circle, of whom Philip, on occasional leave from the Royal Navy, was one.

On his father's side, his connection with the British royal family came through Edward VII's wife, Alexandra of Denmark, sister of the first Greek king, his grandfather; on his mother's side, his ties were closer, for she was one of the Battenbergs who had renounced their German connections in the First World War, taken the surname Mountbatten and identified themselves wholly with British interests. In fact, Philip had left Greece when he was only six months old, when his father, Prince Andrew, had taken the family into exile, and from the age of nine he had been educated in Britain, at the now famous Gordonstoun school, before training for the navy at Dartmouth, as we have seen. As in earlier centuries, international war split royal families, and Philip had sisters in Germany (with husbands in the German forces) and many relations in German-occupied Greece, their only contact via 'neutral' cousins in Scandinavia. Even so, somehow family gossip reached an aunt in Greece in the spring of 1941 that Philip was destined to be 'Prince Consort' to the future Queen Elizabeth—or so a visitor to Athens, Sir Henry Channon, recorded in his now famous diaries. Maybe this hint put 'Chips' Channon on the alert, for a few years later he noted that the name 'Philip' appeared significantly often in a certain royal visitors' book.

As early as March 1944 Prince Philip had asked his cousin King George of the Hellenes to sound out the British King George about a marriage between him and Elizabeth, but, as her father wrote to Queen Mary at the time, he had had to discourage him: ". . . she is too young for that now. She has never met any young men of her own age. . . . I like Philip. He is intelligent, has a good sense of humour and thinks about things in the right way. . . . We are going to tell George [of Greece] that P. had better not think any more about it for the present.'"[2] Whether or not the Princess Elizabeth knew anything of these tentative beginnings is impossible to say, but when her governess 'told all', some years later, she did remark that "Philip said this or that" was always on the girl's lips at the time and that his photograph had a prominent place in her room.

When the Prince proposed to her, in the summer of 1946, at Balmoral, and she accepted, the King and Queen were still reluctant to allow them to marry. The Princess was only twenty years old, still a novice in royal duties, only just 'out' into post-war society. The Prince, moreover, was still a Greek citizen, and even though Greece welcomed back its king after the war, the country's internal politics cast doubts on the future of the monarchy there; add to that his German connections and the fact that the British public were thoroughly xenophobic after six years of war, and the time certainly did not seem ripe for the announcement of Philip and Elizabeth's engagement, all personal considerations apart. Thus it was that George VI insisted that his daughter wait a while longer, first until she was twenty-one—in April 1947, and then, when he found that the family would be away on a foreign tour then, until their return home later that spring.

In fact, it was only a matter of days after their return before Philip (now safely naturalized a British subject and bearing the surname Mountbatten, borrowed from his mother's family) presented himself at Buckingham Palace and won George VI's blessing on the marriage. Then the King left him and sent in Elizabeth—on the pretext that he had left a 'present' for her in the room. Even so, several weeks were to go by before the engagement was announced, on 10th July.

The war in Europe had been over just two years. Britain was still dominated by 'austerity' regulations as to food, clothing, housing—everything, so it seemed, that touched on the lives of 'ordinary' men and women seeking to marry. How then could the King's daughter marry with all the usual royal panoply without offending a nation still denied luxuries of any sort? Someone suggested a 'private' wedding at Windsor, without any sort of extravagant show, but in the end it was decided to turn the wedding into a national celebration. As it transpired, it was a wise choice, for the British people treated the occasion as a bright spot in the midst of grey years and showed that they had no wish for the Princess to lack anything they could give her: she was inundated with gifts from all parts of the kingdom—including the then precious nylon stockings and even clothing-coupons (which she had to return, since it was strictly illegal to give away 'points'). From abroad came jewellery and *objets d'art* but also American food-parcels for distribution to war-widows with children; from India arrived a gift made by Gandhi from yarn he had spun himself: some contemporary accounts called it a tablecloth, some a shawl, others 'crocheted lace'—Queen Mary dismissed it disdainfully as a 'loin-cloth'.

While the Press daily issued reports of the choice of bridesmaids, the preparations in the Abbey, the novel introduction of television cameras (discreetly, by the Abbey entrance, not yet inside) and the baking of the cake in an Army kitchen, and while Parliament was voting to increase the Princess's income to £40,000 a year and to give her husband £15,000 a year (to supplement his navy pay of 22 shillings a week, plus a prospective 18 shillings 6 pence married allowance), a less publicized pre-requisite was being planned in the royal family: the christening of Lieutenant Philip Mountbatten RN in the Church of England (first baptized in the Greek Orthodox Church, he had been worshipping as an Anglican since child-hood). On the eve of the wedding, he had a new title too—His Royal Highness Prince Philip, Duke of Edinburgh—bestowed on him by the King.

20th November 1947 was a wet, dark, dreary day in a bad winter, but still hundreds of people had camped out overnight on the London streets, to see the procession, and damp bunting hung out over other streets, in every town and city of the British Isles, ready for community parties. Meanwhile, that morning there was furore in Buckingham Palace: the bride was being helped into her wedding-dress, a Hartnell creation of ivory silk with an interwoven flower design crusted with pearls and crystal, and then crowned with veil and tiara, when the tiara band snapped, and a jeweller had to be called in to mend it; then suddenly it was found that the bouquet, of white orchids, had disappeared—it was some time before a flustered footman remembered that he had put it into a cool cupboard to keep fresh.

In the Abbey, there was complete calm. The high altar shone with gold plate recently retrieved from war-time hiding-places, and a colourful array of foreign monarchs, Empire and Commonwealth dignitaries, British peers and members of the royal family took their places, flanked by royal servants and guards in historic uniforms. The bride came down the aisle on her father's arm and joined her bridegroom and the mass of clergy at the altar, to go through the wedding service, so ancient in origin, she not omitting the vow to 'obey' but he promising to 'share' with her, not 'endow' her with, his 'worldly goods'.

Then back they drove, in the Glass Coach, to Buckingham Palace, through the crowded, cheering streets, followed by a line of carriages and cars of guests. Once all were safely inside the gates, the police let the crowds surge forward, until the Mall was a seething torrent of people calling for the bride and groom, restless until they appeared, with the King and Queen and the bridesmaids, on the central balcony, when the cheers broke out again. Inside the guests sat down to a meal fit for . . . not for *a* king but for five kings, along with eight queens, eight princes and ten princesses, and including twelve wedding cakes, the main one 9 feet high.

That evening, when the new Duke and Duchess of Edinburgh had left for their honeymoon at Lord Mountbatten's house, Broadlands in Kent,

King George VI sat down to write to his daughter: "I was so proud of you and thrilled at having you close to me on our long walk in Westminster Abbey, but when I handed your hand to the Archbishop, I felt I had lost something very precious. You were so calm and composed during the Service and said your words with such conviction that I knew everything was alright."[3]

Little more than four years remained to George VI, but time enough for him to become certain that everything would always be 'alright': to see his daughter cope with life as a naval officer's wife, in London and in Malta, to greet the two grandchildren she gave him in the first years of her marriage and to watch Prince Philip begin to take his own place among the royal family. Then, in February 1952, he died. Princess Elizabeth, Duchess of Edinburgh, had left for Africa a few days previously; she returned as Queen Elizabeth II.

While the British nation and the Commonwealth looked now to the new Queen and her husband and watched their first steps in government, her sister, Princess Margaret, had her own limelight. In the early 1950s the British and foreign Press avidly followed the antics of the 'Margaret Set', the Princess's night-clubbing, informal, sometimes rowdy friends, and while the occasional voice was raised to inform the world that she was about to marry the exiled King Michael of Romania or some obscure German prince, many more harped on the quantity as well as the quality of her 'boyfriends'. However, if she was seen with Group Captain Peter Townsend, the Press put it down to his being Deputy Master of the Household, an old friend of the family; he was sixteen years older than she anyway—and married. In fact, Townsend was living apart from his wife, awaiting the divorce that was granted early in 1953, and he and Princess Margaret were in love.

Royal advisers left the Queen in no doubt that she should not give permission (necessary under the Royal Marriage Act of 1772) for her sister to marry Townsend—how could the Queen do so, as Head of the Church of England, when the Church still refused to countenance the remarriage of divorcés? In 1955, when Margaret would be twenty-five, she could marry, in a civil ceremony, by giving a year's notice to the Privy Council—but that was a couple of years ahead. In the meantime, Townsend eased what was becoming a tense situation by accepting a post as Air Attaché at the British Embassy in Brussels—just in time, for an American newspaper now led the world with its Margaret/Peter 'scoop'. Two years later, they were still intermittently in the news, with a growing body of opinion that the Princess should be allowed to marry where she loved, but her twenty-fifth birthday came and went, in August 1955, with not a word from the Palace. Then, on 31st October, Princess Margaret released a statement in which she declared her decision not to marry Peter Townsend, not to go through with the possible civil ceremony ("mindful of the Church's teachings that Christian marriage is indissoluble and conscious of my duty to the Commonwealth"). Towards the end came the words: "I have reached this decision entirely alone, and in doing so I have been strengthened by the unfailing support and devotion of Group Captain Townsend."

It is a tragic irony that, having sacrificed one love to duty, because of a divorce, the Princess's second love, and her marriage to Antony Armstrong-Jones, should itself end in divorce—the first in the immediate royal family (by not counting George IV's intent as the deed) since the old days of annulments back in Henry VIII's time.

It all began so well, a real 'true-life romance', the Princess and the photographer (albeit with aristocratic connections and created Earl of Snowdon), the Abbey wedding, the exotic West Indian honeymoon and then a glamorous life among all the 'beautiful people' of the 'swinging sixties'. But as early as 1966 there were rumours of a partial separation, and by 1974 the Princess's biographer had difficulty in reconciling the by-then well known stories of a break-up with a wishful picture of what she called "married fondness". In May 1978 the couple divorced.

While the Queen's children were growing up, the nation's interest in royal romances focussed on her cousins, the Kents and Gloucesters, who were often in the public eye with their share in royal duties. In 1961 the Duke of Kent's wedding, to Miss Katharine Worsley, brought the crowds—and the television cameras—to York Minster, but in April 1963 Westminster Abbey was used again for his sister Princess Alexandra's wedding to the Honourable Angus Ogilvy. Then, in July 1972, the wedding of the future Duke (Richard) of Gloucester to a Dane, Birgitte van Deurs, was a very different affair, reminiscent of Princess Beatrice's miniature wedding on the Isle of Wight: they were married at the little parish church in Barnwell near his home, with members of the royal family flown in by helicopter to attend the ceremony.

By then Princess Anne was in her early twenties, and the Press could lose no chance of offering the public her private as well as her royal moments. Time after time reporters stung the Princess's ready temper to anger when they pestered her at the equestrian events in which she was trying to build a career, and so she could not be blamed for refusing to take them into her confidence at every stage in her 'love life'—as they seemed to expect—and for using subterfuge to keep from them her developing relationship with another show-jumper, and army officer, Mark Phillips. The announcement of their engagement, on 29th May 1973, came only after weeks of firm denials from the Palace Press office.

Inevitably, between then and the wedding, some six months later, the Press ran loose, examining every aspect of the marriage, from the Phillips pedigree (which revealed that a sixteenth-century forbear had invented the lavatory) to the number of rooms in the Sandhurst 'tied' house that had been allocated to them by the Army. In the circumstances, the couple were remarkably restrained when placed before a television camera and interviewer, calmly answering questions that anyone would find prying, even impertinent.

But that is what royal weddings are now: public property, and while on the one hand the public demands 'pomp and circumstance', on the other it insists that a princess should have no special privileges when it comes to her married home and income—except what she is *seen* to earn with her share of 'functions' and ceremonial. As to the wedding itself, the television cameras in Westminster Abbey see almost everything, and what they miss, the 'presenter' tells; with the simultaneous transmission of television pictures, the Queen's subjects thousands of miles away can watch the wedding as it happens. (Fortunately, there has never been a dispute among prelates such as marred Henry I's second wedding, never a royal bridegroom appearing drunk, as the future George IV was, and no bride has ever vomited over a queen's skirt, as Augusta of Saxe-Gotha did back in 1736.) However, the fact that royal weddings do not degenerate into mere television spectaculars is due largely to the fact that the public's curiosity is always tempered, genuinely, sincerely, by a love for the royal family that has just as much to do with what is known of their personalities as with their ceremonial 'glamour'.

Those last words were written on the first day of 1981, and since then 1980's predictions of an engagement between the Prince of Wales and Lady Diana Spencer have been justified.

The announcement has come after years in which all the old clichés of 'rumour being rife' and 'speculation high' have been as much employed as in 1936, 1947, 1955 and 1973, for the Press has been 'linking the name' of the Prince with those of eligible foreign princesses and British aristocrats—and the occasional 'outsider'—since he was in his teens.

At one point, in 1977, there was a Press 'scare' when Prince Michael of Kent married a Catholic, Baroness Marie-Christine von Reibnitz—with the complication that her previous marriage had been annulled by her Church. At that time there were rumours that the Act of Settlement would be amended to allow members of the royal family to marry Catholics—specifically to allow the Prince of Wales to marry Princess Marie-Astrid of Luxembourg. The suggestion drew out of murky depths of prejudice and ignorance a reviling of Popery and papist plots on the one hand, on the other the indignation that the Prince could marry a heathen, an atheist, but not a Catholic. More balanced commentators ignored extremes and asked how the Prince could marry a Catholic if her Church demanded the upbringing of their children as Catholics, when a potential son or daughter must one day become Head of the Anglican Church as well as sovereign.

'The world's most eligible bachelor' has responded to interviewers' questions with frankness and patience. He has confessed to having been in love more than once and admitted that he must be sure of a girl's commitment to their joint career before he can offer her marriage. More than one 'possible', it has been said, withdrew from a developing relationship with him because of the spotlight on her—easy to understand after 1980's hounding of Lady Diana Spencer; another was put out of the running—if she was ever in it—by Press revelations that she had lived with a man as his mistress. Every girl seen with the Prince of Wales was submitted to scrutiny as to her family tree, her character and her looks, her friends pumped for anecdote and scandal.

The future Princess of Wales, one day to be Queen, has not only won the love of the Prince and his confidence in her ability to face up to her future life but emerged from this 'ordeal by newsprint' as one who is so self-controlled, tolerant and courageous as to deserve her bridegroom.

Once before, back in the early eighteenth century, a Prince of Wales came close to marrying a Lady Diana Spencer. She was the granddaughter of the great Duke of Marlborough, the victor of Blenheim in Queen Anne's reign, and of his termagant wife Sarah, Queen Anne's confidante for so many years. Sarah long outlived her husband—and her power, and in 1735 she offered Lady Diana to George II's son Frederick Lewis, Prince of Wales, to be his bride, along with a dowry of £100,000. The Prince himself was apparently on the point of accepting when George II heard of the secret negotiations from his chief minister, Robert Walpole, who pointed out to him that the old Duchess was about to use his son to put her Whig friends into government. That was the end of that. Lady Diana later became Duchess of Bedford; she died, of tuberculosis, childless at the age of twenty-six.

Today's Lady Diana does not look in the least tubercular; nor has her marriage been 'arranged' by anyone but herself and the Prince. If heredity has had any part in moulding her character, no one can find a blemish there: she comes from a family which for centuries has put public service at least as high as their own rural powers, though her cousinship—albeit distant—with Sir Winston Churchill (really Spencer-Churchill) will be sure to over-charge her with supposed heroic potentialities in some quarters. Before the engagement, the most the public saw of her was a shy, almost frightened little face with a wry smile as she scurried to work between pursuing reporters—who had to fall back on eulogies of her car, her flat and her career as a teacher, even references to her step-grandmother, the novelist Barbara Cartland, in lieu of 'hard news'. Now she faces the world, still with reserve and caution but with the confidence of one ordeal over, perhaps the hardest. Her new confidence must surely come from the fact that the Prince of Wales has chosen her, of all the women he has ever met, as the one most worthy to wear the crown as well as the ring.

References

THE MIDDLE AGES
"THE GREAT BOND OF MATRIMONY"
1 Translated from the original by Pamela Ellis.
2 *The Paston Letters*, ed. J. Gairdner (1872–5, 1901), volume II, pp. 150–1.
3 *The Stonor Letters and Papers*, ed. C. L. Kingsford (Camden Society, 1919, third series), volume II, pp. 6–8.
4 *The Paston Letters, op. cit.*, volume I, pp. 89–90.
5 *The Cely Letters*, ed. H. Malden (Royal Historical Society, 1900), volume I, pp. 102–4.
6 J. C. Jeaffreson, *Brides and Bridals* (1872), volume I, p. 280.
7 P. M. Kendall, *The Yorkist Age* (George Allen & Unwin, 1962), p. 375.
8 Ordericus Vitalis, *Ecclesiastical History of England and Normandy*, trs. T. Forester (1853–6), volume II, p. 174.

ANGLO-SAXONS AND DANES
1 William of Malmesbury, *Historia Regum . . .*, in *The Church Historians of England*, ed. J. Stevenson (1854), volume III, part i, pp. 119–20.
2 Fabius Ethelwerd, *Chronicle . . .*, in *Church Historians . . ., op. cit.*, volume II, part ii, p. 550.
3 William of Malmesbury, *op. cit.*, p. 139.
4 *Ibid.*, pp. 185–6.

NORMANS AND PLANTAGENETS
1 *A Journal by One of the Suite of Thomas Beckington . . .*, ed. N. H. Nicholas (1828), p. 62.
2 Jean Froissart, *Chronicles . . .*, trs. T. Johnes (1844), volume II, p. 583.
3 In some cases, these averages were computed on only approximate ages; often there is no record of the birth-date of even a king, let alone his sisters.
4 Ingulph, *The Chronicle of the Abbey of Croyland*, trs. H. T. Riley (1854), p. 265.
5 *Excerpta Historica*, ed. S. Bentley (1831), p. 228.
6 A. Strickland, *Lives of the Queens of England* (1861), volume II, p. 170.
7 M. A. E. Green (Wood), *Lives of the Princesses of England* (1852), volume V, p. 59.
8 J. Leland, *de Rebus Britannicis Collectanea*, ed. T. Hearne (1774), volume IV, p. 262.
9 Roger of Hoveden, *Annals*, ed. H. T. Riley (1853), volume I, p. 414.
10 Roger of Wendover, *Flowers of History*, trs. J. A. Giles (1849), volume III, p. 609.
11 *Ibid.*
12 Matthew Paris, *English History*, trs. J. A. Giles (1853), volume I, p. 8.
13 *Excerpta Historica, op. cit.*, p. 237.
14 J. Froissart, *op. cit.*, volume II, p. 600.
15 J. Stow, *Annals, or a General Chronicle of England* (1631 edition), p. 369.

MEDIEVAL SCOTLAND

1 *Early Sources of Scottish History*, ed. A. O. Anderson (Oliver & Boyd, 1922), volume II, pp. 121–3.
2 William of Malmesbury, *op. cit.*, p. 349.
3 M. Paris, *op. cit.*, volume III, p. 129.
4 *Lanercost Chronicle*, ed. H. Maxwell (James Maclehose & Sons, 1913), p. 23.
5 E. Hall, *Chronicle (The Union of the Two Noble and Illustre Families of Lancastre and Yorke*, 1548), 1809 edition, p. 23.
6 *Ibid.*
7 *Ibid.*, p. 186.
8 *Ibid.*

THE SIXTEENTH CENTURY
"HIS PRETTY PUSSY TO HUGGLE"

1 R. Cleaver, *A Godly Form of Household Government* (1598), not paginated.
2 P. Stubbs, *An Anatomy of Abuses . . .* (1583), ed. F. J. Furnival (New Shakespeare Society, 1877–9), p. 97.
3 *Hastings Papers*, ed. F. Bickley (Historical Manuscripts Commission, 1947), volume IV, p. 332.
4 T. Becon, *Works* (1564), part i, p. dlxiv.
5 *Memorials of the Verney Family*, ed. F. P. Verney (1892), volume I, p. 48.
6 William Cecil, Lord Burghley, *Advice to a Son* (1617), pp. 6–7.
7 T. Deloney, *The Pleasant History of John Winchcombe* (1626 edition), p. 22.
8 J. Stow, *A Survey of London* (1598 edition), p. 87.
9 T. Deloney, *op. cit.*, p. 22.
10 W. Whateley, *A Bridal Bush* (1619), p. 12.
11 *Original Letters Illustrative of English History*, ed. H. Ellis (1827), second series, volume II, pp. 321–4.
12 *The Stradling Correspondence*, ed. J. M. Traherne (1840), pp. 160–1.
13 H. Hall, *Society in the Elizabethan Age* (1882), pp. 242–8.

THE EARLY TUDORS

1 J. Leland, *op. cit.*, volume V, p. 356.

2 *Ibid.*, volume V, p. 358.
3 E. Hall, *op. cit.*, p. 494.
4 J. Leland, *op. cit.*, volume V, p. 362.
5 *Chronicle of King Henry VIII of England*, ed. M. A. S. Hume (1889), p. 8.
6 *Memorials of King Henry VII*, ed. J. Gairdner (Rolls Series, 1858), pp. 223–39.
7 *Letters of Royal and Illustrious Ladies*, ed. M. A. E. Green (Wood) (1846), volume I, p. 197.
8 *Original Letters . . .*, *op. cit.*, second series, volume I, p. 234.
9 *Letters of Royal and Illustrious Ladies*, *op. cit.*, volume I, p. 207.
10 *Ibid.*, volume I, pp. 204–5.
11 *Correspondence Politique de MM de Castillon et de Marillac*, ed. J. Kaulek (1885), p. 81.
12 *Ibid.*, p. 135.
13 E. Hall, *op. cit.*, p. 834.
14 *Ibid.*, p. 835.
15 *Ibid.*, p. 836.
16 *Correspondence Politique . . .*, *op. cit.*, p. 214.
17 F. Strype, *Ecclesiastical Memorials* (1721; 1832 edition), p. 555.
18 *Ibid.*
19 *Correspondence Politique . . .*, *op. cit.*, p. 214.
20 *Ibid.*, p. 218.

THE LATER TUDORS

1 A. Strickland, *op. cit.*, volume II, p. 259.
2 *The Literary Remains of King Edward VI*, ed. J. G. Nichols (Roxburghe Club, 1857), volume II, p.237.
3 *Letters and Papers, Foreign and Domestic, of the Reign of Henry VIII*, ed. J. S. Brewer *et al.* (1862), volume XVII, pp. 220–1.
4 *The Chronicle of Queen Jane and of Two Years of Queen Mary . . .*, ed. J. G. Nichols (Camden Society, 1840), p. 141.
5 *Ibid.*, p. 170.
6 *Calendar of Letters, Despatches and State Papers . . . Spain*, ed. G. A. Bergenroth *et al.* (1862), volume XIII, p. 26.

SIXTEENTH-CENTURY SCOTLAND

1 J. Leland, *op. cit.*, volume IV, p. 296.

2 R. Lindsay of Pittscottie, *Cronicle [sic] of Scotland* (1814 edition), volume II, p. 360.
3 *Ibid.*, volume II, p. 363.
4 *Ibid.*, volume II, p. 364.
5 *Ibid.*, volume II, p. 368.
6 *Ibid.*, volume II, pp. 370–1.
7 *Ceremonial at the Marriage of Mary, Queen of Scots . . .*, ed. H. Ellis (1818), p. 12.
8 A. Strickland, *Lives of the Queens of Scotland . . .* (1858), volume IV, pp. 169–70.
9 *Ibid.*, volume V, p. 293.
10 Sir James Melville, *Memoirs*, ed. T. Thomson (1827), p. 62.

THE SEVENTEENTH CENTURY
'RATIONAL LOVE'
1 *Letters from Dorothy Osborne to Sir William Temple*—hereafter cited as '*Osborne*', ed. E. A. Parry (1888), p. 41.
2 *Ibid.*, p. 73.
3 *The Complete Works of George Savile, 1st Marquess of Halifax*—hereafter cited as '*Halifax*', ed. W. Raleigh (Clarendon Press, 1912), p. 7.
4 J. Cartwright, *Sacharissa* (1893), p. 60.
5 *Osborne, op. cit.*, p. 130.
6 *Memorials of the Civil War*, ed. R. Bell (1849), volume I, p. 320.
7 F. P. Verney, *Memorials of the Verney Family during the Civil War* (1892), volume I, pp. 277–8.
8 R. Baxter, *Christian Directory* (1673), p. 483.
9 *Ibid.*
10 *Osborne, op. cit.*, p. 139.
11 *The Life of Colonel Hutchinson . . . by his widow Lucy* (1885 edition), volume I, p. 43.
12 R. Baxter, *op. cit.*, p. 483.
13 D. Rogers, *Matrimonial Honour* (1642), p. 264.
14 H. Best, *The Rural Economy of Yorkshire, 1641 . . .*, ed. C. B. Robinson (Surtees Society, XXXIII, 1857), pp. 116–17.
15 *The Autobiography of Anne, Lady Halkett*, ed. J. G. Nichols (Camden Society, 1875, new series, volume XIII), pp. 102–3.
16 *Halifax, op. cit.*, p. 8.

THE EARLY STUARTS
1 T. Birch, *Life of Henry, Prince of Wales* (1760), p. 309.
2 James I, *Basilikon Doron* (1616), p. 74.
3 T. Birch, *op. cit.*, p. 311.
4 R. Coke, *Detection of the Court and State of England* (1694), volume I, p. 64.
5 J. Leland, *op. cit.*, volume V, p. 53.
6 J. Nicholls, *The Progresses, Processions and Magnificent Festivities of King James I . . .* (1828), volume II, p. 534.
7 *Ibid.*, volume II, pp. 434–5.
8 *Ibid.*, volume II, p. 588.
9 J. Howell, *Familiar Letters* (1759), p. 133.
10 J. H. Jesse, *Memoirs of the Court of England during the Reigns of the Stuarts* (1855), volume I, p. 160.
11 *Original letters . . ., op. cit*, second series, volume III, p. 198.
12 A. Strickland, *Lives of the last four Princesses of the Royal House of Stuart* (1872), p. 6.
13 *Ibid.*, p. 8.
14 J. Leland, *op. cit.*, volume V, p. 343.

THE LATER STUARTS
1 J. J. Jusserand, *A French Ambassador at the Court of Charles II* (1892), p. 107.
2 G. Burnet, *History of My Own Time*, ed. O. Airy (1897–1900), volume I, p. 315.
3 J. H. Jesse, *Memoirs of the Court of England . . .* (1855), volume III, pp. 6–7.
4 E. Campagna de Cavelli, *Les derniers Stuarts à Saint-Germain en Laye* (1871), volume I, pp. 132–3.
5 *The Diary of Dr Edward Lake*, ed. G. P. Elliott in *The Camden Miscellany* (Camden Society, 1847), p. 6.
6 *Ibid.*
7 *Ibid.*, pp. 9–10
8 *Ibid.*, p. 10.

THE EIGHTEENTH CENTURY
"MARRIAGES PERFORMED WITHIN"
1 E. Chicken, *The Collier's Wedding* (1764), pp. 26–31.
2 *The Early Diary of Frances Burney*, ed. A. R. Ellis (1889), volume I, p. 15.

3 T. Pennant, *Some Account of London* (1813 edition), pp. 309–10.

THE EARLY HANOVERIANS—AND THE LAST OF THE STUARTS
1 R. L. Arkell, *Caroline of Anspach* (Oxford University Press, 1939), p. 270.
2 *Ibid.*
3 John, Lord Hervey, *Memoirs of the Reign of George II . . .*, ed. J. W. Croker (1884), volume I, p. 239.
4 *Letters of Philip Dormer Stanhope, Earl of Chesterfield*, ed. Lord Mahon (1845), volume III, p. 48.
5 John, Lord Hervey, *op. cit.*, volume I, p. 318.
6 *Ibid.*, volume I, p. 319.
7 *The Letters of Horace Walpole*, ed. P. Cunningham (1891), volume III, p. 432.
8 *The Diaries of a Duchess*, ed. J. Greig (Hodder & Stoughton, 1926), p. 31.
9 *The Letters of Horace Walpole, op. cit.*, volume III, p. 432.

THE LATER HANOVERIANS
1 *The Diaries of a Duchess, op. cit.*, p. 63.
2 W. H. Wilkins, *A Queen of Tears* (Longmans Green, 1904), volume I, p. 110.
3 *The Diaries of John Harris, 1st Earl of Malmesbury* (1844), volume III, p. 153.
4 *Ibid.*, volume III, pp. 169–70.
5 *Ibid.*, volume III, p. 218.
6 *Ibid.*
7 *Ibid.*, volume III, p. 219.
8 *Ibid.*, volume III, p. 220.
9 *The Diary of a Lady-in-Waiting . . .*, ed. A. F. Steuart (The Bodley Head, 1908), volume I, p. 23.
10 *Ibid.*
11 *Ibid.*, volume I, p. 197.

THE NINETEENTH CENTURY
'LIE BACK AND THINK OF ENGLAND'
1 Mrs Humphry, *Manners for Women* (1897), p. 37.
2 *Ibid.*, p. 38.
3 *Ibid.*, p. 47.
4 *Useful Toil*, ed. J. Burnett (Allen Lane, 1975), pp. 61 and 75.

5 *The Woman at Home*, October 1896.

VICTORIA AND ALBERT
1 *The Girlhood of Queen Victoria*, ed. A. C. Benson (John Murray, 1904), volume II, pp. 188–9.
2 *Ibid.*, volume II, p. 268.
3 *The Letters of Queen Victoria*, first series, 1837–61, ed. A. C. Benson and Viscount Esher (John Murray, 1907), volume I, pp. 273–4.
4 John Campbell, Duke of Argyll, *VRI: Her Life and Empire* (Eyre & Spottiswoode, 1902), pp. 121–2.
5 *My Dear Duchess*, ed. A. L. Kennedy (John Murray, 1956), p. 72.
6 *Ibid.*, p. 136.
7 *Ibid.*, p. 214.

THE LATER VICTORIANS
1 *The Letters of Queen Victoria*, second series, 1861–85, ed. G. E. Buckle (John Murray, 1926), volume I, p. 632.
2 *The Times*, 14th October 1869.
3 *The Letters of Queen Victoria, op. cit.*, second series, volume III, p. 689.
4 *Ibid.*, third series, 1886–1901, ed. G. E. Buckle (John Murray, 1930), volume II, p. 274.
5 Royal Archives.
6 *Life with Queen Victoria*, ed. V. Mallet (John Murray, 1968), p. 205.

THE TWENTIETH CENTURY
'FOR AS LONG AS YE BOTH SHALL LOVE'
1 M. Young and P. Willmott, *Family and Kinship in East London* (Routledge & Kegan Paul, 1957, here quoted from the Pelican edition), p. 63.

THE HOUSE OF WINDSOR
1 Wallis, Duchess of Windsor, *The Heart has its Reasons* (Michael Joseph, 1956), p. 247.
2 Royal Archives.
3 Wallis, Duchess of Windsor, *op. cit.*, p. 297.

MOUNTBATTEN-WINDSOR
1 Mabel, Countess of Airlie, *Thatched with Gold* (Hutchinson, 1962), p. 112.

2 Royal Archives. 3 *Ibid.*

Works of fiction, plays or poems have been quoted without reference above only when they are out of copyright and appear in several editions.

Further Reading

Many hundreds of books were consulted in the preparation of this book—chronicles, letters, memoirs and diaries, along with general histories, contemporary and modern biographies of monarchs, their consorts and relations, even novels and poems. To give a full list would almost be to compile a bibliography of British history, political, constitutional and social, and another of the love-stories, in poetry and prose, which have been read over the past thousand years—even without any reference to the foreign publications consulted. Instead, here is a list of some recent books on the history of love, courting, weddings and marriage:

M. Baker, *Wedding-customs and Folklore* (David & Charles, 1977)

P. Cunnington and C. Lucas, *Costume for Births, Marriages and Deaths* (Adam & Charles Black, 1972)

N. Epton, *Love and the English* (Cassell, 1960)

J. Harris and A. Wisker, *Marriage* (Batsford, 1976)

P. Laslett, *Family Life and Illicit Love in Earlier Generations* (Cambridge University Press, 1977)

A. Monsarrat, *And the Bride Wore* . . . (Gentry Books, 1973)

B. Murphy, *The World of Weddings* (Paddington Press, 1978)

E. S. Turner, *A History of Courting* (Ian Henry Publications, 1977)

A Royal Genealogy

William, Duke of Normandy (born *c.* 1028), became King of England by conquest in 1066 and reigned until his death in 1087. He married (*c.* 1051, at the Cathedral of Notre Dame at Eu, Normandy) Matilda of Flanders (*c.* 1031–83).

Their children:
    Robert, Duke of Normandy (*c.* 1053–1134), married (1090, in Apulia, Italy) Sybilla of Conversano (d. 1103)
    Richard (*c.* 1054–*c.* 1075)
    William II, King of England (born *c.* 1056, reigned 1087–1100)
    Henry I, King of England—*see below*
    Cecily, Abbess of Caen (*c.* 1055–1127)
    Agatha
    Adelicia
    Constance (*c.* 1057–90) married (1086, at Caen, Normandy) Alan, Count of Brittany (d. 1119)
    Adela (*c.* 1062–1127) married (1080, at Breteuil, Normandy) Stephen, Count of Blois (d. 1101), and was mother of, among others, King Stephen—*see below*
    Matilda (d. *c.* 1080)

Henry I, King of England (born 1068, reigned 1100–35), married first (11th November 1100, in Westminster Abbey) Matilda of Scotland (*c.* 1079–1118) and secondly (24th January 1121, at Windsor) Adelicia of Louvain (1102–51), who was childless.

The children of Henry and Matilda:
    William (1102–20) married (June 1119, at Lisieux, Normandy) Isabelle of Anjou (1107–54)
    Matilda (1102–67) married first (7th June 1114, in Mainz Cathedral,

Germany) the Holy Roman Emperor Henry V (d. 1125) and secondly (22nd May 1127, in the Cathedral of St Julian, Le Mans) Geoffrey, Count of Anjou (1113–51)

At the death of Henry I in 1135, the throne of England was disputed between the King's daughter Matilda and her cousin Stephen of Blois. For almost two decades there was civil war in England, with sometimes Stephen, occasionally Matilda, triumphant. For the most part, however, Stephen was recognized as king.

Stephen, King of England (born 1097, reigned 1135–54), married (c. 1124) Matilda of Boulogne (1103–52).

Their children:
    Baldwin (c. 1126–c. 1135)
    Eustace, Count of Boulogne (c. 1127–53), married (c. 1140, in Paris) Constance of France (c. 1128–53)
    William, Count of Boulogne (c. 1134–59), married (c. 1149) Isabel de Warenne (c. 1137–99)
    Matilda (c. 1133–c. 1135)
    Mary, Countess of Boulogne (1136–82), married (c. 1160—divorced 1169) Matthew, Count of Flanders (d. 1173)

In the last years of his life, King Stephen agreed to pass over his own children's claims to the throne in favour of Matilda's eldest son, Henry (by Geoffrey, Count of Anjou), who at Stephen's death in 1154 became King Henry II.

Henry II, King of England (born 1133, reigned 1154–89), married (18th May 1152, at Poitiers) Eleanor, Duchess of Aquitaine (1122–1204), the divorced first wife of Louis VII, King of France.

Their children:
    William (1152–6)
    Henry (1155–83) married (2nd November 1160, at Rouen, Normandy) Marguerite of France (1158–97)
    Richard I, King of England (born 1157, reigned 1189–99), married (12th May 1191, in the Chapel of St George, Limassol, Cyprus) Berengaria of Navarre (c. 1163–c. 1230)
    Geoffrey, Duke of Brittany (1158–85), married (July 1181) Constance, Duchess of Brittany (1161–1201)
    John, King of England—*see below*
    Matilda (1156–89) married (1st February 1168, in Minden Cathedral, Germany) Henry, Duke of Saxony and Bavaria (1129–95)
    Eleanor (1161–1214) married (September 1177, at Burgos, Spain) Alfonso VIII, King of Castile (1158–1214)
    Joan (1165–99) married first (13th February 1177, at Palermo, Sicily)

William II, King of Sicily (1154–89), and secondly (October 1196, at Rouen, Normandy) Raimond VI, Count of Toulouse (1156–1221)

John, King of England (born 1166, reigned 1199–1216) married first (29th August 1189, at Marlebridge) Isabel (Avisa), Countess of Gloucester (d. *c.* 1217), and divorced her (1200) to marry (24th August 1200, at Bordeaux) Isabelle of Angoulême (*c.* 1187–1246).

The children of John and Isabelle:
Henry III, King of England—*see below*
Richard, Earl of Cornwall, King of the Romans (1208–72), married first (13th March 1231, at Fawley, Berkshire) Isabel Marshall (1199–1240), secondly (23rd November 1243, in Westminster Abbey) Sanchia of Provence (*c.* 1225–61) and thirdly (16th June 1269, in the Stiftkirche, Kaiserslautern, Germany) Beatrix of Falkenburg (*c.* 1255–77)
Joan (*c.* 1203–38) married (18th June 1221, at York Minster) Alexander II, King of Scotland (1198–1249)
Isabel (1214–41) married (20th July 1235, in Worms Cathedral, Germany) the Holy Roman Emperor Frederick II (1194–1250)
Eleanor (1215–75) married first (23rd April 1224) William Marshall, Earl of Pembroke (d. 1231), and secondly (7th January 1239, in West-minster Palace) Simon de Montfort, Earl of Leicester (d. 1265)

Henry III, King of England (born 1207, reigned 1216–72) married (4th January 1236, in Canterbury Cathedral) Eleanor of Provence (*c.* 1217–91).

Their children:
Edward I, King of England—*see below*
Edmund, Earl of Lancaster (1244–96) married first (8th/9th April 1269, in Westminster Abbey) Aveline de Forz (1259–74) and secondly (December 1275/February 1276, in Paris) Blanche of Artois, widowed Queen of Navarre (*c.* 1245–1302)
Richard (*c.* 1247–*c.* 1256)
John (*c.* 1250–*c.* 1256)
William (*c.* 1250)
Henry
Margaret (1240–75) married (26th December 1251, at York Minster) Alexander III, King of Scotland (1241–85)
Beatrice (1242–75) married (22nd January 1260, in the Abbey of St Denis, Compiègne, France) John, Duke of Brittany (1248–1305)
Catherine (1253–7)

Edward I, King of England (born 1239, reigned 1272–1307) married first (13/31 October 1254, at Burgos, Spain) Eleanor of Castile (*c.* 1244–90) and secondly (8th September 1299, in Canterbury Cathedral) Marguerite of France (*c.* 1282–1317).

The children of Edward and Eleanor:

John (1266–71)

Henry (1267–74)

Alfonso (1273–84)

Edward II, King of England—*see below*

Eleanor (1264–98) married first (15th August 1282, by proxy) Alfonso I, King of Aragon (d. 1290) and secondly (20th September 1293, in Bristol Cathedral) Henry, Count of Bar (d. 1302)

Catherine (1271)

Joan (1272–1307) married first (30th May 1290, in Westminster Abbey) Gilbert de Clare, Earl of Gloucester (d. 1295), and secondly (January 1297) Ralph de Monthermer (d. 1325/6)

Margaret (1275–1318) married (8th July 1290, in Westminster Abbey) John, Duke of Lorraine (d. 1312)

Berengaria (1276–9)

Mary (1278–1332), a nun

Alice (1279–91)

Elizabeth (1282–1316) married first (8th January 1297, at Ipswich, Suffolk) John, Count of Holland (d. 1299), and secondly (14th November 1302, in Westminster Abbey) Humphrey de Bohun, Earl of Hereford and Essex (d. 1322)

Beatrice (*c.* 1286)

Blanche (*c.* 1290)

The children of Edward and Marguerite:

Thomas, Earl of Norfolk (1300–1338) married first (*c.* 1316) Alice Halys (d. 1326) and secondly (*c.* 1328) Mary de Braose (d. 1362)

Edmund, Earl of Kent (1301–30) married Margaret, Lady Wake (*c.* 1299–1349)

Eleanor (1306–11)

Margaret

Edward II, King of England (born 1284, reigned 1307–27), married (28th January 1308, at Boulogne, France) Isabelle of France (1292–1358).

Their children:

Edward III, King of England—*see below*

John, Earl of Cornwall (1316–36)

Eleanor (1318–55) married (May 1332, at Nijmeguen, in the Netherlands) Rainald, future Duke of Guelders (d. 1343)

Joan (1321–62) married (17th July 1328, at Berwick-on-Tweed) David II, King of Scotland (1324–71)

Edward III, King of England (born 1312, reigned 1327–77), married (24th January 1328, at York Minster) Philippa of Hainault (1314–69).

Their children:

Edward, Prince of Wales (1330–76) married (10th October 1361, in

Windsor Castle) Joan, Countess of Kent (1328–85), by whom he became the father of the future King Richard II—*see below*

William (1335–6)

Lionel of Antwerp, Duke of Clarence (1338–68) married first (9th September 1342, in the Tower of London) Elizabeth de Burgh, Countess of Ulster (1332–63), and secondly (28th May 1368, in Milan) Violante Visconti (*c.* 1353–86)

John of Gaunt, Duke of Lancaster (1340–99), married first (19th May 1359, in the Queen's Chapel, Reading, Berkshire) Blanche, heiress of Lancaster (1347–69), secondly (September 1371, at Rochefort, near Bordeaux, France) Costanza of Castile (1354–94) and thirdly (13th January 1396, in Lincoln Cathedral) Catherine Swynford (*c.* 1356–1403).

By his first wife, John was the father of, among others, Henry IV, King of England—*see below*, and of Philippa (1360–1415) who married (11th February 1387, at Oporto, Portugal) John I, King of Portugal (d. 1433). By his second wife, John had only one surviving child, Catherine (*c.* 1372–1418) who married (1393, at Burgos, Spain) Henry III, King of Castile (d. 1406). By his third wife the Duke was the ancestor of the House of Beaufort, from which Henry Tudor (King Henry VII—*see below*) derived his claim to the throne.

Edmund of Langley, Duke of York (1341–1402), married first (1st March 1372, probably at Hertford) Isabel of Castile (1355–94) and secondly (4th November 1393) Joan Holland (*c.* 1380–1434)

William (1349)

Thomas of Woodstock, Duke of Gloucester (1355–97), married (*c.* 1375) Eleanor de Bohun (1366–99)

Isabel (1332–82) married (27th July 1365, at Windsor Castle) Enguerrand de Coucy, Earl of Bedford (d. 1397)

Joan (1333–48)

Blanche (1342)

Mary (1344–61) married (1361, at Woodstock, Oxfordshire) John, Duke of Brittany (d. 1399)

Margaret (1346–61) married (19th May 1359, in the Queen's Chapel, Reading, Berkshire) John Hastings, Earl of Pembroke (d. 1375)

Richard II, King of England (born 1367, reigned 1377–99, died 1400)—grandson of Edward III; son of Edward, Prince of Wales—married first (14/20th January 1382, in St Stephen's Chapel, Westminster Palace) Anne of Bohemia (1366–94) and secondly (1st November 1396, in the Church of St Nicholas, Calais) Isabelle of France (1389–1409).

In 1399 Richard was overthrown by his cousin Henry, Duke of Lancaster, son of John of Gaunt, who reigned as

Henry IV, King of England (born 1366, reigned 1399–1413). Henry married first (July 1380/March 1381, at Arundel Castle, Sussex) Mary de

Bohun (c. 1370–94) and secondly (7th February 1403, in St Swithin's Church, Winchester) Jeanne of Navarre, widowed Duchess of Brittany (c. 1370–1437).

The children of Henry and Mary:

Henry V, King of England—*see below*

Thomas, Duke of Clarence (1388–1421), married (1412) Margaret Holland (d. 1349)

John, Duke of Bedford (1389–1435), married first (17th April 1423, at Troyes, France) Anne of Burgundy (1404–32) and secondly (20th April 1433, at Thérouanne, France) Jacquetta of St Pol (c. 1416–72)

Humphrey, Duke of Gloucester (1390–1447) married first (1422— divorced 1428) Jacqueline, Countess of Holland and Hainault (1401–36) and secondly (c. 1431) Eleanor Cobham (d. 1454)

Blanche (1392–1409) married (6th July 1402, in Cologne Cathedral, Germany) Louis, Duke of Bavaria (d. 1436)

Philippa (1394–1430) married (26th October 1406, at Lund, Sweden) Eric X, King of Denmark, Norway and Sweden (d. 1459)

Henry V, King of England (born 1386, reigned 1413–22) married (3rd January 1420, at Troyes, France) Catherine of France (1401–37), by whom he became the father of one child,

Henry VI, King of England (born 1422, reigned 1422–61, 1470–71), who married (22nd April 1445, in Titchfield Abbey, Hampshire) Margaret of Anjou (1430–82), who gave him one son:

Edward, Prince of Wales (1453–71), who married (August 1470, in Angers Cathedral, France) Anne Neville (1456–85)

Henry's right to the throne was challenged by his cousin Richard, Duke of York (descendant of Edward III's sons Lionel and Edmund). Richard was killed in battle (1460), but his claim was taken up by his son Edward, who overthrew Henry VI in 1461 and ruled (apart from a brief period in 1470–71 when Henry was restored) as Edward IV.

The children of Richard, Duke of York, and his wife Cecily Neville (1415–95) included:

Edward IV, King of England—*see below*

George, Duke of Clarence (1449–76) married (11th July 1469, at Calais) Isabel Neville (1451–76)

Richard III, King of England—*see below*

Anne (1439–76) married first (30th July 1447, divorced 1472) Henry Holland, Duke of Exeter (d. 1473) and secondly (1472/3) Sir Thomas St Leger (d. 1483)

Elizabeth (1444–1503) married (October 1460) John de la Pole, Duke of Suffolk (d. 1491)

Margaret (1446–1503) married (3rd July 1468, at Dame, Burgundy) Charles, Duke of Burgundy (d. 1477)

Edward IV, King of England (born 1442, reigned 1461–83) married (1st May 1464, at Grafton, Northamptonshire) Elizabeth Woodville, the widowed Lady Grey (*c.* 1437–92).

Their children:
  Edward V, King of England (born 1470, reigned 1483, died at a date unknown)
  Richard, Duke of York (1472–?), married (15th January 1478, in St Stephen's Chapel, Westminster Palace) Anne Mowbray, Duchess of Norfolk (1472–81)
  George (1477–9)
  Elizabeth (1465–1503) married (18th January 1486, in St Stephen's Chapel, Westminster Palace) Henry VII, King of England—*see below*
  Mary (1466–82)
  Cecily (1469–1507) married first (November/December 1487) John, Viscount Welles (d. 1499), and secondly (1503) Thomas Kyme
  Margaret (1472)
  Anne (1475–1511) married (4th February 1495) Thomas Howard, Duke of Norfolk (d. 1554)
  Catherine (1479–1527) married (October 1495) William Courtenay, Earl of Devon (d. 1511)
  Bridget (1480–1517), a nun

Edward IV was succeeded by his eldest son in 1483, but in the same year the throne was usurped by the late King's brother,

Richard III, King of England (born 1452, reigned 1483–5), who had married (12th July 1472, in St Stephen's Chapel, Westminster Palace) Anne Neville (1456–85), widow of Edward of Lancaster, Prince of Wales.

Their son:
  Edward, Prince of Wales (1473–84)

In 1485 Richard III was overthrown by the Lancastrian claimant to the throne, Henry Tudor (descendant of Edward III through the third marriage of John of Gaunt), who reigned as

Henry VII, King of England (born 1457, reigned 1485–1509), married (18th January 1486, in St Stephen's Chapel, Westminster Palace) the heiress of the rival claim to the throne, Elizabeth of York (1465–1503).

Their children:
  Arthur, Prince of Wales (1486–1502), married (14th November 1501, in St Paul's Cathedral, London) Catherine of Aragon (1483–1536)
  Henry VIII, King of England—*see below*

Edmund (1499–1500)

Margaret (1489–1541) married first (8th August 1503, in Holyrood Abbey, Edinburgh) James IV, King of Scotland (1473–1513), secondly (4th August 1514, at Kinnoull—divorced 1527) Archibald Douglas, Earl of Angus (*c.* 1489–1557) and thirdly (1528) Henry Stewart, Lord Methven (*c.* 1495–1551)

Elizabeth (1492–5)

Mary (1496–1533) married first (9th October 1514, at Abbeville, France) Louis XII, King of France (1462–1515) and secondly (3rd March 1515, in Paris, and 13th May 1515, at the Grey Friars' Church, Greenwich) Charles Brandon, Duke of Suffolk (1484–1545)

Catherine (1503)

Henry VIII, King of England (born 1491, reigned 1509–47), married first (11th June 1509, at the Grey Friars' Church, Greenwich) his brother's widow, Catherine of Aragon (1483–1536), whom he divorced in May 1533, having married (25th January 1533, at Whitehall) Anne Boleyn (*c.* 1509–36); the marriage was declared null in 1536. Henry VIII took as his third wife (30th May 1536, at Wolf Hall, Wiltshire) Jane Seymour (*c.* 1509–37) and as his fourth (6th January 1540, at Greenwich) Anne of Cleves (1516–57), whom he divorced in 1540. Henry then married (28th July 1540, at the Palace of Hampton Court) Catherine Howard (*c.* 1521–42) and (12th July 1543, again at Hampton Court) Catherine Parr (*c.* 1512–48).

Henry's children were: by Catherine of Aragon, Mary I, Queen of England—*see below*; by Anne Boleyn, Elizabeth I, Queen of England—*see below*; by Jane Seymour, Edward VI, King of England—*see below*, who succeeded his father.

Edward VI, King of England was born in 1537 and reigned 1547–53. At his death the throne was usurped by his cousin **Jane Grey** (Dudley) who reigned only a few days before the rightful queen, Mary, was proclaimed.

Mary I, Queen of England (born 1516, reigned 1553–8), married (25th July 1554, in Winchester Cathedral) Philip II, King of Spain (1527–98). Childless, she was succeeded by her half-sister,

Elizabeth I, Queen of England (born 1536, reigned 1558–1603). At Elizabeth's death, the crown devolved to her cousin James VI, King of Scotland, who was descended from Henry VII. Thus the crowns of England and Scotland were united.

THE ROYAL HOUSE OF SCOTLAND 1058–1625

Malcolm III, King of Scotland (born *c.* 1031, reigned 1058–93), married first (*c.* 1059) Ingeborg of Halland and secondly (*c.* 1069, in Dunfermline

Abbey) St Margaret (*c.* 1046–93), one of the last representatives of the Anglo-Saxon royal dynasty of England.

The children of Malcolm and Ingeborg included:
Duncan II, King of Scotland (born 1060, reigned May–November 1094), married (*c.* 1090) Ethelreda of Northumberland and Dunbar, by whom he had issue passed over in the royal succession.

The children of Malcolm and Margaret included:
Edgar, King of Scotland (born 1074, reigned 1098–1107)
Alexander I, King of Scotland (born *c.* 1074, reigned 1107–24) married (*c.* 1107) Sybilla (d. 1122), illegitimate daughter of Henry I, King of England
David I, King of Scotland—*see below*
Matilda, otherwise Edith (1079–1118), married (11th November 1100, in Westminster Abbey) Henry I, King of England (1068–1135)
Mary (*c.* 1082–1116) married (1102) Eustace, Count of Boulogne (d. 1125)

Malcolm III was succeeded by his brother **Donald III Bane,** who, after reigning a few months, was overthrown by Malcolm's eldest son, Duncan II. Donald engineered Duncan's murder and continued to reign until 1097, when he was overthrown by another nephew, Edgar. Both the latter and his successor, his brother Alexander I, were childless and were succeeded by a fourth son of Malcolm III, David I.

David I, King of Scotland (born *c.* 1084, reigned 1124–53), married (1113/1114) Matilda, heiress of Huntingdon and Northampton (*c.* 1074–1131).

Their children included:
Henry, Earl of Huntingdon (*c.* 1115–52) married (1139) Ada de Warenne (d. 1178), whose children included:

Malcolm IV, King of Scotland (born 1142, reigned 1153–65)
William I, King of Scotland—*see below*
David, Earl of Huntingdon (1144–1219), married (26th August 1190) Maud, heiress of Chester (d. 1233), by whom he became the ancestor of the Scottish kings John Balliol and Robert Bruce—*see below*
Ada (*c.* 1143–1212) married (1161) Florent III, Count of Holland (d. 1190)
Margaret (*c.* 1145–1201) married first (1160) Conan IV, Duke of Brittany (1125–71), and secondly Humphrey de Bohun, Earl of Hereford

William I, King of Scotland (born *c.* 1143, reigned 1165–1214), married (5th September 1186 at Woodstock, Oxfordshire) Ermengarde de Beaumont (d. 1234).

Their children:

Alexander II, King of Scotland—*see below*

Margaret (d. 1259) married (1221, at York) Hubert de Burgh, Earl of Kent (d. 1243)

Isobel married (1225) Roger Bigod, Earl of Norfolk (d. 1270)

Marjorie (d. 1244) married (1st August 1235, at Berwick-on-Tweed) Gilbert Marshall, Earl of Pembroke (d. 1241)

Alexander II, King of Scotland (born 1198, reigned 1214–49) married first (18th June 1221, at York Minster) Joan of England (*c.* 1203–38), who was childless, and secondly (15th May 1239, at Roxburgh) Marie de Coucy. The only son of Alexander and Marie was

Alexander III, King of Scotland (born 1241, reigned 1249–86), who married first (26th December 1251, at York Minster) Margaret of England (1240–75) and secondly (1st November 1285, at Jedburgh Abbey) Yolande of Dreux (d. 1323), who was childless.

The children of Alexander and Margaret:

Alexander (1264–84) married (15th November 1282, at Roxburgh) Marguerite of Flanders (d. 1330)

David (1273–81)

Margaret (1261–83) married (31st August 1281, at Bergen, Norway) Eric, King of Norway (d. 1299), whose only child became **Margaret, Queen of Scotland** (born 1283, reigned 1286–90)

At Queen Margaret's death in 1290, the Scottish throne was claimed by more than a dozen descendants of David, Earl of Huntingdon (*see above*). Edward I, King of England, was called upon to arbitrate the claims and awarded the crown to **John Balliol** (b. *c.* 1250), who reigned 1292–6. He married (January 1281) Isabel de Warenne and died in 1313. The throne was seized by Robert Bruce (*see below*), but John Balliol's son **Edward** reigned briefly in 1332 and spasmodically between 1333 and 1346. He married Marguerite of Anjou-Taranto and died in 1363.

Robert Bruce, King of Scotland (born 1274, reigned 1306–29) married first (*c.* 1295) Isobel of Mar and secondly (1302) Elizabeth de Burgh (d. 1327).

The only child of Robert and Isobel was:

Marjorie (d. 1316), who married (1315) Walter Stewart (d. *c.* 1326) and whose son became Robert II, King of Scotland—*see below*

The children of Robert and Elizabeth:

David II, King of Scotland (born 1324, reigned 1329–71). He married first (17th July 1328, at Berwick-on-Tweed) Joan of England (1321–62) and secondly (20th February 1364, at Inchmurdach, Fife—divorced 1370) Margaret Drummond, the widowed Lady Logie (d. 1375)

John

Matilda (1353) married Thomas Isaac

Margaret (d. *c.* 1346) married William, Earl of Sutherland (d. 1370/71)

Robert II, King of Scotland (born 1316, reigned 1371–90), married first (1347) Elizabeth Mure (d. *c.* 1355) and secondly (1355) Euphemia of Ross, widowed Countess of Moray (d. 1387)

The children of Robert and Elizabeth:

Robert III, King of Scotland—*see below*

Walter, Earl of Atholl (d. 1362), married Isobel, Countess of Fife (d. 1389)

Robert, Duke of Albany (*c.* 1340–1420), married first (9th September 1361) Margaret, Countess of Menteith (d. 1380), and secondly Muriel Keith (d. 1449)

Alexander, Earl of Buchan (d. *c.* 1405–6), married (July 1382) Euphemia, Countess of Ross (d. *c.* 1394)

Margaret married (1350) John Macdonald, Lord of the Isles (d. 1387)

Marjorie married first (1370) John Dunbar, Earl of Moray (d. 1392), and secondly (*c.* 1403) Sir Alexander Keith

Elizabeth married (1372) Thomas de la Haye, Lord Erroll (d. 1406)

Isobel married first (1371) James, Earl of Douglas (d. 1388), and secondly (*c.* 1390) Sir John Edmondstone

Jean married first Sir John Keith, secondly (*c.* 1376) Sir John Lyon (d. 1382) and thirdly (1384) Sir James Sandilands

The children of Robert and Euphemia:

David, Earl Palatine of Strathearn, Earl of Caithness (*c.* 1356–*c.* 1390), whose wife's name is unknown

Walter, Earl of Atholl (d. 1437), married (1378) Margaret de Barclay

Egidia married (1387) Sir William Douglas

Catherine married (1380) David Lindsay, Earl of Crawford

Robert III, King of Scotland (born 1337, reigned 1390–1406), married (1366/7) Annabella Drummond (d. 1401).

Their children:

David, Duke of Rothesay (1378–1402), married (February 1400, at Bothwell) Marjorie Douglas

Robert

James I, King of Scotland—*see below*

Margaret married Archibald, Earl of Douglas, Duke of Touraine (d. 1424)

Mary (d. 1458) married first (1397) George Douglas, Earl of Angus (d. 1402), secondly (1405) Sir James Kennedy (d. 1408), thirdly (13th November 1413) William, Lord Graham (d. 1424), and fourthly (1425) Sir William Edmondstone

Elizabeth married (1387) James Douglas, Lord Dalkeith (d. 1441)
Egidia

James I, King of Scotland (born 1394, reigned 1406–37), married (2nd February 1424, in the church of St Mary Overy in London, now Southwark Cathedral) Joan Beaufort (d. 1445).

Their children:
Alexander (1430)
James II, King of Scotland—*see below*
Margaret (1424–45) married (25th June 1436, at Tours, France) the
    future Louis XI, King of France (1423–83)
Isobel (d. 1494) married (30th October 1442, at Aurai Castle, Brittany)
    François I, Duke of Brittany (d. 1450)
Joanna married (1459) James Douglas, Earl of Morton (d. *c.* 1445)
Eleanor (d. 1480) married (12th February 1449) Sigismund, Duke of
    Austria (d. 1496)
Mary (d. 1465) married (1444, at Sandenburg in the Netherlands)
    Wolfaert van Borselen, Count of Grandpré (d. 1487)
Annabella married first (14th December 1447—divorced March 1456)
    Louis, Count of Geneva (d. 1482) and secondly (1459—divorced July
    1471) George Gordon, Earl of Huntly (d. 1501)

James II, King of Scotland (born 1430, reigned 1437–60), married (3rd July 1449, at Holyrood Abbey, Edinburgh) Marie of Guelders (d. 1463).

Their children:
James III, King of Scotland—*see below*
Alexander, Duke of Albany (*c.* 1453–85), married first (divorced 1478)
    Catherine Sinclair and secondly (10th February 1480) Anne de la
    Tour of Auvergne (d. 1512)
David, Earl of Moray (*c.* 1455–7)
John, Earl of Mar (1459–79)
Mary (d. 1488) married first (1467) Thomas Boyd, Earl of Arran (d. *c.*
    1474), and secondly (1476) James, Lord Hamilton (d. 1479)
Margaret married William, Lord Crichton

James III, King of Scotland (born 1452, reigned 1460–88), married (13th July 1469, at Holyrood Abbey, Edinburgh) Margaret of Denmark (1457–86).

Their children:
James IV, King of Scotland—*see below*
James, Duke of Ross (1476–1504)
John, Earl of Mar (1479–1503)

James IV, King of Scotland (born 1473, reigned 1488–1513), married (8th

August 1503, at Holyrood Abbey, Edinburgh) Margaret of England (1489–1541).

Their children:
    James, Duke of Rothesay (1507–8)
    Arthur, Duke of Rothesay (1509–10)
    James V, King of Scotland—*see below*
    Alexander, Duke of Ross (1514–15)

James V, King of Scotland (born 1512, reigned 1513–42), married first (1st January 1537, in the Cathedral of Notre Dame, Paris) Madeleine of France (1520–37) and secondly (12th June 1538, at St Andrews) Marie of Guise, widowed Duchess of Longueville (1515–60).

The children of James and Marie:
    James, Duke of Rothesay (1540–41)
    Arthur, Duke of Albany (1541)
    Mary, Queen of Scotland—*see below*

Mary, Queen of Scotland (born 1542, reigned 1542–67, died 1587), married first (24th April 1558 in the Cathedral of Notre Dame, Paris) the future François II, King of France (1544–60), secondly (29th July 1565, in Holyroodhouse, Edinburgh) Henry Stuart, Lord Darnley (1545–67), and thirdly (15th May 1567, in Holyroodhouse, Edinburgh) James Hepburn, Earl of Bothwell (*c.* 1537–78). Mary's only child, by Lord Darnley, succeeded to the throne on her abdication as

James VI, King of Scotland (born 1566, reigned 1567–1625)—*see below*.

THE ROYAL HOUSE OF ENGLAND AND SCOTLAND 1603–1707

James VI, King of Scotland (born 1566, reigned 1567–1625) and **I, King of England** (1603–25) married (23rd November 1589, at Oslo, Norway) Anne of Denmark (1574–1619).

Their children:
    Henry Frederick, Prince of Wales (1594–1612)
    Charles I, King of England and Scotland—*see below*
    Robert, Duke of Kintyre (1602)
    Elizabeth (1596–1662) married (14th February 1613, in the Chapel Royal, Whitehall) Frederick V, Elector Palatine, later King of Bohemia (1596–1632), from whom descended King George I—*see below*
    Margaret (1598–1600)
    Mary (1605–7)
    Sophia (1606)

Charles I, King of England and Scotland (born 1600, reigned 1625–49) married (13th June 1625, in Canterbury Cathedral) Henrietta Maria of France (1609–69).

Their children:
    Charles, Duke of Cornwall and Rothesay (1629)
    Charles II, King of England and Scotland (born 1630, reigned 1660–85), married (21st May 1662, at Portsmouth, Hampshire) Catherine of Braganza (Portugal, 1638–1705)
    James II, King of England, VII, King of Scotland—*see below*
    Henry, Duke of Gloucester (1640–60)
    Mary, Princess Royal (1631–60) married (2nd May 1641, in the Chapel Royal, Whitehall) William II, Prince of Orange (1626–50) and became the mother of the future King William III—*see below*
    Elizabeth (1635–50)
    Anne (1637–40)
    Catherine (1639)
    Henrietta Anne (1644–70) married (31st March 1661, in the Chapel of the Palais Royal, Paris) Philippe of France, Duke of Orleans (1640–1701)

James II, King of England, VII, King of Scotland (born 1633, reigned 1685–8, died 1701) married twice before coming to the throne, first (24th November 1659, at Breda, and 3rd September 1660, at Worcester House, London) Anne Hyde (1638–71) and secondly (21st November 1673, at Dover) Mary (Maria Beatrice) of Modena (1658–1718).

The children of James and Anne:
    Charles, Duke of Cambridge (1660–61)
    James, Duke of Cambridge (1663–7)
    Charles, Duke of Kendal (1666–7)
    Edgar, Duke of Cambridge (1667–71)
    Mary II, Queen of England and Scotland—*see below*
    Anne, Queen of England and Scotland/Great Britain—*see below*
    Henrietta (1669)
    Catherine (1671)

The children of James and Mary:
    Charles, Duke of Cambridge (1677)
    James Francis Edward, 'Prince of Wales/King James III' (1688–1766), married (3rd September 1719, at Montefiascone, Italy) Maria Clementina Sobieska (1702–35), by whom he became the father of the last Stuart claimants to the throne,
        Charles Edward (1720–88) who married (17th April 1772, at Macerata, Italy) Louise of Stolberg-Gedern (1752–1824)
        Henry Benedict, Cardinal York (1725–1807)
    Catherine Laura (1675)

Isabella (1676–81)
Charlotte Maria (1682)
Louise Marie (1692–1712)

When James II was overthrown and driven into exile in 1688, the throne was taken by his elder surviving daughter and her husband,

Mary II, Queen of England and Scotland (born 1662, reigned 1689–94) who had married (4th November 1677, in St James's Palace) her cousin William III, Prince of Orange, who reigned as **William III, King of England, II, King of Scotland** (born 1650, reigned 1689–1702). Childless, they were succeeded by Mary's sister

Anne, Queen of England and Scotland, under whom the Act of Union was effected in 1707, which created her Queen of Great Britain (born 1665, reigned 1702–14). She had married (28th July 1683, in the Chapel Royal, St James's) George of Denmark (1653–1708). From some fourteen babies, the Queen reared only one son:

William, Duke of Gloucester (1689–1700)

THE ROYAL HOUSE OF GREAT BRITAIN 1707–today

Anne, the last monarch of the House of Stuart, was succeeded by her cousin George of Hanover (descended from James VI and I's daughter Elizabeth), as

George I, King of Great Britain (born 1660, reigned 1714–27), who had married (21st November 1682, at Celle, Germany—divorced 1694) Sophia Dorothea of Celle (1666–1726).

Their children:
    George II, King of Great Britain—*see below*
    Sophia Dorothea (1687–1757) married (17th November 1706, in Berlin)
        Frederick William I, King of Prussia (1688–1740)

George II, King of Great Britain (born 1683, reigned 1727–60), married (22nd August 1705, at Hanover, Germany) Caroline of Anspach (1683–1737).

Their children:
    Frederick Lewis, Prince of Wales (1707–51), married (27th April 1736, in the Chapel Royal, St James's) Augusta of Saxe-Gotha (1719–72)—*see below*
    George William (1717–18)
    William Augustus, Duke of Cumberland (1721–65)

Anne, Princess Royal (1709–59), married (25th March 1734, in the Chapel Royal, St James's) William IV, Prince of Orange (1711–51)

Amelia (1711–86)

Caroline (1713–57)

Mary (1723–72) married (28th June 1740, at Cassel, Germany) Frederick, Landgrave of Hesse-Cassel (1720–85)

Louisa (1724–51) married (11th December 1743, at Altona, Denmark) Frederick V, King of Denmark (1723–66)

The children of Frederick Lewis, Prince of Wales:

George III, King of Great Britain and Ireland—*see below*

Edward Augustus, Duke of York (1739–67)

William Henry, Duke of Gloucester (1743–1805), married (6th September 1766, in Pall Mall, London), Maria Walpole, the widowed Lady Waldegrave (1739–1807)

Henry Frederick, Duke of Cumberland (1745–90), married (2nd October 1771, in Hertford Street, London) Anne Luttrell, the widowed Mrs Horton (1743–1808)

Frederick William (1750–65)

Augusta (1737–1813) married (16th January 1764, at St James's Palace) Charles, Duke of Brunswick-Wolfenbuttel (1735–1806)

Elizabeth Caroline (1740–59)

Louisa Anne (1749–68)

Caroline Matilda (1751–75) married (8th November 1766, at Christianborg, Denmark) Christian VII, King of Denmark (1749–1808)

George III, King of Great Britain and Ireland (born 1738, reigned 1760–1820), later also King of Hanover, married (8th September 1761, at St James's Palace) Charlotte of Mecklenburg-Strelitz (1744–1818).

Their children:

George IV, King of Great Britain and Ireland, King of Hanover (born 1762, reigned 1820–30), married (with the most dubious legality, on 21st December 1785, in Park Street, London) Maria Smythe, the widowed Mrs Fitzherbert (1756–1837), and (8th April 1795, in the Chapel Royal, St James's) Caroline of Brunswick-Wolfenbuttel (1768–1821), whose only child was

Charlotte (1796–1817) who married (2nd May 1816, at Carlton House, London) Leopold of Saxe-Coburg-Saalfeld, future King of the Belgians (1790–1865)

Frederick, Duke of York (1763–1827), married (28th September, in Berlin, and 2nd November 1791, at Buckingham House, London), Frederica of Prussia (1767–1820)

William IV, King of Great Britain and Ireland, King of Hanover (born 1765, reigned 1830–37) married (11th July 1818, at Kew Palace, Surrey) Adelaide of Saxe-Meiningen (1792–1849) and had two daughters:

Charlotte (1819)

Elizabeth (1820–21)

Edward, Duke of Kent (1767–1820), married (29th May 1818, at Schloss Ehrenburg, Coburg, and 11th July 1818, at Kew Palace, Surrey) Victoire of Saxe-Coburg-Saalfeld, widowed Princess of Leiningen (1786–1861). Their only child was:

Victoria, Queen of Great Britain etc—*see below*

Ernest Augustus, Duke of Cumberland, King of Hanover (born 1771, reigned 1837–51), married (29th May 1815, at Strelitz, and 29th August 1815, at Carlton House, London) Frederica of Mecklenburg-Strelitz, widowed Princess of Solms-Braunfels (1778–1841), from whom descends the House of Hanover/Cumberland

Augustus Frederick, Duke of Sussex (1773–1843), married first (4th April 1793, in Rome, and 5th December 1793, in St George's Church, London—annulled 3rd August 1794) Augusta Murray (1768–1830) and secondly (May 1831, in Great Cumberland Place, London) Lady Cecilia Underwood, the widowed Lady Cecilia Buggin (1785–1873)

Adolphus Frederick, Duke of Cambridge (1774–1850) married (7th May 1818, at Cassel, and 1st June 1818, at Buckingham House, London) Augusta of Hesse-Cassel (1797–1889)

Octavius (1779–83)

Alfred (1780–82)

Charlotte, Princess Royal (1766–1828), married (18th May 1797, in the Chapel Royal, St James's Palace) Frederick I, King of Württemberg (1754–1816)

Augusta (1768–1840)

Elizabeth (1770–1840) married (7th April 1818, at Buckingham House, London) Frederick, Landgrave of Hesse-Homburg (1769–1829)

Mary (1776–1857) married (22nd July 1816, at Buckingham House, London) her cousin William, Duke of Gloucester (1776–1834)

Sophia (1777–1848)

Amelia (1783–1810)

Victoria, Queen of Great Britain and Ireland (born 1819, reigned 1837–1901), Empress of India (1877–1901), married (10th February 1840, in the Chapel Royal, St James's Palace) Albert of Saxe-Coburg-Gotha (1819–61).

Their children:

Edward VII, King of Great Britain etc—*see below*

Alfred, Duke of Edinburgh and Saxe-Coburg-Gotha (1844–1900), married (23rd January 1874, at the Winter Palace, St Petersburg, Russia) Marie of Russia (1853–1920)

Arthur, Duke of Connaught (1850–1942), married (13th March 1879, in St George's Chapel, Windsor) Louise of Prussia (1860–1917)

Leopold, Duke of Albany (1853–84), married (27th April 1882, in St George's Chapel, Windsor) Helen of Waldeck (1861–1922)

Victoria, Princess Royal (1840–1901), married (25th January 1858, at Buckingham Palace) the future German Kaiser Frederick (1831–88)

Alice (1843–78) married (1st July 1862, at Osborne House on the Isle of Wight) Louis, future Grand Duke of Hesse (1837–92)

Helena (1846–1923) married (5th July 1866, in the Private Chapel, Windsor Castle) Christian of Schleswig-Holstein (1831–1917)

Louise (1848–1939) married (21st March 1871, in St George's Chapel, Windsor) John Campbell, future Duke of Argyll (1845–1914)

Beatrice (1857–1944) married (23rd July 1885, at Whippingham, Isle of Wight) Henry of Battenberg (1858–96)

Edward VII, King of Great Britain and Ireland, Emperor of India (born 1841, reigned 1901–10) married (10th March 1863, in St George's Chapel, Windsor) Alexandra of Denmark (1844–1925).

Their children:

Albert Victor, Duke of Clarence (1864–92)

George V, King of Great Britain etc—*see below*

Alexander (1871)

Louise, Princess Royal (1867–1931), married (27th July 1889, at Buckingham Palace) Alexander Duff, future Duke of Fife (1849–1912)

Victoria (1868–1935)

Maud (1869–1938) married (22nd July 1896, at Buckingham Palace) the future King Haakon VII of Norway (1872–1957)

George V, King of Great Britain and Ireland, Emperor of India (born 1865, reigned 1910–36) married (6th July 1893, in the Chapel Royal, St James's Palace) Mary of Teck (1867–1953).

Their children:

Edward VIII, King of Great Britain and Ireland, Emperor of India (born 1894, reigned 1936, died 1972), married (3rd June 1937, at the Château de Candé, France) Bessie Wallis Warfield, Mrs Simpson (born 1896)

George VI, King of Great Britain etc—*see below*

Henry, Duke of Gloucester (1900–1974) married (6th November 1935, at Buckingham Palace) Alice Montagu-Douglas-Scott (born 1901)

George, Duke of Kent (1902–42) married (29th November 1934, in Westminster Abbey) Marina of Greece (1906–68)

John (1905–19)

Mary, Princess Royal (1897–1965) married (28th February 1922, in Westminster Abbey) Henry Lascelles, Earl of Harewood (1882–1947)

George VI, King of Great Britain and Ireland (born 1895, reigned 1936–52), Emperor of India (1936–48), married (26th April 1923, in Westminster Abbey) Elizabeth Bowes-Lyon (born 1900).

Their children:

Elizabeth II, Queen of Great Britain and Ireland—*see below*

Margaret (born 1930) married (6th May 1960, in Westminster Abbey—divorced 1978) Antony Armstrong-Jones, Earl of Snowdon (born 1930)

Elizabeth II, Queen of Great Britain and Ireland (born 1926, succeeded to the throne 1952) married (20th November 1947, in Westminster Abbey) Philip Mountbatten, Duke of Edinburgh (born 1921).

Their children:

Charles, Prince of Wales (born 1948)

Andrew (born 1960)

Edward (born 1964)

Anne (born 1950) married (14th November 1973, in Westminster Abbey) Mark Phillips (born 1948)

A NOTE ON NAMES

Historians always have a problem as to whether to anglicize the names of foreign-born consorts of the royal family (Marguerite or Margaret for Edward I's second wife and Henry VI's consort, for instance). This book is unashamedly inconsistent, using English or foreign forms where one or the other has been used in the majority of past histories.

Index